ANCIENT COIN COLLECTING

COLLECTING

2ND Edition

WAYNE G. SAYLES

© 2003 by

Wayne G. Sayles

Published by

 **krause publications**
An F&W Publications Company

700 East State Street • Iola, WI 54990-0001
715-445-2214 • 888-457-2873
www.krause.com

Please call or write for our free catalog.
Our toll-free number to place or obtain a free catalog is 800-258-0929
or please use our regular business telephone 715-445-2214
for editorial comment and further information.

Library of Congress Catalog Number: 95-82428

ISBN: 0-87349-515-2

Printed in the United States of America

For Sabrina, Brendan and Anwen

PREFACE

Since publication of the first edition of this book in 1996, literally thousands of collectors have joined the ancient coin collecting fraternity. The primary reason for this impressive migration is the advent of the Internet, with its worldwide reach and ease of access to information. In that first edition, we presented a chapter dealing with what was then a relatively new phenomenon. Today, the Internet is for many people a part of everyday life. From the comfort of one's home, it is possible to learn more about ancient coins than one might ever have imagined. In fact, one web site even offers interactive courses about ancient coins (read on). With any new technology, change is inevitable and much of the information about the Internet in our first edition is already outmoded. This revision will update that information and add to it. We have also added a few topical areas of general interest to collectors and have greatly expanded some of the reference sections found in the earlier edition. We have corrected a few errors that crept into the first edition and clarified a few points, adding some perspective gained in the intervening years. We have also expanded the section that explains how value is affected by various factors. A number of important books have been released in the past seven years and we have updated the bibliography herein to reflect these additions. In response to requests from readers, we have also indexed this edition. Aside from these changes, the contents and style of this edition are very much the same as in the earlier edition.

Technology has made a tremendous impact on ancient coin collecting in the past decade. The influx of new collectors spawned by the rising popularity of the Internet was matched by a sudden and dramatic increase in the number of ancient coins coming onto the market. This was due in large part to the development of sophisticated metal detecting equipment. At the same time, political and economic instability in several source countries created situations where controls on the export of antiquities were either relaxed or unenforced. The market for certain types of coins became saturated and prices plummeted to levels not seen in the past twenty years. Of course, rare and exquisite coins are as much in demand as ever, but common generic coins of Roman rulers, for example, are bargain priced today. This is an excellent time for beginning collectors of ancient coinage because one can develop a fascinating collection at a relatively modest cost.

In generations past, the study of antiquity was a core element of one's education—often made easier through examination of coins from the ancient world. These coins were the newspapers of their day. They announced the rise of political leaders, the winning of great victories and the artistic triumphs of proud cultures. Is it any wonder that they

iv

have served well to illuminate the history of civilization? With the focus on technology which characterizes our age, many schools have drifted from the basic "classical" education. The current focus is on "education for employment" and classicists are not in great demand. Even in the hallowed halls of academia, numismatics, as a science, is becoming passé. In spite of this, our society remains rooted in traditions which we have inherited from earlier civilizations. Though we are not consciously aware of these links, it is natural that we hold a special feeling for our classical heritage, and that we are attracted to the coins and artifacts which speak to us about past civilizations. Discovery of these historical time capsules is usually an exciting experience for the uninitiated. A new and fascinating world is opened to them—but it is also a bewildering world filled with strange names and places.

One of the obstacles to collecting coins from antiquity is that the beginner often finds it difficult to obtain information about the hobby, still less about the coins themselves. David R. Sear, author of the now famous guides to ancient coins and their values, once remarked that ancient coin collectors suffer from "the Robinson Crusoe syndrome". That is, they often feel alone on a vast and uncharted island. The purpose of this book, and of those in the series which follows, is to help the newcomer discover, like Robinson Crusoe, a set of footprints in the sand.

This is not a guide to attribution, but it will introduce you to the process of attributing coins from each major series. It is not a price list, but it will show you how and where to obtain information about ancient coins and current market values. It is not a scientific study of ancient metals, but it should help you to understand how ancient coins were made and how that knowledge can help you to judge authenticity. It is not an encyclopedia of ancient history, but it may help you to understand the relationships between ancient civilizations and to focus your collecting interest in a sensible way. It certainly is not an investment guide, but hopefully it will help you to understand the ancient coin market and prepare you or your heirs for the eventuality of liquidation.

In the first edition, we parted with tradition in two areas of particular note. The coinage struck in the Roman provinces during the first half of the imperial period had for many years been referred to as *Greek Imperial*. Today, numismatists have generally accepted, and we also have adopted, the more appropriate title *Roman Provincial*. A similar, but even more incongruous, situation exists within the field of "Byzantine" coins. As explained in the text, the term *Byzantine* is totally inappropriate. The term *Romaion*, which appears on the coins themselves, is far more accurate in describing the people of this culture. Recognizing that this is a radical departure from tradition, and that most traditions die hard, we nevertheless feel compelled to abandon the specious title Byzantine in favor of Coins of the Romaioi, or Romaion coinage. We do not consider this in any way to be a crusade to change current convention, it is simply a matter of personal preference. Readers are encouraged to decide for themselves which is preferred.

Some of the material offered here is a reflection of the author's personal experiences over the past 30 years and is consequently subjective in nature. All opinions offered are intended to provide insight and to shorten the learning curve for new collectors. They are, however, opinions, and should be regarded as such.

Due to the type of material, manner of presentation and intended purpose of this book, we have thought it admissible to forego footnotes. Instead, we have included a bibliography of particular sources consulted, and a comprehensive bibliography of works which are regularly used in the field for attribution. Likewise, we have included a glossary of specialized terms that are commonly used in the field, as well as in the text. Although many of our sources delve into these topics at great length, we will have touched only briefly on their subject matter. The reader is urged to further explore subjects of interest by consulting the works listed.

Throughout this book, one will find suggestions which are offered as an aid to the new collector of ancient coins. They should not in any way be considered professional advice about buying specific coins either as collectibles or as an investment. It is our hope that this introductory survey will make ancient coin collecting easier and more enjoyable, and that it will serve the needs of those who have dreamed but never dared to give ancient coin collecting a try.

Gainesville, Missouri 2003   W.G.S.

ACKNOWLEDGMENTS

This book is not the result of new discoveries or revolutionary new ideas, it is a synthesis of the thoughts and experiences of those who have travelled this path before us. The author, much more a journalist than a scholar, is indebted to a whole fraternity of academic, professional and amateur numismatists who have shared their knowledge of ancient coins and culture through books, articles and lectures. It is not possible to acknowledge all of them, but the reader will, over time, become aware of their many contributions.

A few special acknowledgments, however, are necessary. Marvin Tameanko has kindly allowed the abstraction of information from his *Celator* articles about the depiction of Homer on ancient coins, and about the coins of Saba and Himyar. We are grateful to Clifton R. Fox, whose persuasive arguments encouraged us finally to break with tradition in the substitution of *Romaion* for *Byzantine*. Cartoons, also from *The Celator*, are reproduced here with the permission of the artist, Parnell Nelson. Kerry Wetterstrom, Peter Lampinen and Barry Murphy, all professional numismatists, helped with proofing of the first edition and offered many useful suggestions which are embodied herein. A final proofing of this edition by Kandy Bruce, of Krause Publications, saved us from numerous inconsistencies. Mrs. Bruce has played an important part in the finalization of text for each volume of the *Ancient Coin Collecting* series. Victor England and Eric J. McFadden, Senior Directors of Classical Numismatic Group, Inc., graciously allowed the reproduction of photographs from catalogs of auctions held by their firm, as well as reproduction of their technical bibliography—which has been updated in this volume. The majority of coin illustrations used in this volume were derived from that source. The line drawings used in this work have been extracted mainly from Victor Duruy's *History of Greece* (1890) and *History of Rome* (1894). It is difficult to name the contributions of the many correspondents who have shared their interest and expertise on Internet chat sessions, particularly on Moneta-L. The community of collectors resident on the Internet is becoming an important part of the ancient coin collecting community at large and the interaction between this element and the traditional fraternity is growing daily.

The acknowledgments to Doris J. Tobalske in the first edition of this book should also be updated. Doris (now Sayles) proofread manuscripts and made numerous suggestions for improvement in this edition, as she has in every volume of this series. As always, her support and encouragement were invaluable. Doris and I were married at our home in the Missouri Ozarks, with many numismatic friends and family members in attendance, on August 9, 1997.

TABLE OF CONTENTS

H ow old is ancient? This may seem like a crazy question, but it's amazing how many people today have a very poor understanding of ancient history. We have a natural interest in things that are old, but how old is ancient? For that matter, where was the ancient world? In one recent survey of graduating high school seniors, 45% could not locate Japan on a map of the world. Heaven forbid they should be asked to locate Characene. Is this a problem? Probably not for the majority of the world. But if you want to collect ancient coins, it would be nice to know when they were made and where they came from.

It would be convenient if there were some monumental event that marked a transition from the ancient world to the medieval world, but we are not so fortunate. Actually, from the coin collector's viewpoint, the distinction between ancient and medieval coins is determined more along cultural lines than by chronology. For example, the coinage of Charlemagne struck in the late 8th and early 9th centu-

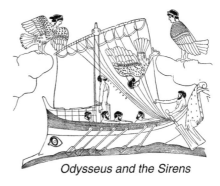

Odysseus and the Sirens

ries is generally regarded as being medieval. Conversely, coinage of the Romaion or "Byzantine" empire struck during the 15th century is typically regarded as being ancient. The latter example is, however, an anomaly and most coinage struck after the fall of the Western Roman Empire is looked upon as being more medieval than ancient.

Another perplexing question involves the geographical boundaries of the world we call "ancient." Western civilization is generally regarded to have evolved along the rim of the Mediterranean Sea. Notwithstanding Homer's description of that "wine dark sea" as being fraught with perils, it was overall a friendly environment. The Mediterranean climate is favorable throughout most of the year, and navigation is encouraged by fairly predictable winds. Remember that it was the predictable *Meltemi*, funneling through the Aegean Sea off the barren steppes of Russia, that set Odysseus wandering for ten years. Nevertheless, dependable land and sea breezes, coupled with a virtual absence of tides, nurtured a prosperous maritime trade. People who lived along the Mediterranean coast became seafarers and, as their civilizations developed, they ventured into distant lands and established new

1

communities. The Greeks developed prosperous cities from Spain to the Oxus and from the Crimea to the upper reaches of the Nile. As they tamed these new lands, they also became exposed to civilizations on the fringe of their world. This exposure led to trade and eventually to the international use of coinage which greatly aided the growth of commerce.

We would be remiss to limit our discussion of the ancient world only to lands affected by classical culture. The production of coins in antiquity extended to lands well beyond the control of Greece or Rome—to such distant places as China, India, Arabia, Africa and even to tribes of Northern Europe who were at the time thought of as "uncivilized". However, let us begin in the West where coinage as we know it today began.

Lydian EL-1/3 stater, late 7th-early 6th c. BC.

From the earliest days of recorded time, the Mediterranean has also been a center of conflict. The annals of history are filled with tales of triumph and devastation as the East and West clashed at the shores of this great sea. It has been argued by some modern numismatists that the invention of coinage in the West was inspired by the need to pay large numbers of mercenaries. Which leads one to ponder why coins would be of any use to mercenaries if they were not useful in commerce? As massive armies and migrations swept back and forth over these lands, a great mixing of cultures occurred. This is especially evident in the art and artifacts of the people who labored under one conqueror after another. The coinage which survives from these historic peoples and places is visual testimony to this fusion. Consequently, it is impossible to think of the ancient world in quite the same way as we think of nations in our age.

The Roman Eagle universally understood symbol of power

Since coins are the product of a political system, we can view them in that context. This, to some degree, defines geographical boundaries and groups. To a greater extent, however, the political systems of the ancient world reflect the fortunes of rising and declining cultures, not just of individual kings and emperors.

Civilization in the Mediterranean predates the Greeks by several thousand years, but we are concerned here only with the western civilizations that produced coinage—and the *Greeks* were the first. The actual date ascribed to the origin of coinage is a matter of continuing debate, but it is generally agreed that the first coins originated in western Asia Minor

2

Cameo of Augustus,
first emperor of Rome, crowned
with oak and olive leaves

(modern Turkey) during the late 7th century BC. We will examine the evolution of coinage a bit later, but let it suffice for the present to say that the rise of Greek culture and the development of coinage as a form of artistic and political expression go hand in hand. The study of numismatics, from the 7th to the 3rd centuries BC, is really an exploration of Greek civilization.

As Greek influence in the Mediterranean declined, the rising dominance of Rome took its place. The transfer of power and cultural diffusion that marked this event was more evolutionary than revolutionary, and much of the Greek way of life was adopted by their Roman conquerors. For all practical purposes, Greek autonomy died with Cleopatra in 30 BC.

Romans were not new to the Mediterranean world. They had been developing as a political and military power since the overthrow of their monarchy in 510 BC. As the **Roman Republic** grew in strength and ambition, during the second and first centuries BC, the Hellenistic Kingdoms became increasingly fragmented and ineffectual. The period is alternately marked by conflicts and alliances, with Rome asserting greater and greater pressure on the few remaining Greek strongholds. Internal conflicts raged between great Roman generals during the 1st century BC, ushering in a relatively short period that we refer to as the **Imperatorial Period.** Following an intense civil war, Julius Caesar prevailed over the forces of Pompey and became perpetual dictator. Caesar's subsequent assassination threw the Roman world into another period of internal conflict, out of which emerged his nephew Octavian as undisputed leader and "emperor."

Traditionally, the acceptance of Octavian as *Augustus* in 27 BC is considered the beginning of the **Roman Empire.** Prior to this date, the Roman Republic

Anastasius I, AE 40 nummia

and the political alliances of the Imperatorial period are treated by numismatists as separate entities. The Romans embarked upon a program of colonization as ambitious as that of the Greeks, and their influence spread from the north of Britain to the Indian Ocean. In conquered lands, the Romans often retained local monetary customs which led to the

3

development of a distinct provincial coinage. This series of coins, which lasted late into the third century AD, has often been referred to as "Greek Imperial" because of the many types which embody a fusion of Greek and Roman legends or motifs. The more modern, and certainly more accurate, term for this series is **Roman Provincial.** Surviving nearly constant challenge for some 500 years, the Roman Empire finally was splintered by external pressure and internal decay. The fall of the western empire in AD 476 marked the end of an era, but the political system established by Rome in its eastern provinces survived and developed in its own unique way.

From Constantinople, the surviving Roman emperors—referred to in modern times as "Byzantine"— presided over a modified form of Roman law and civilization that lasted for another millennium. The term *Byzantine,* like *Greek Imperial,* is outdated and we prefer the more recently popularized term Romaion. The date that numismatists generally accept as the beginning of the **Romaion Empire** is AD 491, which marks the beginning of the reign of Anastasius I. This is a convenient dividing point numismatically, because Anastasius initiated a major reform of the coinage which took on a distinctive character after that. Romaion art and coinage were extremely conservative and reflected the close ties of church and state. The exceptional longevity of the Romaion Empire causes numismatists some problems. It spans, without interruption, the period from the fall of Rome to the rise of modern Europe. Constantinople fell to the Franks in AD 1204, but the Romaions continued their empire in exile at Nicaea and Thessalonica. Romaion coins struck in the 15th century are generally thought of as ancient coins, while coins struck as early as the 8th or 9th century in Western Europe, oddly enough, are regarded as Medieval coins. Perhaps this is because the Romaion series is so distinctly uniform in its iconography and minting practices that it is easy to find a thread of continuity in the series. In this work, we include as ancient only those western issues struck prior to the coronation of Charlemagne in AD 800.

The term "Classical" is often applied to certain coinage from the ancient world, and may cause some confusion. This term, by definition, describes the coinage of the Greeks and Romans (we would include the Romaions). Along with these are included the coinage of local or eastern dynasties subservient to these classical cultures. There are many other civilizations which struck coins in ancient times, and there are subdivisions of infinite variety. For lack of a better term, we will refer to them within the broad framework of **Non-Classical.**

Some Non-Classical coins form mainline collecting areas in themselves—especially those of the Persians, Baktrians, Indo Scythians, Parthians and Sasanians. We also consider Islamic coins issued up to the Mongol conquest, and early coins of India, as ancient. Each forms a

4

very large and important series. In fact, Islamic coinage presents such a large series that in variety of types, it rivals classical coinage. There are simply too many small kingdoms of the ancient world to name here, but the collector with true grit will find them, learn about them and maybe become an expert in one of them.

Consequently, the main divisions of ancient coinage that we encounter today, and that we will be discussing in this book, are Greek, Roman Republican (including Imperatorial), Roman Imperial, Roman Provincial, Romaion (Byzantine) and Non-Classical. The period encompassed by these coins is from about 625 BC to AD 1453.

Major Categories of Ancient Coins

GREEK: ca. 625 BC to 30 BC (death of Cleopatra)

ROMAN REPUBLIC: ca. 289 BC to 41 BC (last moneyer issues)

IMPERATORIAL: ca. 60 BC to 27 BC (1st Triumvirate to Augustus)

ROMAN: 27 BC to AD 491 (accession of Anastasius I)

ROMAN PROVINCIAL: 27 BC to AD 297 (last coinage of Roman Egypt)

ROMAION (BYZANTINE): AD 491 to AD 1453.

NON-CLASSICAL: ca. 550 BC to AD 1258 (Mongol conquests)

Timeline of Numismatic History

Date	Greek / RP	Roman / Romaion	Non-Classical
600 BC			
550 BC			
500 BC	*Greek*		
450 BC			*Persian*
400 BC			
350 BC			
300 BC			
250 BC			*Baktrian*
200 BC		*Roman Republic*	*Armenian*
150 BC			
100 BC			
50 BC			
0			
AD 50			*Parthian*
AD 100			
AD 150	*Roman Provincial*		
AD 200			
AD 250			
AD 300		*Roman Empire*	
AD 350			
AD 400			*Sasanian*
AD 450			
AD 500			
AD 600			
AD 700			
AD 800		*Romaion (Byzantine)*	*Islamic*
AD 900			
AD 1000			
AD 1100			*Armenian in Cilicia*
AD 1200			
AD 1300			
AD 1400			
AD 1500			

Before discussing the origins of coinage, we should define exactly what the term "coin" implies. For thousands of years, goods were acquired through trade using a system called barter. If one person has a surplus of milk and a shortage of eggs, and another has eggs but no milk, the two can trade one for the other and mutually benefit. Of course they need to determine how many eggs are exchangeable for a jug of milk. As one's surplus mounts from improved production, and other needs increase, there are widening opportunities for barter. There are also greater incentives to assign value— for example, how much are six chickens worth? Finding something of common value, against which commodities can be measured, is the essence of establishing a monetary system. Money does not need to be in the form of coins. In fact, early forms of money included such unlikely objects as sea shells and oxen.

While other objects may work as a medium of exchange, metal has distinct advantages. It is durable, portable and constant in weight and size. An added consideration in ancient times, was that metal was relatively rare and everyone needed it—more so at least than sea shells. Not surprisingly, metal became a form of money very early in the evolution of western civilization. Lumps of gold, silver and bronze were exchanged by weight for a wide variety of commercial goods and services. Under this system every transaction required a cumbersome weighing and testing for purity. What looked like silver on the outside might not be silver on the inside! As political authorities became involved in the management of commerce (taxation) it became possible and advantageous for governing bodies to certify and guarantee the value of a predefined quantity of metal.

This guarantee was assured by the application of a stamp of recognizable design which became known and accepted by traders and neighboring rulers. In this fashion, wealth could be accumulated and relocated, because the problems associated with storage and transportation were greatly reduced.

Lydian Electrum,
first coins of the West

The first precious metal "coins" were actually neither gold nor silver. In the streams of Lydia, in western Asia Minor, alluvial gold and silver washed out of the ore-rich mountains and was gathered by local inhabitants much like placer gold is panned yet today. The natural amalgam of these two metals, pounded together as they tumbled down the mountain streams, is light yellow in appearance and is called *electrum.*

At some point in the late seventh century BC, electrum pellets were acquired by traders or rulers and stamped with the intention of using them for exchange. The dating of the first Greek coins has been a matter of controversy for some time. The issue hinges on the dating of a deposit of coins, including some of the earliest types, found in the early 1900s at Ephesos during an archaeological excavation. The coins were apparently buried as an offering beneath a foundation stone at the Temple of Artemis. The temple itself was built in 625 BC, so the dating of these coins was determined to be earlier than that time—with some estimates pushing the envelope backward to 650 BC. By the middle of the twentieth century, a review of the excavation of the Artemesion had determined that the foundation beneath which these coins were found was actually from a later addition to the temple. This prompted scholars to rethink the dating of these coins and it became accepted practice to rather loosely date the first coins as being struck "before 561 BC". The precise date is unknown, but it seems based on current information that 650 BC is perhaps too early and 561 BC is too late.

The earliest stamped electrum specimens that we are aware of do not exhibit designs of any distinguishable type. They simply have striations on their surfaces and incuse marks from being struck by a crude punch. Before long, however, designs began to appear with some

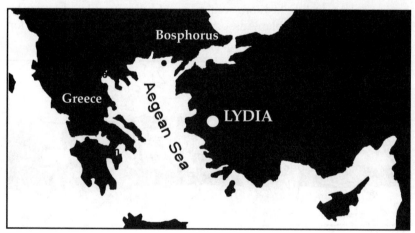

regularity. Among these are images of animals, and particularly of the Bull and Lion which were culturally symbolic in Lydia. It has been suggested that the earliest of these images were the personal badges of important officials. One early stater bearing the im-

AR Double Siglos of Croesus,
ca. 560-546

age of a stag was inscribed with the words "I am the badge of Phanes". The concept of marking coinage with representative designs was quickly adopted by cities within and beyond Lydia, including many places in the islands. Shortly thereafter, cities on the Greek mainland began striking their own coins in silver.

King Croesus ascended the throne of Lydia in 561 BC, acquiring substantial wealth and power. Early in his reign he issued electrum coins, but soon realized the advantage of dividing the two metals and producing separate denominations of pure gold and silver. Before long, this "bi-metallic" system of coinage was adopted throughout the Greek world.

The bi-metallic system of coinage was also adopted by the Persians, who had conquered the armies of Croesus in 546 BC and by the end of the sixth century controlled most of Asia Minor. They struck gold "Darics," named after the great king Darios, and the corresponding silver coin called a "Siglos," in huge quantities. The Daric became a standard trade coin east of the Bosphorus. Naturally, authorities who struck coins and guaranteed their acceptability also took steps to control their production. Therefore, from a very early date, the authority to strike coins was a carefully protected

Persian gold Daric
5th century BC
(enlarged)

right and a privilege bestowed by great rulers on favored cities. Among the Greeks, autonomy was a highly coveted status. Coins struck by these honored cities often heralded their autonomy and propaganda became commonplace in the coin designs as well as in the inscriptions that were to follow. When autonomy was not possible, coin inscriptions usually paid homage in some fashion to the ruling power of the moment.

The coins of Aigina, an island in the Saronic Gulf which separates Attica from the Peloponnesus, were among the earliest issued in Greece proper. The island was very successful in commerce, and their coins were widely distributed as the result of a growing trade. The characteristic device used on early coins of Aigina was a sea turtle, which reminded everyone who came into contact with the coins that the island was an important maritime center. Other mainland cities quickly followed

9

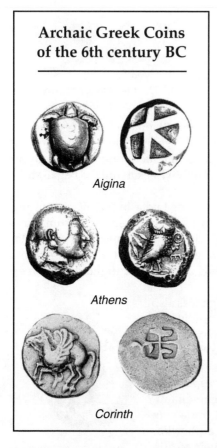

Archaic Greek Coins of the 6th century BC

Aigina

Athens

Corinth

suit and within the short span of less than a century Greece was a hotbed of numismatic activity. The Turtles of Aigina, Owls of Athens, Colts of Corinth, and a variety of other distinctive blazons became well known and respected throughout the ancient world.

The early issues of these Greek cities are characterized by incuse punches on the reverse and by an archaic style of representation in the imagery. Rather quickly, the crude punch mark reverse gave way to increasingly sophisticated punch mark designs and then to images on both sides of the coin. Concurrently, the development of art led to more realistic or "classical" renderings of coin images. This phenomenon will be discussed in a later section.

Another notable characteristic of the earliest coins is the nature of the coin module itself, which numismatists refer to as "fabric". The fabric of early archaic issues is usually thick and crude or "dumpy". As the artistic execution of images on coins improved, so too did the mint's technical ability. Dumpy flans were gradually replaced by thinner, more uniform, flans which offered better surfaces for the transfer of sophisticated images.

One thing that even the most novice of collectors will notice is that every ancient coin is different from the next. Even two coins struck from the same pair of dies will be different. This is because each coin was struck by hand, with differing alignment, different pressures, and sometimes at different temperatures. When everything went smoothly, the result was an individual work of art. When things did not go smoothly, it could be very interesting, to say the least.

The earliest coins were marked with a single punch. In order to keep the lump of metal (planchet) from sliding around, lines were scratched into the anvil. Someone, either with an artistic flair or a need to identify specific pieces, devised the scheme of placing a design on the punch. This led quickly to the engraving of complex designs and images into the punch. In order for the designs to be visible on a coin, they needed to be raised off the surface. This required the engraving of the image into the die in reverse, which is called *intaglio*. Thus, dies were born. If one punch can produce an image on a coin, why not two? Within only a few years of the advent of coinage, obverses and reverses appeared. Normally, the obverse die was anchored in a solid anvil, and the reverse die was engraved into the face of a punch—but there are notable exceptions and the obverse or more important image was not necessarily engraved into the anvil die. Dies were sometimes made of iron, but iron is not easily engraved. Bronze is much softer and easier to work. When

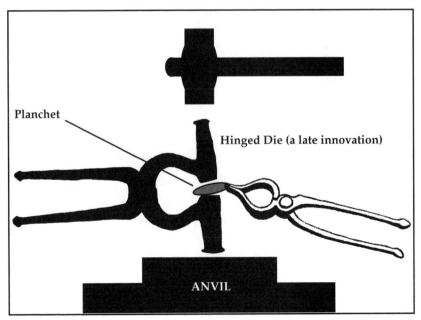

Planchet

Hinged Die (a late innovation)

ANVIL

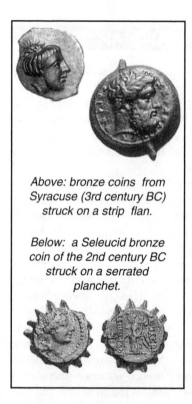

Above: bronze coins from Syracuse (3rd century BC) struck on a strip flan.

Below: a Seleucid bronze coin of the 2nd century BC struck on a serrated planchet.

AR Denarius
of T. Carisius, 46 BC,
with tongs, hammer
and anvil—mint tools.

annealed (heated and cooled slowly) it becomes stronger and less brittle. This proved to be a workable metal for almost all die-engravers.

The striking process was simple enough. Planchets were made by pouring molten metal into a mold. When the mold cooled, the planchets were extracted and saved until needed. Sometimes they were hammered flat on top and bottom to make the striking easier. The prepared surface of a planchet, or the surface (particularly the edge) of a coin after it is struck, is referred to as the *flan*. The planchet was reheated to a point slightly lower than the melting point of the metal, and it was placed with tongs between the anvil and punch dies. The punch die was then struck with a hammer to squash the metal between the dies. If the temperature was right, and the dies were aligned properly, and the planchet was placed in the center of the dies, and the hammer found its mark squarely, and the planchet didn't stick to the die, there was a fairly good chance that the images would transfer cleanly from the dies to the planchet.

In one minting process, planchets were cast in strips of round blanks connected by a narrow bridge. These strips would then be reheated and each blank would be struck between obverse and reverse dies. When all of the blanks had been struck, they would be chopped or twisted apart creating separate coins. This technique is especially apparent in the remaining sprues seen on certain coins of southern Italy and Sicily, as well as on some bronze coins of Judaea, Roman Egypt, and of some Islamic dynasties. Planchets were also cast in particular shapes, especially with bevelled or serrated edges, and they were prepared for striking by a variety of hammering, grinding, and polishing techniques. The bevelled edge on a cast planchet made removal of the cooled blank from the mold much easier. Circulating coins were sometimes recalled and used as blanks. The result is called an *overstrike.* If the new strike was well placed, the *undertype* may have been completely erased, but often the strike was weak and the undertype still shows through. It is a challenge sometimes to identify the undertype from the remaining evidence.

No doubt, with the demands for coinage being very great, mint supervisors pushed workers to produce as many units per day as possible. That any at all turned out well is surprising. That many turned out beautiful, is amazing. Mint workers must have been talented and adequately motivated. In cases where they were not, it becomes obvious.

The alignment of obverse and reverse dies was not a concern for run-of-the-mill token coinage. But it *was* a concern for semi-precious metal coins that circulated around the ancient world and visually demonstrated the level of a society's technological expertise. Keeping dies aligned manually must have proven difficult, but eventually an inventive mint worker devised the hinged die. This kept the obverse and reverse dies in perfect alignment for every strike. This alignment is referred to as *die axis,* and is a subject of great interest to numismatists studying mint production.

There were, of course, times when things did not go well at the mint. Dies had to be replaced on a regular basis because they tended to shatter when they got old and brittle. If an errant worker missed placing a planchet on the die, and his companion hit the die with a hammer, it tended to make a mess of things. If the die didn't actually shatter, the reverse die became a punch and its image was transferred to the obverse die. This is called a *clashed die.* Coins struck after the clash will exhibit a faint impression of the reverse die on the obverse of the coin— or vice-versa. If the die started to break up, and pieces of metal disappeared, the coins struck from that die would show the deterioration. Sometimes, we can trace the deterioration of a die through specimens found together in a hoard. This is especially useful for analyzing the

sequence of use between different obverse and reverse dies. If a die was simply worn, and not badly damaged, it was sometimes pulled off line and re-engraved. A coin struck from a reingraved die can usually be spotted with careful examination with a high power loupe.

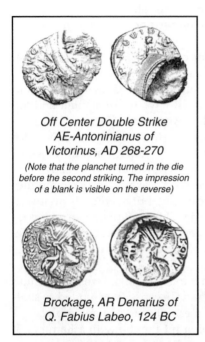

Off Center Double Strike AE-Antoninianus of Victorinus, AD 268-270

(Note that the planchet turned in the die before the second striking. The impression of a blank is visible on the reverse)

Brockage, AR Denarius of Q. Fabius Labeo, 124 BC

Occasionally, in the rush of business, the hammer wielder hit the die twice before a planchet could clear—causing a *double strike*. If the planchet did not move very much, the result was simply a shadow around the image. If the coin was half way out of the die when the hammer fell the second time, another strike was registered, but very much off center. Another problem that occurred with some frequency, was a struck coin sticking to the obverse or reverse die. When this happened, another planchet could easily be placed on top of or beneath the struck coin. This, in effect, made the first coin a die. When the hammer fell again, the images were transferred, but the image transferred from the first coin would be *incuse*. That is, it would be indented into the surface rather than raised. This mint error is called a *brockage,* and ancient brockages are encountered from time to time. In rare instances, one may encounter a brockage and double strike on the same specimen. There are many other mint problems that can be detected by studying the surface of a coin, and this is one of the charming things about *hammered* coins. As with error coins of all periods, ancient errors are highly collectable.

Another activity of the mint was the *counter-marking* of coins which had previously been in circulation. This was done in order to re-tariff coins whose value had changed, or to indicate acceptance of coins produced by another regime. Counter-marks may take the form of simple letters, or elaborate tiny images. They usually were created by punching the detail into the surface of a coin, without regard to the quality of execution. Therefore, they appear in

Bronze coin of Numidia (2nd-1st c. BC) countermarked with a caduceus symbol

the most objectionable places—like the face of a ruler or deity. Some mints actually tried to place the countermarks in a preferred spot, and met with limited success. For example, coins of Tarkondimotus, the King of Cilicia, often bear an anchor counter-mark which is invariably placed beneath the portrait. Sometimes countermarks appear with regularity on either the obverse or reverse of the host coin, other times they appear indiscriminately. Countermarks are very important to the historian, especially in the Roman period, as the movement of Legions and magistrates is traced. Virtually every ancient culture used counter-marks in some form, and they are, like errors, very collectable.

There are other marks on coins that were not produced by the mint, including *banker's marks* and *graffiti*. Banker's marks are usually tiny punch marks that served like the assayer's marks of the early American West. They may be tiny circles or letters or simply little chop marks. Graffiti is simply the scratching of letters on a coin by someone who owned it along the way.

During shortages of coinage in general, or of particular denominations, coins were cut into segments. These *cut coins* are typically found in halves and quarters. Some were clearly cut with a tool, as the edges are very straight. They are usually well worn, indicating a shortage of coins in circulation. Others, like the coins of Nemausus which are often found broken in half, do not show chisel marks. Furthermore, they are always broken precisely between the two portraits. These coins may have been

AE as of Augustus and Agrippa Nemausus, ca. AD 10-14 divided for revaluation

divided by Roman officials as part of a monetary revaluation. For an interesting article explaining this theory see Marvin Tameanko, *The Celator,* September 1996, pp. 6-11. It would seem, however, that the majority of cut coins were created in commerce as a matter of necessity.

Sometimes, a whole issue of coins was restruck over a particular host coin. Most of the Bar Kochba War denarii, for example, were struck over circulating Roman denarii. Ironically, the portrait of a Roman emperor is sometimes visible beneath the design of this coin of the Jewish rebellion against Rome. The ultimate example of this is a specimen struck over a Vespasian Judaea

Bar kochba, AR zuz, year 3 (CE 134/5) overstruck on a Judaea Capta denarius

Capta denarius issued after the Roman victory in the First Jewish War. This specimen was the subject of articles by Harlan J. Berk and David Hendin in *The Celator*, February 1992, pp. 6 and 7.

Nearly all of the conditions mentioned above, since they have to do with the physical characteristics of a coin, will be considered again in the later section about factors affecting coin value.

Studying mint practices, and tracing the development of minting technology can be quite interesting. Relatively few artifacts remain from actual mint operation. The tools of their trade were carefully protected—for the obvious reason that unauthorized coins could be made with stolen dies—and mintmasters were undoubtedly charged with destruction of the dies and tools in an emergency. Nevertheless, actual dies have survived. Cornelius Vermeule compiled a catalog of existing ancient coin dies in an article titled "Some Notes on Ancient Dies and Coining Methods" (*Numismatic Circular*, Spink & Son, London, 1954). This was updated by William Malkmus in The Journal of the Society of Ancient Numismatics, *SAN*, XVII and XVIII.

Much of what we know about minting practices comes from examination of the coins themselves, especially when intact hoards are available for study. The publication of hoards is important to future as well as present study, and several recent hoards have been documented with excruciating care. The Royal Numismatic Society, in London, publishes a continuing series of books and articles recording all known coin hoards and details of their publication.

There have been many excellent articles and books written about the technology of coin production. Elvira Clain-Stefanelli's bibliography, for example, contains six pages of titles on this subject alone. A good general introduction is Denis R. Cooper's *The Art and Craft of Coinmaking: A History of Minting Technology* (London, 1988).

Roman obverse die for an aureus or denarius of Vespasian (AD 69-79) found in Yugoslavia, type of RIC 123-124 struck AD 74-79

The Perfectly Designed Coin

The design of a die has much to do with its success in producing coins of beauty, but it must also take into consideration the technical aspects of coin production. The transfer of an image from the die to a hot planchet (P) requires a great deal of force, and the distribution of that force is important to the integrity of the image as well as the life of the die. If the force is unbalanced, metal will not flow properly into the detail areas of the die. The resulting stress will cause the die to fragment and gradually disintegrate. This process is sometimes seen on the surface of a coin in the form of lines or lumps of extraneous metal as voids in a disintegrating die are filled. Remember that the die is engraved with an intaglio image so that the coin image is positive.

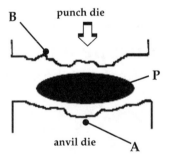

This Hellenistic Greek coin from Myrina, in Aeolia (ca. 165 BC), was struck in very high relief. This required a large amount of metal to fill the center of the obverse die (A). For this reason, the obverse die was placed on the anvil. The highest point of relief, by design, is at the center of the obverse, where the maximum amount of metal will flow when the reverse die is struck with a hammer. The lowest relief is at the center of the reverse. The result is a slightly concave reverse. In order to reduce flatness on the edges of the reverse design, from striking and wear, the artist has reduced the size of the image and placed the letters bearing the city name within a protective wreath of higher relief (B). The effect is subtle, but noticeable when compared to other specimens of the same type that were not so expertly designed.

I t is not the purpose of this volume to detail the coinage of various cultures from antiquity; a set of companion volumes will serve that need. But it may be helpful to introduce the various cultures that produced the coinage we plan to explore. The following capsules do not do justice to the complexity of each collecting area, but they will at least present the general categories of ancient coins that we have touched on earlier and that one will typically see offered for sale. Suggestions about how to identify these coins more precisely are included in a later chapter.

The Greek and Roman worlds, and to some extent the later Romaion Empire, overlap in many respects. Although political boundaries are not necessarily the same, most countries that came under Roman rule also produced coinage during the period we refer to as *Greek*. The term Greek in this sense is not really Greek in the ethnic sense. Included in the Greek section of most catalogues or commercial price lists will be coinage of many peripheral cultures that have no real connection ethnically or politically with the people that settled in mainland Greece or its many colonies. This is a matter of expediency in cataloguing and not a reflection of any historical link.

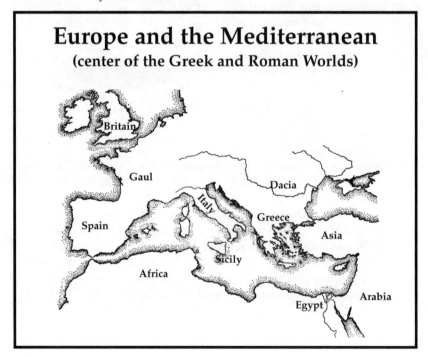

Europe and the Mediterranean
(center of the Greek and Roman Worlds)

The coinage of the Greeks is divided into three main chronological phases. The earliest of these, the Archaic Period, spans the years from the invention of coinage down to the Greek victory over Persia in 479 BC. From that date to the accession of Alexander the Great as King of Macedon in 336 BC is known as the Classical Period. The last phase of Greek cultural dominance, known as the Hellenistic Period, ended in 30 BC with the death of Cleopatra. The Greeks (Hellenes) derived their name

Sicily, Himera - AE Hemilitron
before 407 BC
actual size 17mm

from Hellen, the mythical son of Pyrrha and Deucalion (the Greek "Noah"). These "periods" of Greek culture are arbitrary and are a creation of the modern mind. One will also see references to transitional periods, and other creative divisions, but the primary periods are Archaic, Classical and Hellenistic. Although the dates are tied to major political events, these periods actually reflect a recognition of changes in artistic style and cultural adjustments. It is probably not coincidental that these artistic and political milestones converge.

Many Greek cities struck coins continuously from the Archaic Period down to the Roman conquest and then continued to strike coinage in the name of Rome and its emperors. Through the coinage of these cities, it is interesting to observe the changes that occurred over a span of six or seven hundred years. When examining the Greek series of coinage, there is a natural tendency to think in artistic rather than political terms. Looking at the popular tetradrachms from Athens, one can see early, middle and late styles—but we seldom think of Pericles or Demosthenes. Because they are appreciated as works of art, it is easy to forget the political aspects of Greek coinage. Even the minor coinage of the Greek world can wonderfully illustrate the celator's skill. A fine example is the tiny bronze coin illustrated above. Changes in artistic style are discussed in the later chapter about connoisseurship, but we will briefly examine here the political changes that occurred during this same time frame.

Greek society reflected a strong individualism and sense of self-determination. This is the origin of our concept of democracy. Consequently,

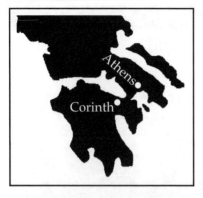

Greek cities and colonies were fiercely independent and resisted centralized controls. Even their coinage was produced on a variety of different weight standards. Cities as close to each other as Athens and Corinth maintained their own distinct monetary systems.

The most important factor in uniting the Greeks was a threat from outside the Hellenic world. In 547 BC, Cyrus the Great with his united Persian forces overthrew King Croesus of Lydia and assumed control of Asia Minor. This was a concern to mainland Greeks, because of the number of Greek colonies established there. The real threat did not emerge, however, until 490 BC when the Persians advanced on Greece itself. The Athenian victory at Marathon boosted the morale of the entire Greek world, but the Persians under Xerxes launched another invasion of Greece in 480. Although hard pressed, the Greeks prevailed in an epic

naval battle near Salamis and on land at Plataea. These victories, which assured the independence of Greek cities, also liberated the pent-up energy of a society ready to bloom. The resulting Golden Age of Pericles and its flourishing of the arts is evident in virtually every trade and industry. Colonization of southern Italy and Sicily was expanded, and it was during this period that the Parthenon, with its monumental sculptures, was completed.

The peace was not to be enjoyed for long. Lacking a common enemy, the Greeks reverted to their individualism and began feuding amongst themselves. The Peloponessian War (431-404 BC), between Athens and Sparta, each with its allies, was devastating emotionally, as well as economically. The strain is evidenced in the coinage of the period, especially in that of Athens whose demands for external trade were very great. At the

Syracusan Decadrachm
ca. 385-380 BC
by the artist Euainetos

same time that Athens was struggling, Sicily was enjoying a period of unexcelled creativity. Coinage from Syracuse, Catana, Naxos, Akragas, Gela, Selinos, Messana and Himera captured the essence of the classical age and these cities competed against each other to produce the most spectacular examples of numismatic art that the world has ever seen. Artists were held in such regard that they were allowed to engrave their names into the designs. These "signed" types are extremely popular with collectors today.

In the fourth century, Philip II of Macedon undertook a program of military conquest that once again united the Greeks. Under the leadership of his ambitious son, Alexander the Great (ruled 336-323 BC), conquest became a way of life. Alexander expanded the Greek world to the edge of China, and his successors ruled his fragmented empire for centuries after his death. Egypt was added to the Greek world, and would remain a Greek territory under the Ptolemaic Dynasty for nearly three hundred years.

The third century was marked by wars in the East among Alexander's successors, but important events were also taking shape in the West. The prosperity of Magna Graecia, the Greek colonies in southern Italy, drew attention from all quarters—especially from their northern neighbors, the Romans, and their southern neighbors across the sea at Carthage. Tarentum, one of the most important cities in southern Italy, fell to the Romans in 272 BC.

Siculo-Punic tetradrachm ca. 305-295 BC

They later revolted and allied with Hannibal, but were harshly repressed by Rome. The Punic wars between Carthage and Rome, which engulfed these Greek city-states, left behind a beautiful and interesting series of coins. As the armies of Hannibal, and other Carthaginian generals, captured cities and set up camps in Sicily and Italy, they struck coins with images of Phoenician gods and goddesses, war elephants, palm trees and the like. The Punic Wars weakened the Greek populace, and opened the door to further invasions from Rome. By 210 BC, the Romans were in complete control of Magna Graecia and Sicily. Early in the second century, we see a Romanization of the coinage of southern Italy and Sicily in style and iconography. These coins might actually be considered the first Roman Provincial coins.

By the middle of the second century, the Romans had conquered all of Italy and northern Greece, and had set their sights on lands to the east. There were still autonomous Greek cities and kingdoms in the first century BC, but they were falling fast under Roman expansion. Those cities that maintained some semblance of autonomy usually did so by agreeing to pay tribute to the Romans, both politically and financially. In a few places, traditional kingdoms were allowed to stay in place under Roman supervision and direction. These "Client Kings" were a bridge between the Greek way of life and that of the Romans. Although a few lasted into the third century AD, most had disappeared by the time of Octavian's accession as Emperor of the Romans and assumption of the title Augustus.

The Romans

In contrast to Greek coinage with its artistic attraction, Roman coinage is more historically appealing. That is not to say that Roman portraiture, with its stark realism is not beautiful in its own way, but the series is most often collected for historical reasons.

According to legend, Rome was founded in 753 BC by Romulus—who, along with his twin brother Remus, was raised by a she-wolf. The early history of the city recounts the struggles between contending powers in Italy, but it is not until the Republican period that coinage appears. Prior to 290 BC

Romulus and Remus being suckled by a She-Wolf

the currency of central Italy consisted of irregular lumps of bronze referred to as *Aes Rude*. Like the earliest monetary instruments of the Greek states, this metal was exchanged purely by weight and bore no marks of identification. This is remarkable in light of the wonderful, and apparently plentiful, coinage which had been circulating in southern Italy for 200 years. The isolation between Greeks and Romans during this period could not be better exemplified. The transformation of Roman bronze coinage from bullion to a purely token instrument progressed steadily over a half millennium and is a subject which has drawn much scholarly and collector interest.

In about 290 BC, cast bronze ingots called *Aes Signatum* appeared with designs which seem to have been indicative of a specific value. These ingots were used concurrently with a cast bronze coinage, *Aes Grave*, which was produced at various times in up to seven denominations. At about the same time, die-struck gold, silver and bronze coins began to appear as anonymous issues. That is, they were not struck in the name of a particular official or moneyer, but simply as coins of "Roma." About 211 BC, the denarius appeared as the standard silver coin, with its value preestablished by a closely controlled measure of the precious metal.

The Roman Republican series, especially in the denarii, is fertile collecting ground for the lover of mythology. Countless mythological allusions and references appear as types issued by moneyers who were authorized by the Senate to produce coinage. Often, these moneyers chose imagery which honored their lineage. Since it was considered inappropriate for a living Roman to place his own image on a coin, moneyers frequently portrayed their ancestors and heralded memorable deeds (real or imagined) of honor, virtue or bravery.

The strength of the Republic was severely challenged in the middle of the first century BC as great generals like Pompey and Julius Caesar amassed incredible wealth and power. A period of political turmoil, which we refer to as the "Imperatorial Period," lasted for more than 30 years with several alliances and wars inspiring propagandistic coin types.

Anepigraphic aureus of Augustus issued 32-29 BC

Following the assassination of Julius Caesar, and the subsequent victory by Octavian over Marc Antony, stability returned in the form of an Imperial mandate. Endowed by the Roman Senate with the title *Augustus,* Octavian became sole master of the Roman world in 27 BC. The rise of Roman power is a subject that can fill a library in itself. If the Greeks were the inventors of Democracy, the Romans were the inventors of Bureaucracy. Their centralized system of government generated a tremendous variety of coinage, and its subject matter is filled with intriguing details for the collector. Students of economic history will find that the coins are a reliable and accurate source of information. Inflation caused the gradual debasement of the monetary standard both in weight and purity. For example, a denarius of relatively pure silver that weighed nearly four grams during the time of Julius Caesar was less pure and weighed only about three grams during the reign of Nero. Several

Roman personification of Victory, on a coin of C. Valerius Flaccus

reforms were attempted and new denominations were devised in an effort to shore up the Roman economy in times of financial crisis—but the general trend toward debasement continued relentlessly. In spite of this, the denarius retained its popularity well into the late third century AD, at which time it became essentially a bronze coin with hardly a trace of silver.

The progress of military campaigns, civil construction programs and political alliances may also be studied from these primary sources that are so readily available to the collecting fraternity. Snapshots of Roman customs and traditions are also presented on their coins. For example, one can find representations of wedding ceremonies, the traditional giving of gifts to the people, and the apotheosis (raising to heaven) of the deceased. The rise of Christianity took place in the shadow of Roman power, and there are many references on later Roman coinage to Christianity as a state religion. The subject is a fascinating one for many, since the great persecutions of Christianity were initiated by emperors whose numismatic portraits are readily available.

Reading about the reigns of the emperors, one is struck by the violence that usually accompanied their end. Many were murdered by their Praetorian Praefects, the head of the imperial guard. Others were murdered by their wives or other family members. Some were dragged through the streets of Rome and a few were abandoned to their enemies in the field. A lucky few died of disease or exhaustion. Rarely, they died of natural causes at a respectable age.

It was often the case that emperors ruled until they died, but there were exceptions. Valerian I, who was proclaimed emperor in AD 253, was captured in the field by the Sasanian king Shapur I. Although this ended his reign as emperor, he lived in captivity for many years afterward. It is written that Shapur kept Valerian at hand in order to use him as a foot stool for mounting his horse. In AD 273, Tetricus I abdicated his throne and his military forces to Aurelian, and was given a post in the government where he served as a private citizen in a position of honor. Diocletian, Maximian and Vetranio also abdicated their titles. In fact,

Maximian abdicated twice. The third time, he was killed. Maximus (AD 409-411), a usurper in Spain, received a pardon from Honorius and also retired to private life. Late in the empire, several rulers outlived their positions. Priscus Attalus was deposed to the island of Lipara, Avitus became bishop of Placentia, Glycerius became bishop of Salona and Romulus Augustus, the last emperor of the west, retired to a villa in Campania.

The fortunes of Rome declined severely in the fourth and fifth centuries AD. The strains of maintaining a huge bureaucracy, coupled with a serious influx of unskilled "citizens," sent the Roman economy into serious stages of inflation. The result can be seen in their coinage. There were many attempted monetary reforms, but the situation became progressively worse. By the end of the fifth century, bronze coinage had degenerated to a point where the standard unit was about six or seven millimeters in diameter. These are very crude issues and are only recognizable today because of the monograms which are still readable. Gold coinage remained fairly stable, but the general population had little access to gold. It certainly was not a coin which normally circulated in commerce. All coinage of the emperors claiming authority in the West after AD 476 is rare, but some at least are obtainable in silver or bronze. A few are obtainable only in gold.

The Roman Empire survived for more than 500 years at its capital in the West. Its citizens in the East, the Romaions (Byzantines), survived another 1,000 years. Much of our civilization today, including our language, laws, and bureaucracy is modeled after the Romans. The influence of Rome was so great, even in conquered lands (and some that never were conquered), that languages changed, architecture and technology were imitated, and Roman religious customs were adopted. Their roads and bridges are still seen throughout Europe today, and some are still in use. Their calendar is universally accepted and their alphabet is the basis of most written languages in the West. Clearly, they were achievers.

As the Romans consolidated power in central Italy and became a conquering nation, their influence spread widely and quickly. It was common practice for the Romans, upon seizing control of an area, to appoint a local magistrate or suppliant king under the supervision of a Roman military governor. Local inhabitants were inducted into the Roman army, which proved doubly advantageous. Not only were the ranks of the army swelled, the native populations were slow to challenge Roman authority for fear that their sons would suffer retaliation. As long as provincial cities fulfilled their tax and military levies, they were left with a great degree of latitude in managing their own affairs. The Romans, being extremely pragmatic, even supported local religious practices and carried some of the gods from conquered lands back to the pantheistic temples of Rome.

Mytilene, Valerian I
Artemis in biga of stags

In keeping with this relative freedom, many cities were granted the privilege of striking coins. In fact, titles and honors of various kinds were bestowed by the emperor in order to keep provincial cities productive and competitive. These titular grants were propagandized on local coinage and form a very interesting series for research by the political historian.

Since provincial coinage was struck mainly for use within the confines of a single city or district, it is relatively scarce in comparison to general coinage of the same period. In addition to its characteristically local flavor, Roman provincial coinage is distinguished by its comparative irregularity. Where Imperial coinage is easily recognized by denomination and type, Roman provincial is not. Certain issues appear to parallel Imperial denominations, but the diversity in this series is tremendous.

Kevin Butcher, in his recent monograph *Roman Provincial Coins*, suggests that these coins are the same as Roman imperial coins except for their place of minting and circulation. In general terms, this is true enough. But long before identifying a mint city, the collector will notice other differences between provincial and imperial coins of the Romans. For one thing, portrait styles and legends are much less refined on most provincial coinage. Flan preparation and methods of striking also vary. Immediately apparent, and sometimes a cause of frustration to the beginner, is the unique set of characters and abbreviations found in the inscriptions. The legends themselves are unusual in the sense that they typically include full mint names and a multitude of honorific titles. For many, the appeal of Roman provincial coinage is primarily in its propagandistic themes and art historical or mythological imagery.

Roman provincial coins are a collector's dream, because they lend themselves so well to organization. Many of the coins were struck bearing a series of regnal or foundation dates. These dates run consecutively from the founding of a city and are generally indicated on coins by a combination of Greek letters. Another reason that these coins are great collector material is that they often are quite inexpensively priced. Large diameter specimens with mythological or historical reverses tend to be very popular, and consequently more dear, but unappreciated rarities abound in the smaller diameter and lower grade coins.

For many years, these coins have been known as *Greek Imperial*. The term is still used by many who resist change. This term recognizes the Greek influence on most provincial coins struck east of Italy. There are, however, a number of provincial coins which do not bear Greek inscriptions. These come mainly from Spain and Gaul.

Within the general category of Roman Provincial coins exists the wonderful group of coins struck in Egypt by Roman emperors from Augustus through Galerius. This coinage is so coherent and complete, and has such a distinctive style, that it is basically a series unto itself. The fabric of coins from Roman Egypt is completely different from that of any other Roman province. This in itself is tribute to the tremendous influence and power of Egypt as a supplier of food to Rome and much of its empire. From the time of Octavian's victory over Antony and Cleopatra, Egypt was considered the personal property of the emperor and from it the emperors derived incredible wealth.

AE Drachm of Roman Egypt
Antoninus Pius, year 6 (AD 142/3)
"Hercules capturing the Cretan bull"
(Kerry K. Wetterstrom Collection — CNG XIII lot 201)

The Romaioi (Byzantines)

For over two hundred years, historians and numismatists have been perpetuating a misguided attempt to rename the Eastern Romans surviving after the fall of Italy. An article by Clifton R. Fox in The Celator, *March 1996) suggests a simple solution that is accurate, unbiased and logical. His argument is presented here in abridged form.*

"By modern convention, the phrase "Byzantine Empire" refers to a political entity that once existed in the Mediterranean world. The city called Constantinople or, on today's maps, Istanbul, served as capital of the empire. The Byzantine Empire originated with the founding of Constantinople in the fourth century A.D. on the site of the far more ancient Greek colony of Byzantium. The Roman emperor Constantine I (died A.D. 337) called the site New Rome or Constantinople; Constantine placed his capital in the new city named after himself. A long succession of emperors who followed Constantine I also lived in Constantinople. These monarchs and their subjects experienced and endured centuries of change and struggle. Emperors reigned almost nine centuries over the empire without interruption, until 1204. In that year, Crusaders from Western Europe, diverted from the path to Jerusalem, captured and looted Constantinople. They held the city until 1261. The "Romaioi" restored the Byzantine Empire at Constantinople after the Franks were expelled. In 1453, the Ottoman Turks stormed Constantinople and the Byzantine Empire ceased to exist.

Bronze coin (AD 334) issued by Constantine the Great, commemorating the founding of Constantinople. Note the Christian Chi-Rho symbol in the field.

The role of the Byzantine Empire in European history is not sufficiently understood by the educated public of today. Constantinople stood at the economic, political, and cultural heart of Europe from its founding until its wanton sacking by the Crusaders. The "New Rome" withstood the assault of many attackers, protecting all Europe against the flood of invasion. The Byzantine Empire flourished in the same era that found Western Europe ensnared by poverty and violence. One cannot omit the fact that Constantinople yet remains the religious lodestar of Orthodox Christians: the predominant faith of Russia and other lands is rooted in the Byzantine experience. In spite of its rich heritage and significant role, the achievements of the Byzantine civilization have often been given short shrift and denigrated: the very name is, in fact, an insult.

The phrase "Byzantine Empire" was coined by the eighteenth century French scholar Montesquieu. He was the same author whose seminal volume *The Spirit of the Laws* did much to inspire the founding

Europe

Byzantium

Asia Minor

fathers of the United States in their writing of the Constitution. Like other thinkers of his time, Montesquieu admired the ancient Greeks and Romans with immoderate enthusiasm—as masters of politics and culture to be emulated. Following a Western European tradition that extended back to the early Middle Ages, Montesquieu regarded the empire at Constantinople as corrupt and decadent. Although he wrote a long history of the empire at Constantinople, Montesquieu could not bear to refer to it with the noble names of "Greek" or "Roman." From the obsolete name Byzantium, Montesquieu coined the word "Byzantine." The word Byzantine denoted both the empire and its supposed characteristics: dishonesty, dissimulation, and decadence.

The people who lived in the Byzantine Empire never knew nor used the word Byzantine. They knew themselves to be Romans, nothing more and absolutely nothing less. By transferring the Imperial capital from Rome on the Tiber to the "New Rome" on the Bosphorus, Constantine I had transferred the actual identity of Rome to the new location. Long before Constantine I, the idea of "Rome" had become dissociated from the Eternal City on the Tiber. Before the Imperial period, in 89 B.C., a Roman law had granted Roman citizenship to people throughout Italy. Afterwards, citizenship was granted to an increasing number of people in different parts of the empire. In A.D. 212, the emperor Caracalla declared all free persons in the empire to be Roman citizens, entitled to call themselves Roman, not merely subject to the Romans. Within a few decades, people began to refer to the entire empire less often (in Latin) as "Imperium Romanorum" (Domain of the Romans) and more often as "Romania" (Romanland).

In the provinces close to Constantinople, where the Greek language predominated over the Latin of old Rome, the idea of Roman citizenship and identity appealed to a broad segment of the population. Greek speaking citizens were proud to be Romans: in Latin, "Romani," or in Greek, "Romaioi." The word "Romaioi" became descriptive of the Greek speaking population of the empire; the old term "Hellene" fell into disuse. In ancient times, "Hellene" had meant Greek: this was the case from the seventh century B.C. onward—if not earlier. Pericles, Plato, and Alexander were "Hellenes," as were Greek speaking inhabitants of the Roman Empire in the first and second centuries A.D. In the fourth century A.D., as the empire became Christianized, the term "Hellene" became redefined by common convention to include people who still worshipped the old gods and studied philosophy in hopes of resisting the new faith of Christianity. Emperor Julian II (A.D. 361-363), an emperor who tried to stop the Christian tide, described himself as a "Hellene." By "Hellene," Julian signified his combination of Neo-Platonic philosophy and worship of the Olympians.

In the final years of the fourth century A.D., the emperor Theodosius I (A.D. 379-395) made Christianity the sole state religion after subduing the rebellion of a "Hellene" usurper. After Theodosius' fateful decision, fewer and fewer people were willing to call themselves "Hellenes." For centuries, the word "Hellene" remained in bad repute, associated with outlawed religious ideas and disloyalty to the state. Greek speakers found the identity of "Romaioi" in place of "Hellene" to be a safe refuge in changing times. Greek speaking Romaioi inhabited the empire until its end in the fifteenth century.

AR Miliaresion of Michael II (AD 820-821) with legend describing the emperor as "Basileus Romaion" [Emperor of the Romans]

The empire at Constantinople should not, perhaps, be called the Byzantine Empire at all. If it requires a special name, we might better associate the empire at Constantinople with the title "Romaion Empire" (Empire of the Romaioi).

Medieval westerners referred to the territory of the Romaion Empire with the name "Romania" (Roman-land). They did not call themselves Romans, or refer to their homeland as Romania. These words were conceded, albeit grudgingly, to Constantinople. When the Franks of the Fourth Crusade stormed Constantinople in 1204, these adventurers elected their own emperor, and established their own Frankish or Latin empire. The Imperial title was "Imperator Romaniae" (Emperor of Romania).

In the eleventh century, a branch of the Seljuk Turks established a Sultanate in Asia Minor carved out of lands of the Romaioi. The Sultanate's territory had been severed from the empire after the Battle of Manzikert (1071) in which emperor Romanus IV fell into the hands of the Turks as a prisoner. This Turkish state was called "Rum" [Rome]. The Sultanate of Rum continued until after 1300, with its capital at Konya (Iconium). Later, the Ottoman Turks adopted the term "Rumelia" to designate the portions of the Balkan Peninsula that they acquired from the Romaioi in the fourteenth century.

One might wonder why the name "Romania" became applied to the present nation of that name. The association actually stems from nineteenth century politics and diplomacy. In light of the late date at which modern Romania acquired its name, it appears clear that earlier, the term Romania referred to the territory where the Greek speaking Romaioi lived. For more than a millennium, the state that we call, inaccurately, the Byzantine Empire was Romania. After the end of the empire, Greek speaking inhabitants of the Ottoman Empire continued to call themselves Romaioi.

The names by which things are called are important in shaping our interpretation of reality. People are often surprised to discover that historical labels which define the past are inventions of later scholarship and ideology, not parts of the past itself. Men and women of the Middle Ages did not know that they lived in the Middle Ages: people who lived in Classical Athens or Renaissance Italy suffered the same disability. The people of the "Byzantine Empire" had no idea that they were Byzantine. They regarded themselves as the authentic continuators of the Roman world: the Romans living in Romania.

Numismatics permits us to view primary evidence of the past with our own eyes. We read the names of peoples, places, and institutions as they were known in the languages and thoughts of the past, unfiltered by the needs and ideologies of later ages."

The most notable and consistent feature of Romaion coinage is that it is dominated by Christian iconography. As the Eastern capital developed politically, it also matured as the seat of the most important leaders of the Christian church. The fusion of church and state occurred officially during the reign of Constantine the Great, when he accepted Christianity as *one* of the state religions, and was cemented by Theodosius I when he extended those ties by making Christianity the *sole* state religion. This fusion led to a conservative program of religious art that is manifested on the earliest of Romaion coins and continues through the fall of Constantinople to the Turks.

Portrayals of the cross and of the saints are common, but no figure appears so regularly as that of Christ himself. From bold nimbate portrait busts to

The earliest numismatic portrait of Christ, on a gold solidus of Justinian II (AD 685-695)

standing or enthroned figures, the representation of Christ is far and away the most common theme in Romaion numismatic art.

There was a period, however, when images of Christ were not allowed. This period of Iconoclasm (destruction of religious images) lasted from AD 726 to 842. It was, in part, a reaction to the successful rise of Islam, which rejected a reverence of pictures. The Romaions seemed, for a time, to be following suit just in case there was something offensive to the Almighty. They questioned that if victory comes through the intervention of God, why was He helping the Muslims? During this period, religious images are absent from Romaion coinage, and most artists and craftsmen fled to Italy where they were able to work. The accession of the Macedonian Dynasty marked the end of this philosophy and, like a phoenix, the rebirth of imagery shows clear signs of classical inspiration, even though the subjects remained conservative. This golden age lasted nearly until the Latin sack of Constantinople in AD 1204.

In that year, a group of Crusaders, on their way to the Holy Land, decided instead to lay siege to Constantinople. They invaded the Golden Horn by capturing the garrisoned fortification at Galata and lowering the huge chain that sealed off the entrance to the strait—thus allowing their ships to enter. These Franks accomplished what invading armies for centuries were unable to achieve. The sack of Constantinople was a barbarous act, with many people put to the sword. During the seige, a 1,600-year-old bronze statue, cast by Pheidias in the fourth century BC, was torn down by an angry mob and destroyed—thinking that it had beckoned the invaders. Great buildings were razed and libraries were burned.

Although the city was eventually recovered, and the Romaion Emperors restored their residence, the strength of the empire was dissipated. Nearing the final fall of Constantinople, Romaion coinage suffers technically and artistically, as abstraction of every element becomes

John VIII AD 1423-1448
AR Stavraton
bust of Christ/bust of John

commonplace. If coins reflect the prosperity of a nation, the Romaions were due for a disaster in 1453.

As a sequel, the conquering Turks actually treated the city with much greater respect than the Latins had in the 13th century. Christians were allowed to continue their worship and buildings of great antiquity were restored by the Ottoman Sultans. Ironically, Constantinople again became the jewel of the Bosphorus—and the crossroads of the East and West—but not as a Roman or Romaion capital.

Musa, Parthian Queen
2 BC-AD 4
AR Tetradrachm

There were so many coins struck by Non-Classical cultures in the ancient world that one could hardly list them all. The most evident ones are those that appear regularly in sale catalogues. But this is not really a good indication of the complexity of the field. Many of the coins seldom appear in a catalog, because they are difficult to attribute, there is not a stable market, and often they do not sell for enough money to warrant the expense of listing them.

Occasionally, someone will write a book about coins of an obscure series and enthusiasm will be rekindled at least for a time. Mostly, however, the collecting interest in these coins is too marginal to cause them to be highlighted. This is a somewhat bittersweet situation. It may be hard to locate such coins, even if they are very common. And, it is hard to learn the series because little is written about them. The advantage, however, is that any collector with persistence can become *the* world expert. This is truly the essence of numismatics as a science, and anyone can play. You don't need a PhD, or a curatorial position. You probably *do* need access to a good university library though. It is amazing how much information is buried in obscure articles. The nineteenth century was a very productive one for numismatists, and they wrote about some of the most obscure coins and cultures that one can imagine. Locating those articles is the catch. Armed with the knowledge of a century past, one can easily begin to apply the corrections and additions that time has given us. Another advantage to collecting coins in a field that is underappreciated is that specimens will usually cost much less than equivalent rarities in one of the more popular collecting areas.

The coins of a few Non-Classical cultures have enjoyed great popularity and their coins are very well published. Judaean coins, for example, appear in virtually every auction. Coins of the Celts and Armenians are also very popular. Others like the Aksumites, Sabaeans and Turkomans are fairly well published, but not generally as popular or prevalent in the market. Coinage of the various Germanic Kingdoms that ruled Western Europe after the fall of Rome is not as well published, and seldom appears on the market in any quantities.

There has been a resurgence in recent years of interest in coins of the Persians and their successors. This is due partly to a migration of educated Iranians to the West. Along with their skills, they have brought an intense interest in their cultural heritage. Thus, the market for ancient Persian, Parthian and Sasanian coins is becoming quite well developed, and there are many offerings at the moment. Another field of rather limited, but increasing, interest is Islamic coins. Islam has interacted with so many cultures that one cannot help but find correlations, no matter what series one collects. The coinage of India is so vast, and the written history is so sparse, that it has never been fully catalogued. The Kushan coins of ancient India, especially in gold, are readily obtainable. Later minor coinage of India is very diverse and relatively inexpensive.

Listed on the following page are some of the popular collecting fields that fall under the general category of Non-Classical cultures. A short description of each is offered in the chapter *Identifying Ancient Coins.* The collector who discovers an interest in any one of these fields should locate a copy of the recommended introduction and examine the bibliography in that work. This is the fastest and easiest way to find valuable source material.

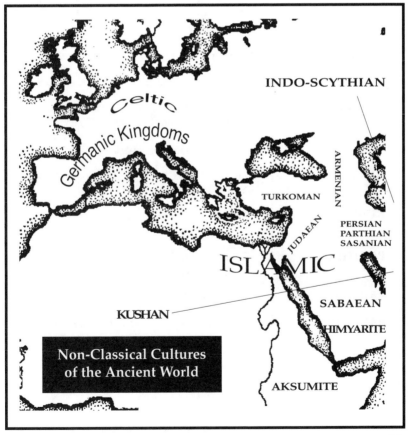

INDO-SCYTHIAN

Celtic

Germanic Kingdoms

ARMENIAN

TURKOMAN

JUDAEAN

PERSIAN
PARTHIAN
SASANIAN

ISLAMIC

KUSHAN

SABAEAN

HIMYARITE

Non-Classical Cultures
of the Ancient World

AKSUMITE

List of Non-Classical Ancient World Cultures

Culture	Recommended Introduction
AKSUMITE	Munro-Hay, and Juel-Jenson. *Aksumite Coinage*, London, 1995.
ARMENIAN	Nercessian, Y.T.. *Armenian Coins and Their Values*, Los Angeles, 1995
BARBARIAN	Grierson and Blackburn. *Medieval European Coinage*, Cambridge, 1986.
CELTIC	Van Arsdell, Robert D. *Celtic Coinage of Britain*, London, 1989.
CHINESE	Schjoth, F. *Chinese Currency, The Schjoth Collection at the University of Oslo*, Oslo, Norway, 1929.
HIMYARITE	Mitchiner, Michael. *Oriental Coins ..as above*
INDO-SCYTHIAN	Mitchiner, Michael. *Oriental Coins ..as above*
ISLAMIC	Album, Stephen. *Marden's Numismata Orientalia Illustrata* New York, 1977, along with *A Checklist of Popular Islamic Coins* by the same author, Santa Rosa, CA 1993.
JUDAEAN	Hendin, David. *Guide to Biblical Coins*, New York, 2002.
KUSHAN	Göbl, R. Münzprägung des Kusanreiche, Vienna, 1974.
PARTHIAN	Shore, Fred B. *Parthian Coins and History: Ten Dragons Against Rome*, Quarryville, PA, 1993.
SABAEAN	Mitchiner, Michael. *Oriental Coins ..as above*
SASANIAN	Sellwood, Whitting and Williams. *An Intro–duction to Sasanian Coins*, London, 1985.
TURKOMAN	Spengler and Sayles, *Turkoman Figural Bronze Coins and Their Iconography*. 3 vol. (2 in print). Lodi, WI, 1992, 1996.

THE ANTIQUARIAN TRADITION
Our Place in History

W e are not the first to walk this path, nor will we be the last. The allure and romance of the past is timeless and compelling. Humans are an egocentric species. We tend to see ourselves at the center of the universe, and it takes real focus for us to realize and understand that what we know and feel has been known and felt before. Fortunately, as humans, we also have a tendency to record our discoveries and our experiences. The preserved records of the past are today's history. The historical record does not tell us only about kings and emperors or great deeds, it tells us about the interests of people just like us. It tells us about their prejudices and perceptions, and about their hobbies.

Collecting probably did not start out as a hobby, but more as a pack-rat mentality to accumulate anything useful. Cave inhabitants were certainly accumulators if not collectors. However, when we find items of beauty in a burial site we have to wonder if these things were not appreciated as more than something that was simply useful. When we find several such things, we must wonder if they were collected.

Recorded history is more illuminating. We know that people from ancient civilizations were collectors, because they tell us so. We also know that collectors have always enjoyed discourse with other collectors, because we can read the letters that they exchanged. These letters reveal an awareness and level of scholarship that often shocks our modern egocentric minds. How often have we heard that the ancients thought the world was flat? Coins tell us otherwise. In fact, Krates of Mallos was commissioned in the 2nd century BC by the Pergamene King Atallus to erect a ten foot diameter world globe at Pergamum. Not only did the globe portray a spherical earth, but the existence of three unexplored continents across the seas. The thought that great libraries existed before the invention of the Dewey Decimal System is somehow alien to us—but they did. If only we could have back the great libraries of Pergamum and Alexandria! If only we could have back the books burned during

Modern Reconstruction
The Globe of Krates

the Holy Inquisition! What is lost is lost forever, but we do enjoy a rich legacy of antiquarian studies, compiled over hundreds of years by some very great minds. These antiquarians are part of an ongoing tradition that as ancient coin collectors we are privileged to inherit.

The Celator journal runs a monthly feature titled "Profiles in Numismatics" which presents a short biography of an important contributor in the history of ancient numismatics. The journal has thus far honored nearly 200 great numismatists and is not close to having run out of candidates.

There is a certain responsibility that goes with this inherited tradition. If we are to call ourselves antiquarians, we should honor the title by making ourselves as informed as possible, and by adding, whenever possible, to the corpus of knowledge that we have acquired as guardians. This is not a burden, it is a joy that reflects the very essence of our desire to collect. We should also be mindful that the next generation will have incredible research tools at their disposal. Will they use these tools to advantage in the many cloudy areas of numismatic research? Only if they have an interest and a sense of the questions that time has thus far left unanswered. It is up to us to provide the catalyst through our own enthusiasm.

The History of Ancient Coin Collecting

Justus Lipsius
17th century classicist

Ancient coin collecting enjoys a rich and interesting history in and of itself—never mind for a moment the history of the coins. Each generation of collectors looks through its own window on the hobby, and is acquainted with its own luminaries. Each generation experiences its own collecting trends and sways to its own rhythm. There was a time, not many generations past, when classical studies were prevalent in our educational systems—students actually majored in Greek and Latin! Ancient coins were collected as an adjunct to these studies, primarily because of their historical or geographical context. Conversely, there was a time, even less distant, in which ancient coins were touted as investment vehicles. A market characterized by rising prices led many to the belief that all ancient coins were undervalued and would increase in value at a favorable rate. Today, we enjoy a stable market in which an appealing coin of the Roman Empire can be purchased for less than the cost of a modest dinner. True, one can spend hundreds of thousands of dollars on a masterpiece of Greek numismatic art, but few of us will fly that close to the sun.

Before we discuss the particulars of ancient coin collecting today, a look at the history of the pursuit might help to instill an appreciation of the tradition which we have inherited. The very fact that these lines are being read indicates an enthusiasm for (or at least a curiosity toward) collecting in general. Why do we collect ancient coins? The reason why a person collects objects from any one of myriad categories is actually very basic if one accepts the premise that collecting is a natural human instinct. The most enlightening discussion of this subject that we have seen is in Joseph Alsop's *The Rare Art Traditions*. Alsop demonstrates that humans have been collectors even from the days of cave habitation. Anyone bitten by the "collecting bug" would find this easy enough to believe. Humans seem to harbor an instinctive drive toward the discovery and acquisition of things which fascinate. While the breadth of collecting interest seems boundless, coins are among the most commonly collected objects. Although there are many different reasons for, and ways of, collecting coins, they seem to generate a more or less universal attraction. One will find coin collectors (numismatists) *in* virtually every corner of the globe. And, one will find numismatists who collect coins *from* virtually every corner of the globe. Therefore, it should not be a surprise that some collectors seek coins from the past. Edward T. Newell, the famous American numismatist, once remarked that ancient coins are appealing because not everything of interest is already known.

Coins from the ancient world, from the cultures of Greece and Rome in particular, hold a special appeal for collectors in the West. They serve as a chronograph of western civilization and a visual link to the roots of our legal, moral and political systems and values. They also provide a register of the richly symbolic and allegorical imagery which we borrow from past civilizations. It is easy enough to understand why these coins are collected, but we sometimes overlook the fact that the enchantment luring us today also attracted collectors in times past.

Ancient writers have given us some insight into collecting as a pastime in antiquity. In the fourth century BC, the Greek philosopher Aristotle collected works of art, and probably coins as well. In some of his writings he described the images on coins from distant lands. The early Ptolemies of Egypt, and King Attalus I of Pergamum (241 BC) were also avid art collectors. Pliny the Elder (AD 23-79), in his monumental *Historia Naturalis*, included several chapters on the history of art. One of the many things that this contemporary work reveals is widespread collecting interest in Rome. Pliny reported, for example, that a famous collection assembled by King Mithradates of Pontus—which included countless objects of art and probably coins—was transferred to Rome after his defeat by Lucullus and Pompey in 65 BC. He also related how Augustus, the first Roman emperor (27 BC - AD 14), collected gems and seals, and was fond of coins from distant lands—often giving them as gifts to his friends. The "friends" probably did not buy bread with these gifts, so we might assume that they were collected, or at least saved as mementos. Pliny further recounts the habit of Romans who collected counterfeit coins (fourrés) and paid higher prices for them than for genuine coins.

In addition to literary suggestions of coin collecting in antiquity, there is a strong argument for the case from archaeological finds. In ancient times, since they had no banks, coins were buried or hidden in some other way whenever danger threatened. These groups of coins are called hoards. Usually, a hoard consists of fairly homogeneous coins. That is, most of the coins will have been struck at regional mints, or in some cases the burial will contain standard trade coins which too are rather homogeneous. It would be unusual for a typical hoard to include coins of a wide variety of types and mints, but it would not be unusual for a collection to reflect this diversity. A hoard containing 114 silver tetradrachms from the third century BC was found during an excavation at the ancient site of Gordion in Asia Minor. The group contained practically no duplication and represented over 50 ancient cities or rulers from Parthia to Macedon and Phoenicia to the Black Sea. An even earlier dated group of 17 ancient Greek coins from very widely separated mints, and without duplication, was found in Afghanistan in the 1960s. Leonard Forrer, in *The Art of Collecting Coins*, reported another archaeological find, this one of 72 Roman gold coins, which was found some years ago in Switzerland. Again, a large number of diverse types, without duplication, were found buried together. Some of this may be coinci-

Roman bracelet
with coins inset

dental, but there are enough similar examples to suggest that collecting was a pastime in antiquity as it is today.

There are many other indicators which tell us that coins were "collected" in ancient times. One of the more obvious of these are so-called "restitution" coins. This form of political propaganda, usually an attempt to legitimize one's power, occurred when a ruler imitated the coin motif of an illustrious ancestor or a popular ruler from the past. The interval between issuance of the original coin and the restitution coinage was, in some cases, as much as two hundred years. While it is theoretically possible for a coin to have remained in circulation for this length of time, the fidelity with which these restitution coins were issued suggests that Roman mintmasters or die-engravers (celators) may have had access to an "official" collection of older coins. Another indicator of collecting activity may be found in ancient jewelry, which often included coins in its design. For example, a Roman bracelet found by archaeologists in Germany was made from seven late Roman gold coins—each of a

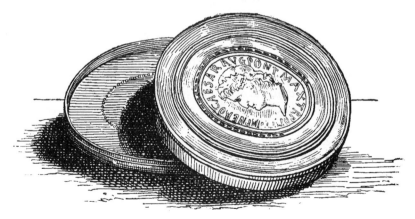

Roman bronze mirror box with a sestertius of Nero inset

different emperor—which were arranged in chronological order around the bracelet. The arrangement of coins in this manner suggests that the jeweler, and perhaps the patron who commissioned the piece, recognized their historical importance—saving (collecting) them for that reason. These coin bracelets were fairly common, and were made over a wide span of time (see illustration). Similar arrangements of coins or coin designs may be seen on a variety of Greek and Roman plates, vases and lamps. Many of these compositions convey an appreciation of the historical or artistic aspects of the coin motifs themselves.

Even during the "Dark Ages," which we now realize were not so dark, ancient coins were used as decorative devices in jewelry and on utilitarian objects. For instance, the Lexdan pendant—which was crafted from a silver denarius of the first Roman emperor, Augustus—was found buried in Britain with the remains of a barbarian chieftain. Notwithstanding the seven or eight centuries separating these two leaders in time, the respect of the latter is obvious. It is hard to imagine that any king would take to his grave a pendant bearing the image of a man about whom he knew nothing.

A moneyer striking coins for one of the Merovingian kings of France, in the late sixth or seventh century, demonstrated not only a Christian influence, but a knowledge of the history of Christianity. In addition to the unmistakable meaning of the crosses on obverse and reverse, the portrait seems clearly to be modeled after the Roman coin portrait of Constantine the Great looking heavenward. According to the Christian bishop Eusebius, who chronicled the life of Constantine, this Roman coin was struck in commemoration of the emperor's "vision," which supposedly led to his conversion to Christianity.

Merovingian
AU Tremissis
ca. AD 570-670

To this day, there seems to be a vague impression among people of our generation that following the collapse of the Roman Empire all knowledge and cultural activity in the West vanished. This simply was not the case. As more research has been done on this period, a recognition of artistic and cultural evolution in the West is beginning to replace the old view of the Renaissance as a spontaneous revival. Among the primary instruments which transfer culture from generation to generation or civilization to civilization (literature, art and oral tradition), numismatics should be included.

Ancient coins are often credited for providing inspiration to Renaissance artists and Humanists. It is common knowledge that archaeological discoveries in the 14th century, including coin finds, provided images and inscriptions which were "deciphered" by the brilliant scholars of that day. Looking at numismatic evidence, however, we find that

Humanism (the intellectual movement that stemmed from the study of Greek and Latin classics) began much earlier than previously thought.

In 12th century Mesopotamia, a complex series of coins bearing classically inspired images was designed and struck for the Turkoman dynasties of the region. These coins copied, in amazing detail, the images on ancient coins dating as early as the fourth century B.C. The images were not random copyings, but reveal a calculated program of numismatic art. They seem likely to have been designed for their Islamic patrons by Nestorian Christians who maintained an important monastic school at the city of Nisibin. The images that they produced make it clear that the die engravers of these coins obtained their inspiration from a significant collection of ancient coins. Contemporary records from the Nestorian monastery at Nisibin confirm that many classical works were

Artuqid AE Dirhem
AD 1176-1184
inspired by a Roman coin

included among the manuscripts maintained in their library at this time. They understood classical Greek and Roman culture, and respected it.

On one of these coins designed for the Artuqid ruler of Mardin, Qutb al-Din Ghazi II, the celator copied the familiar Christian theme of Constantine the Great looking up to the heavens. This copy of the Roman motif is not unlike the Merovingian copy mentioned earlier. It was, and still is, a powerful symbol of the rise of Christianity.

In pre-Renaissance Italy, classical images appear on the coins of Frederick II, Hohenstaufen (AD 1212-1250). This ruler issued a gold coin called the "Augustalis," which was clearly modeled after a solidus of one of the Roman augusti. At about this same time, a monastery in Spain recorded a list of the ancient coins in its collection—providing perhaps the earliest verifiable record of an actual collection.

Along with the 14th century, and the Italian Renaissance, came a new and important change in the nature of ancient coin collecting. No evidence of an organized and competitive market for ancient coins exists prior to this time. With the demand for antiquities of all kinds on the rise, ancient coins became increasingly popular and were actively sought by buying agents for the nobility of Italy and northern Europe.

One of the first entrepreneurs to satisfy this growing penchant for coins from antiquity was Cyriac d'Ancona. He might, in fact, be considered the first "dealer" in ancient coins. In the late 1300s, Cyriac made regular trips from Italy to Greece to acquire coins for his patrons in Florence, Genoa and Venice. As the wave of Humanism grew, one of the greatest minds of the Renaissance, Francesco Petrarch (1304-1374) wrote about his love of collecting ancient coins and encouraged their study to others. By the mid 15th century huge collections were starting to appear in Italy; amassed by the powerful Sforza, Medici, Farnese and Gonzaga families, wealthy bankers and merchants, and several Papal rulers. It was only a matter of time before the trend spread to northern and eastern Europe. In France, John, the Duke du Berry, brother of King Charles VI, assembled the most important collection of coins and antiquities in Europe. By the end of the century, nearly every royal house in Europe had displayed an interest in collecting ancient Greek and Roman coins.

The antique coin market in 16th century Italy was growing at a feverish pace. A Roman coin of the emperor Nero, for example, was reportedly offered to Isabella d'Este's agent for 25 ducats—about 25% of the cost of a major painting by a top Renaissance master. Isabella, who was well educated in the classics as a child, became the Marchioness of Mantua in 1490, when she

Isabella d'Este 1474-1539

married Francesco Gonzaga at the age of 16. Ancient coin collecting had become the hobby of kings, and it took a king's (or queen's) purse to indulge. The decendents of Isabella were avid collectors themselves, and the Gonzaga cachet was inset on many of their coins. It is still possible to find these interesting specimens offered at auction today.

Philip II, AE sestertius struck AD 248, with Gonzaga silver eagle cachet

Serious scientific study of ancient numismatics began in the 17th century, through the initiative of professional numismatists. Individuals like Jean Foy Vaillant in France and Ezechiel Spanheim in Prussia not only acquired coins for their patrons, but wrote important treatises on ancient numismatics. Collections grew larger and larger. In one transaction alone, Peter Paul Rubens—the famous (and rich) Flemish painter— negotiated the sale of 18,000 ancient coins which had belonged to his friend Charles Du Croy, the Duke of Aershot. Rubens and Du Croy were both collectors of ancient coins, and members of an antiquarian group in Antwerp. The group regularly met with and took inspiration from Justus Lipsius—who taught at Louvain and was one of the most famous Latinists of the time. Many of the collections formed during this period ultimately became the basis for the large institutional collections of today. It was also during this period that professional researchers and cataloguers were employed to manage these collections.

The 18th century became an age of specialization, and it was during this period that many of the pioneering studies in ancient numismatics were undertaken. Joseph Eckhel, for example, developed in Vienna the geographical system of arranging Greek coins that is still in use today. It was also a century in which many large and important private collections were dispersed, while institutional collections grew even larger. Toward the end of the century, with competition for coins declining and more coins becoming available, the field began to attract a new class of collector. The independent and educated professional, arising from a relatively new middle-class social strata, began to buy and collect ancient coins. This broadened collector base led to even greater research efforts and to well established markets in the major centers of Europe.

The nineteenth century was marked by an expansion of the common man's participation in ancient coin collecting. Doctors, lawyers, clergy, politicians, military officers, diplomats and bureaucrats—all possessed the means to purchase ancient coins and build modest (or in some cases not so modest) collections. The expanded collector base led to the birth of numismatic societies, as well as for the growth of professional numismatic firms which sold coins at auction. Improved communication systems and transportation made contact between numismatists easier, and information was disseminated to large groups of collectors through periodicals published by the

Friedrich Imhoof-Blumer
19th century numismatist

new and popular numismatic societies. In some cases, foreign duty in a government post offered opportunities to acquire coins within source countries and wonderful private collections emerged. By this time, most of Europe's royal collections had been turned over to state organizations, and placed under the management of professional museum curators. This was a period of great research and many of the world's most important collections were catalogued for the first time. Numismatists like Head, Lane-Poole, Imhoof-Blumer and many others made tremendous contributions to the hobby. Their work is still highly respected and useful a century later.

The face of collecting is changing dramatically in the twentieth century—as the world continues to grow smaller, publication of research becomes easier, and ancient coins become more accessible to the general public. Due to the appearance of new marketing strategies and an increased supply, brought about by such wonders as international express mail and the metal detector, the ancient coin market has evolved into a supply versus demand environment. The collecting fervor of the 50s and 60s turned into an investment fever in the 70s and 80s, only to retrench as a collector market in the 90s.

The interaction between collectors has also increased significantly, with symposia, conventions, seminars, club meetings, popular journals, a variety of social functions, and e-mail, all helping to draw collectors nearer to each other.

Finally, back to the original question: Why do we collect ancient coins? As we have acknowledged, collecting in general seems to stem from a natural and innate drive that probably originated in prehistoric times. It has been suggested that collecting, in our age, is primarily a form of escapism. It may be true that the mental pressures of modern society and of the modern work environment could cause one to seek escape, but it would be an overstatement to suggest that the need to escape is a major factor in one's decision or inclination to collect.

The typical collector pursues his or her hobby in a recreational context which hopefully provides a satisfying balance in one's life. If the focus becomes too intense, and the hobby becomes overtly compulsive, there are dangers. Surely, one *could* turn ancient coin collecting into a vehicle to escape the real world. Aren't we all armchair travelers in some sense?

Fortunately, the act of collecting is, in and of itself, a harmless activity. It has provided countless hours of joy and satisfaction to millions of people over eons of time. Collecting ancient coins is a very high form of that activity and we should happily embrace it, not as a form of escapism but as a cultured and refined expression of our innate Humanistic tendencies. While we explore the mysteries of numismatics, learn about ancient cultures, and gather our collected treasures in a basket (or a cabinet, for the more fortunate), we should keep in mind, always, that collecting is something we do because it is fun.

FOOTPRINTS IN THE SAND
Finding Ancient Coins and Ancient Coin Collectors

One of the initial things that a potential collector of ancient coins seeks is contact with others who can offer advice, counsel and encouragement. One of the common bonds of people who collect ancient coins is a sense of fraternalism with those who hold a similar interest. Finding others may seem difficult at first, but take heart because help is right around the corner. In spite of the long history of collecting, contact between fellow enthusiasts has not always been easy. In the past, a few societies were located in the larger metropolitan centers, but they served only a limited number of members. Most dealers in ancient coins attended only the larger metropolitan area coin shows, and mail order offerings were infrequent at best. Today the situation is quite different. Well over 100 ancient coin dealers in the United States alone maintain active show schedules and produce regular mailings of fixed price lists and auction sale catalogues to serve a growing clientele.

There has also been a proliferation of Ancient Coin Clubs in recent years, and many collectors today will be able to find one within travelling distance of their home. On the following pages is a list of non-profit societies or groups which are chartered to serve collectors of coins from antiquity. Many of these organizations produce newsletters which range in size from one or two pages, to scholarly perfect-bound journals. Their membership rolls vary from a few local collectors who meet in a member's home, to national societies with several thousand members and a full-time staff. One thing that almost all of these organizations seem to have in common is that they are continually seeking new members. The smaller organizations typically hold monthly meetings at which a program is arranged by one of the members. This might consist of "show and tell" or a lecture either by a member or a guest speaker. Before or after the program, a period is generally set aside for socializing. Some clubs hold mini-auctions in which members can offer their extra coins, books or what-not. Club members are usually quick to share information or to help attribute an unidentified coin. They are, after all, there for the same reason—to interact with other collectors. This is also a good place to ask other collectors about their experiences with particular shows or with firms that they have dealt with.

In this age of the Information Superhighway, it was inevitable that collectors of ancient coins would begin to congregate on the Internet. There are several locations where ancient coin "groupies" hang out and share coin stories. A few dealers have invaded the net and, with a little searching, one can now find advertisements for a variety of ancient coins without leaving home.

Clubs, Societies and Associations

American Israel Numismatic Association
12555 Biscayne Blvd. #733, No. Miami, FL 33181
http://amerisrael.com
A non-sectarian cultural and educational organization dedicated to the study and collection of Israel's coinage, past and present, and all aspects of Judaic numismatics.

American Numismatic Association (ANA)
818 N. Cascade Ave., Colorado Springs, CO 80903-3279
http://www.money.org
Museum, Library, Summer Seminars, Video and Audio tapes, etc. Extensive membership and full staff but greater orientation toward modern coins than ancients.

American Numismatic Society (ANS)
Broadway at 155th, New York, NY 10032
http://amnumsoc.org
Museum, Library, Grants and Seminars, Publications. Large membership and full staff including curators of ancient coins. A must for any serious collector of ancients.

Ancient Coin Club of Chicago
P.O.B. 641825, Chicago, IL 60664-1825,
http://www.sknapp.net/accc/
Meets monthly in downtown Chicago.

Ancient Coin Club of Los Angeles
P.O.B. 730, Lomita, CA 90717,
http://mjconnor.home.mindspring.com/accla/
Meets 2nd Sunday of every month at The Balboa Mission "Town Hall", located at 16916 San Fernando Mission Blvd., Granada Hills, CA.

Ancient Coin Study Group
5005 South Grand Blvd., St. Louis, MO 63111
Jointly sponsored by the Missouri Numismatic Society and the World Coin Club of Missouri. Meetings are at 7:30pm 3rd Friday, MNS Library, 5005 S. Grand Blvd. Program/lecture at each meeting.

Ancient Numismatic Society of Washington
P.O. Box 2495, Gaithersburg, MD 20886
Monthly meetings, 3rd Sunday at 2pm at the home of a volunteer member. About 50 members, usually 10-20 at each meeting.

Armenian Numismatic Society
8511 Beverly Park, Pico Rivera, CA 90660,
150 Members, dues $8 ($10 first year), junior $6, life $100. Publishes quarterly Armenian Numismatic Journal. Y.T. Nercessian, secretary.   →

Australian Society of Ancient Numismatists
229 Macquarie St., Sydney, Australia
In care of Noble Numismatics Pty Ltd.

Baltimore Coin Club
P.O. Box 5100, Laurel Centre Station, Laurel, MD 20726
Monthly newsletter, *The Coin Courier.*

Canadian Numismatic Association
4936 Yonge Street, Suite 601
North York, ON M2N 6S3
http://www.nunetcan.net/cna.htm
The primary organization of coin collectors in Canada.

Chicago Coin Club
P.O. Box 2301, Chicago, IL 60690
http:/www.chicagocoinclub.org/
Large active club with diverse interests.

Classical and Medieval Numismatic Society (CMNS)
P.O. Box 704, Station B, Willowdale, Ontario, Canada M2K 2P9
http://home.cogeco.ca/~tczerned/cmns/
Bi-Monthly newsletter, annual journal, lectures, strong membership.

Classical Numismatic Society of the Delaware Valley
P.O. Box 531, Moorestown, NJ 08057-0531
Meets on the 2nd Saturday of each month at 1pm at the Camden County Library on
MacArthur Blvd. in Westmont, NJ. Speakers at every meeting.

Hellenic Numismatic Society
A.Metaxa 28, 106 81, Athens Greece
http://www.helicon.gr/hellenum/
Nomismatika Khronika published annually (bilingual, Greek and English).

NC ANCIENTS (North Carolina Ancients)
Location: Hillsborough, NC
Informal meeting, discussion, latest acquisitions
Contacts: paul_landsberg@yahoo.com or join group below
Yahoogroup: nc_ancients@yahoogroups.com

Numismatics International (NI)
P.O. Box 570842, Dallas, TX 75357-0842
http://www.numis.org
Monthly bulletin, often with articles about ancients.

Numismatic Literary Guild (NLG)
http://www.numismaticliteraryguild.org/
Guild of writers and publishers in the numismatic field.

Oriental Numismatic Society (ONS)
Dr. A. Schweitzerstraat 29
2861 XZ Bergambach, Netherlands
http://www.onsnumis.org/
Worldwide membership, quarterly newsletter.

Pacific Ancient Numismatists
P.O. Box 60283, Shoreline, WA 98160-0283
About 12 active members and mailing list of 26. Usually have a presentation at the meetings. Meetings are monthly, at the Bellevue Public Library.

Professional Numismatists Guild
3950 Concordia Lane, Fallbrook, CA 92028
An association of dealers organized to promote integrity and responsibility within the hobby.

Royal Numismatic Society (RNS)
Dept. of Coins & Medals, British Museum, London WC1B 3DG
http://www.users.dircon.co.uk/~rns/
Venerable society for serious scholars and collectors. *Numismatic Chronicle* annually.

Royal Numismatic Society of New Zealand
PO Box 2023, Wellington 6015
http://www.geocities.com/rnsnz/index.htm
Non-profit organization founded in 1931.

Sacramento Valley Ancients Society
2255 Watt Avenue, Suite 125, Sacramento, CA 95825
Small friendly group, seeking new members.

San Francisco Ancient Coin Club
Paul Henkin, Secretary, 1820 Spruce St. #7, Berkeley, CA 94709
Very well organized and supported club, with active program.

San Diego Ancient Coin Club
Location: San Diego County
Rotation of meetings to various members' homes
Members: approximately 13 who meet on regular basis

Society for Ancient Numismatics (SAN)
P.O. Box 2830, Los Angeles, CA 90078-2830
International membership. SAN Journal is of interest, but published irregularly.

Society Historia Numorum -- Boston

The Society Historia Numorum was organized in 1965 for the benefit of collectors and scholars of ancient coinage in eastern Massachusetts. Membership in SHN is by invitation and includes the Regular Members, who host the monthly meetings of the organization in their homes, and Associates, who generally live at some distance from the greater Boston area. Monthly newsletter.

Swedish Numismatic Society
Banérgatan 17 nb, 115 22 Stockholm

http://www.users.wineasy.se/snf/

Founded in 1873, the largest society of its kind in the Scandinavian countries.

Swiss Numismatic Society

c/o Régie de Fribourg S.A., Rue de Romont 24, CH-1700 Fribourg, Switzerland.

International membership, quarterly and annual reviews.

Twin Cities Ancient Coin Club

Steve Antonello, President

StevePsyck@aol.com

Meets monthly in St. Paul. Coin and book auction at each meeting.

Club bulletins and numismatic society journals, although educational, never seemed to satisfy the hobby's need for a clearing house where ideas could be exchanged and opinions could be aired. In 1987, a "popular" journal burst onto the scene and was immediately embraced by both the collector and dealer

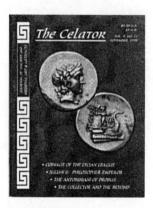

fraternities. Named after the artists from antiquity who carved dies for the striking of ancient coins, *The Celator* became a forum for expression, a vehicle for sharing market news, and a source of basic collector information. Today, with a subscriber base of more than 2,000 collectors worldwide, and over 100 regular advertisers, this monthly magazine has become a recognized fixture in the hobby. Other English language periodicals which frequently offer articles about ancient coins include two British publications—*Coin News* and *Minerva*—along with *Coinage, World Coin News,* and *Coin World* from the United States. The British magazine *Antiquity* , which we had mentioned in the earlier edition of this book, struggled editorially after the passing of its founder, George Lambor and was eventually forced to discontinue publication. Producing a periodical for a relatively small readership requires a delicate balance of editorial and financial management. Usually, this type of publication is very much dependent on the passion of a few indispensable people.

Dealer sponsored "in-house" publications like the *Classical Numismatic Review, Historia Numismata* and the *Spink Numismatic Circular* also include a variety of articles along with their offerings of coins for sale. Although published more frequently, none of these commercial publications match the scholarly level of *The Numismatic Chronicle,* the *Revue Suisse de Numismatique* or the *American Journal of Numismatics.* These are the annual reviews published by the Royal Numismatic Society, Swiss Numismatic Society and the American Numismatic Society respectively. Part of the reason for this is that these professional journals

are "refereed." That is, articles submitted for publication are subjected to the scrutiny of a panel of experts before they are accepted. This helps to assure high standards, but it also requires a great deal of time and effort.

The trade-off is that one issue per year is about all that the staffs of these organizations can manage. Most collectors, craving a steady flow of information, will feast upon the more frequent offerings of commercial periodicals and include the professional journals in their reference libraries.

Some numismatic associations publish periodicals for their membership. These typically focus on articles dealing with the main focus of the organization. Examples of this type of publication include *The Shekel,* a group periodical about Jewish coins published by the

American Israel Numismatic Association; *NI Bulletin* issued by Numismatics International and the *ONS Newsletter* distributed to members of the Oriental Numismatic Society. The latter periodical generally focuses on coinage of Islam and Central Asia, with some coverage of Far East issues as well. All of these organizations have members interested in ancient coinage and consequently offer related articles in their publications. Newest on the scene of association periodicals is the *American Numismatic Society Magazine,* published three times a year. This high quality magazine replaces the former newsletter of the society and includes im-

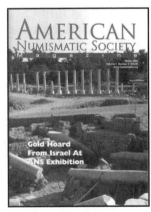

portant notices and information for members. It also presents very timely and well produced articles on a variety of numismatic topics including ancient coinage.

The articles offered in periodicals of the type shown here are usually written by amateur or semi-professional numismatists. One of the great joys of ancient coin collecting is the opportunity that the hobby affords for independent research. Often, particularly in an obscure series, private collectors have access to a depth and breadth of coinage that is not found in public institutions. Therefore, the sharing of information through periodical articles is a benefit for the collector as well as for the professional scholar. Although the standards are generally more relaxed than in the scholarly journals, periodicals can be a wonderful source of educational and entertaining material.

English-language Commercial Publications or dealer lists with frequent editorial content

The Celator (Monthly)
P.O. Box 839, Lancaster, PA 17608-0839
(717) 656-8557 , Independent popular journal about ancient and medieval coins, magazine format.

Classical Numismatic Review (Semi-annual)
Subscription includes several auction catalogues.
P.O. Box 479, Lancaster, PA 17608 • (717) 390-9194
"In-house" publication of Classical Numismatic Group, magazine format.

Coin News (Monthly)
P.O. Box 20, Axminster, Devon EX13 7YT, U.K.
(01404 831878)
Independent popular journal, magazine format.

Coinage (Monthly)
4880 Market St., Ventura, CA 93003-7783 • (805) 644-3824
General numismatic publication, magazine format.

Coin World (Weekly)
P.O Box 150, Sidney, OH 45365-0150 • (513) 498-0800
General numismatic publication, tabloid format.

Minerva (Bi-Monthly)
14 Old Bond St., London, W1X 4JL • (0171) 495-2590
Independent antiquarian journal, magazine format.

Historia Numismata
P.O. Box 131040, Ann Arbor, MI 48113
Ancient to Medieval coins, "in-house" publication of Pegasi Numismatics, magazine format.

Spink Numismatic Circular (Monthly)
Spink & Son Ltd, 69 Southampton Row, Bloomsbury, London WC1B 4ET, England • Tel: +44 (0) 20 7563 4000
Dealer "in-house" publication, magazine format .

World Coin News (Monthly)
700 E. State St., Iola, WI 54990
World coins (ancient-modern), tabloid format (see also *Numismatic News*—same address— for their annual Show Directory supplement).

Coin Shows and Numismatic Conventions

One of the most thrilling, yet intimidating, experiences is a new collector's first visit to the numismatic bourse. The word bourse is of French derivation, and is a term used for the monetary market. It comes from the Latin word *bursa* which is also the root for purse. The bourse of a convention or coin show consists of row upon row of tables lined up end-to-end forming aisles. The bourse of a local show may include as few as a dozen dealers, or as many as 1,000. Shows are held virtually everywhere, from the hills of Kentucky to downtown Manhattan or the L.A. Airport. Although many of the smaller shows offer coins along with stamps, baseball cards and a variety of other collectibles, diligence and perseverance will generally ferret out an ancient coin or two.

With the number of ancient coin dealers on the rise, it is becoming more common, even at the small club shows, to find dealers who specialize in, or at least carry a selection of, ancient coins. The terms "show" and "convention" are used rather indiscriminately within the hobby, so don't place too much stock in the terminology used. Generally speaking, a convention is a gathering promoted by a specific organization, and it will include a schedule of events or program for the benefit of its members and visiting guests. A convention bourse is identical with a show bourse. If you have already been to a few coin shows, and can't seem to find much in the way of ancient coins, don't despair! There are major conventions which cater specifically to collectors of ancient and foreign coins. These shows are called "Internationals."

The major Internationals held in the U.S. are The Chicago International, held in the Spring, and the New York International which is currently held in January. International shows at Boston and San Francisco have been organized from time to time, but are not currently on a firm schedule. At these shows, dealers are often restricted in the kind of material offered for sale. That is, the sale of modern U.S. coins is prohibited. The resulting focus on ancient and foreign coins is a tremendous help to the collector of these. In addition to the Internationals, a regular convention circuit brings together dealers who carry stocks of ancients. A list of shows which tend to attract dealers specializing in ancient coins is included here as a general guide. This is not an inclusive list and the dates are only tentative. For precise show dates, it is important to check current show listings in the numismatic press. World Coin News, a Krause publication, produces an annual "Show Directory" which comes to subscribers free as an insert. This is a very useful guide, but it does not indicate what kinds of coins might be found at a listed event. *The Celator* includes a monthly, but much more limited, "Coming Events" feature which lists major shows and auctions of interest primarily to ancient coin collectors.

Major Shows Featuring Ancient Coins

F.U.N. — Florida United Numismatists, Orange County Convention Center, Orlando, Florida. January.

Long Beach Expo — Long Beach Convention Center, Long Beach, California. Three times a year: February, June, October.

Numismatic & Antiquarian Bourse — Cathedral Hill Hotel, San Francisco, California. Spring and Fall.

Seattle Coin Show — Seattle International Trade Center, Seattle, Washington. March.

C.S.N.A. — Central States Numismatic Association Convention. Rotates among Midwest cities. Spring.

C.I.C.F. — Chicago International Coin Fair, Rosemont, Illinois. March/April.

N.Y.I.N.C. — New York International Numismatic Convention, Waldorf Astoria, New York City. January.

A.N.A. — American Numismatic Association convention. Rotates among major cities. Early Spring and Summer.

Bay State Coin Show — Radisson Hotel, Boston, Massachusetts. March and November.

COINEX — British Numismatic Trade Association annual show. Marriott Hotel, London, England. October.

London Coin Fair — Cumberland Hotel, Marble Arch, London, England. February, June, September and November.

Basel World Money Fair—Basel, Switzerland. January/February.

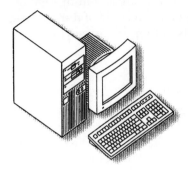

Members of the academic community were the first to use the Internet as a research tool, and early methods of access were not all that user friendly. In the past decade, the situation has changed dramatically. Computers have become so easy to operate that the general public has embraced computers and the Internet in almost every facet of their lives, including their numismatic pursuits. Although one immediately thinks of the Internet as a vehicle for shopping and communicating, an increasing number of scholarly or historical references are available to the public. Virtually every day, complete texts of classical works (often in translation) are added to the data pool. Huge image databases now make it possible for ancient coin collectors to search, compare and attribute many of their coins accurately and without the need to purchase obscure references or visit a major public library.

The benefits of using computers, combined with the continuing development of collector oriented areas and services, are enough to entice a good number of collectors and dealers to the Information Superhighway. In this chapter, we'll examine some of the ways that numismatists are making use of computers, and provide some information on where to "surf."

But first, some caveats. This chapter assumes a rudimentary knowledge of computers and the Internet. Furthermore, the material and services available through the Internet are still growing at a rapid pace. Changes occur frequently, and some areas will always be under development. The Web sites and services outlined here were correct as of this writing, and in no way constitute a complete list, but rather a sampling of available sources.

E-Mail

Communicating via electronic mail is the first place to start. Ever increasing numbers of collectors and dealers are going online, and the advantages of e-mail are fairly obvious. Foremost among these is the speed with which messages—and digital documents—can be sent and received. Customers can send orders or inquiries via e-mail, and even bid in some mail bid auctions, quickly and easily. Additionally, finding other collectors online who have similar interests can help relieve the isolated feeling that some ancient coin enthusiasts experience. Through e-mail, you can also communicate with some of the foremost authorities in the field of ancient numismatics. Becoming active online and developing a good circle of numismatic contacts can help to make your numismatic pursuits surprisingly effective and enjoyable.

Mailing Lists

Subscribing to mailing lists is a good way to communicate with a large group of numismatists. To subscribe, simply send an e-mail message to the List Server, a computer site that controls the list. Then, at regular intervals the List Server deposits all the current postings in your e-mail box. You can usually select either continuous or digest form delivery. In the latter option, postings are grouped and sent once a day, or whenever the backlog exceeds a specified point. You can read the postings, respond to those that interest you, or post your own questions or comments. There are no fees involved with subscribing.

In the previous edition of this book, we briefly mentioned the forums provided by online services like AOL, CompuServe and Prodigy in their own consumer areas. With the universal access now available, these have pretty much disappeared. Although some Internet Service Providers still host their own forums (e.g. http://groups.aol.com) the most active venue today for group interaction among amateur numismatists is the Yahoo Groups forum (http://groups.yahoo.com) which can be accessed with an ordinary browser or by e-mail. A recent survey of Yahoo Groups identified some 34 Mailing Lists which cater to collectors of ancient coins—and this excludes those which are primarily commercial. This is obviously a much different situation than it was ten years ago. The question today is not whether a collector will find a discussion about ancient coins, it is whether the collector will have time to read all of the discussions that are posted every day. These groups provide more than just a means of communicating with like-minded hobbyists, they also offer archival capability for text and photos.

Some Mailing Lists are intended to be for informational purposes only, and commercial transactions are either frowned upon or forbidden; violators are subject to being removed from the list by the list owner. In the past, these lists were usually created or sponsored by someone in the academic community, and their content was generally for intermediate or advanced collectors and scholars. Today, the majority of list moderators or founders are amateur collectors. Consequently, the ban on commercial transactions is less rigidly enforced and some lists like ACM-L even encourage commercial posts. Although on most lists everyone is free to participate in discussions, it is usually prudent to follow the threads for a time and get the feel of a list before jumping in with questions or opinions. Like everything else on the Internet, Mailing Lists are not necessarily immortal. What is popular at the time of this writing may not be in existence five years from now. We will discuss here a few of the currently successful lists, and those which because of their unique sponsorship are likely to be around for a while. If you do not find some of these, try a simple search for "groups" on any major search engine.

The most active list today is **MONETA-L**, which is one of the series of Yahoo Groups. The list enjoyed a membership roll of nearly 1100 at the time of this writing, and was more than twice the size of any other group with an orientation toward ancient coins. Like all Yahoo lists, this one can be accessed through http://groups.yahoo.com by following the links. The range of subject matter varies greatly, from requests for attribution help to notices of fraudulent activity, with long running threads on topics covering every conceivable phase of numismatics and collecting. Most of the remaining Yahoo Groups related to ancient coin collecting are quite specialized. Two of the largest and most active are lists oriented toward collectors of Islamic Coins and Uncleaned Coins.

Another Yahoo group that is like MONETA-L but oriented more toward commercial messages and direct offers of coins for sale by list subscribers is the **ANCIENT COIN MARKET LIST** (ACM-L).

ISLAMIC COINS GROUP (http://groups.yahoo.com/group/Islamic_coins/)is a place for collectors to share knowledge and information about Medieval Islamic coins. This Yahoo group is for the novice and the experienced alike. A place to meet, exchange the latest news, and address the latest concerns.

UNCLEANED COINS GROUP (http://groups.yahoo.com/group/Uncleanedcoins/) is by their own description a place for "bottom feeders" to share information and experiences about cleaning and collecting coins from bulk lots of coins right out of the ground. One of the rules of this group is that anyone with a negative attitude will not be allowed.

PARTHIA-L is established as a forum specifically oriented toward collectors of Parthian coins. One may subscribe by e-mail to Parthia-L-subscribe@yahoogroups.com, or go to the Yahoo Groups sign up page at Yahoo.com.

The **American Numismatic Society** hosts a group for discussion of ANS issues. This is not really a chat list, and topics of a general collecting nature are seldom seen. The list was hosted on the Society's server for a while but recently has taken up residence as one of the Yahoo Groups mentioned above.

The above are only a few of the mailing lists of interest to numismatists. Others include groups specializing in particular types of coinage like Roman Provincial, Parthian, Celtic, Persian, Biblical and more.

Institutional mailing lists are operated independently, and are hosted on the provider's inhouse servers. The venerable **NUMISM-L** is one of the few institutional lists that is entirely focused on ancient and medieval coinage. To subscribe, send an e-mail message to "LISTSERV@LISTSERV.SC.EDU". In the message area, type "SUBSCRIBE NUMISM-L" and your name. You will be subscribed under the e-mail address from which this message is sent and will be able to post items to the list only from that address. Traffic on this list is not as high as it once was, but the quality of postings is generally high and the membership includes many numismatists of very respectable credentials. These institutional lists exist for related fields as well, including history, archaeology, and various antiquarian subjects. The adjacent table provides a sampling of those which may be of interest to the collector of ancient coins. Interested parties can subscribe to the lists by sending an e-mail message to the appropriate List Server. The body of the e-mail message should follow this format: Subscribe <list name> <your name> (e.g. "Subscribe CELTIC-L John H. Doe").

USENET Newsgroups

A USENET group works in a very similar fashion to the above online forums. The only active USENET newsgroup for coin collectors on the Internet is rec.collecting.coins. To search for Newsgroups or to access one, the easiest method is to point your browser to http://groups.google.com and follow the links. A good place to start is with the link labled "Group Help". News readers, like Outlook Express and Netscape Messenger, can also be used to access Newsgroups. Rec.collecting.coins has an active participation, but its content encompasses the entire field of numismatics. Ancient coins are only a small part of the traffic, but some useful information and interesting, if sometimes heated, debate can be found there.

Institutional Mail Lists

Mailing List	List Server
AEGEANET (early Aegean)	majordomo@acpub.duke.edu
AIA (archaeology)	listserv@cc.brynmawr.edu
ANCIEN-L (ancient history)	listserv@listserv.louisville.edu
ANE-L (ancient Near East)	ane@listhost.uchicago.edu
ANSAX-L (Anglo-Saxons)	listserv@wvnvm.wvnet.edu
ARCH-L (archaeology)	listserv@tamvm1.tamu.edu
ARTHURNET (Arthurian studies)	listserver@morgan.ucs.mun.ca
BIBLIONUMIS-L (Books)	majordomo@majordomo.netcom.com
BMCR-L (classical reviews)	listserv@cc.brynmawr.edu
BMMR-L (medieval reviews)	listserv@cc.brynmawr.edu
BYZANS-L (Byzantium)	listserv@mizzou1.missouri.edu
CELTIC-L (Celtic)	listserv@irlearn.ucd.ie
CLASSICS (Classics)	listproc@u.washington.edu
GREEKARCH (Greek archaeology)	majordomo@rome.classics, lsa.umich.edu
INTERSCRIPTA (medieval)	listserver@morgan.ucs.mun.ca
ISLAM-L (Islam)	listserv@ulkyvm.louisville.edu
LATIN-L (Latin language)	listserv@psuvm.psu.edu
LT-ANTIQ (late antiquity)	listserv@univscvm.csd. scarolina.edu
MEDEVLIT (medieval literature)	listserv@siucvmb.siu.edu
MEDIEV-L (medieval)	listserv@ukanvm.cc.ukans.edu
MEDTEXTL (medieval)	listserv@uiucvmd.bitnet
NUMISM-L (numismatics)	listserv@listserv.sc.edu
ROMARCH (Roman archaeology)	majordomo@rome.classics, lsa.umich.edu

Note: These addresses, although active at the time this list was assembled, can and do change from time to time. If the address posted above does not connect you with the list desired, try a search on any major search engine for the name or subject area of the list. Some of these mail lists, like The American Numismatic Society, have started changing from their own institutional servers to the efficient and versatile "Groups" service hosted by Yahoo.com.

PDF, FTP and Gopher Sites

Gopher sites, which once offered information on an almost unlimited number of topics for those with the patience and persistence to unravel their mysteries, have all but vanished in the past decade. The information that once could be found only in these raw data sites is now available in transfer protocols that virtually every browser can interpret. File Transfer Protocol (FTP) has also been incorporated into modern browsers so that the user does not need to launch a separate application in order to download information files from online storage. Most users today would hardly realize that a download is taking place except that a file with the desired information subsequently appears on their computer's hard drive. Also incorporated seamlessly into most browsers is the ability to read Portable Document Format (PDF) files. This innovative format integrates text and graphics into simple pages, with relatively small memory requirements, that can easily be sent from one place to another by e-mail or downloaded from Web sites. PDF files are printable and searchable, so they have become quite popular with citizens of the World Wide Web. Among other valuable uses, PDF is particularly well suited to the conversion of print based books into electronic media. Because the technology is easy to understand and use, scores of amateurs have reproduced reference works that are no longer copyright protected and made them freely available for online reading or download. The transfer of information from an internet source to one's home computer is now an easy task.

World Wide Web

The World Wide Web includes access to an unimaginable number of Web sites, each with its own unique address. These sites are accessed using a Web browser like Microsoft's "Internet Explorer" or Netscape's "Navigator". Several different types of sites are found, ranging from purely informational offerings to commercial ventures. The Web continues to grow very rapidly, and new sites are constantly under development. What once was the land of "dot com" has now blossomed with dot info, dot tv, dot biz, dot org and a seemingly endless stream of address possibilities. The diversity of information available on the Web, combined with the use of hypertext links, makes it one of the most useful areas for numismatists. Hypertext links, which are usually shown in the form of underlined text, allow the user to jump to other Web pages containing related information, usually with just a single mouse click.

The most remarkable advances of the past decade have been in the development of powerful search engines that bring the entire world of Web data to the desktop of users who have virtually no technical experience or special aptitude.

Search Engines

Search engine technology is advancing at such a rapid pace that one can hardly describe the changes in real time. The focus as of this writing is on relevance. Not only can modern search engines determine which of the millions of searched files contain a pertinent word or phrase, they can evaluate the relevance of the search term(s) to the overall document and order the returns by degree of relevance. This process, which once took minutes, now takes only seconds and is no longer limited only to text. Image searches are possible as well. Unless the search is for something really esoteric, the problem these days is not finding material, it is finding time to read all of the material that exists.

Informational Sites

The Internet serves many useful purposes for the collector, but one of its most valuable features is the presentation of massive amounts of general and specific information. Articles on practically any subject can be read, copied and forwarded to others. Hypertext links (underlined text that you can simply click on and "go to") are extremely useful tools for finding additional resources, and many informational sites include comprehensive lists of links to related sites. Finding one useful site is very likely to result in leads to several others of value. One such example is the Resource Center hosted by *The Celator* magazine (at http://celator.com/cws/resource.html) where links to a great variety of informational sites are organized by topical area. The "Learning Place" at Celator.com is a great place for ancient coin collectors to broaden their horizons. Also included in the many *Celator* links are addresses of well established and reputable dealers who advertise in the monthly journal and who host a presence on the Web.

One Web site mentioned in our first edition, still features the same sections on frequently asked questions, glossaries, biographies, news, articles, stories, reviews, trivia, humor, and references. However, the latest items in "Recent News" are dated to 1996. So, even though sites may be around for a long time, the maintenance of a site is critical to its continued value. The sites discussed below were active at the time of this writing, but it is impossible to say what the landscape of the World Wide Web will look like in another five to ten years.

For those interested in the ancient Greek world, visiting the Perseus Project (http://www.perseus.tufts.edu/) site is an absolute must. This Web site, organized by the Classics Department of Tufts University, includes a large database of information.

The main page is broken up into categories: What's New, Art & Archaeology, Searching Tools, English Texts, Greek Texts, Greek Lexica, and Secondary Sources. Users can search the database texts using English or Greek keywords, and the Greek Lexica section is valuable for those doing research utilizing ancient literature sources.

Using the Search Tools, researchers can choose from five subject groupings: Architecture, Sites, Coins, Vases, and Sculpture. Digital images are very effective in these areas and they are generally of very good quality. For example, searching the Sites area, looking for ancient Olympia, users can choose from a variety of views of the ancient stadium and surrounding buildings. Each photo is accompanied by informational text, as well as hypertext links to related images and areas.

The section on Coins features a catalog of the Dewing Collection, with images of 450 coins. Collectors can search the coin catalog using keywords—such as mint, region, period, denomination, etc.—to locate and view pertinent examples. The incredible wealth of information presented in the Perseus Project Web page is an excellent example of the usefulness of the Internet in the areas of numismatics and classical history.

Many Web sites are in the process of being developed, and some are not quite complete, but the progress in the past decade has been extraordinary and the outlook for the future is very bright.

Organizational Sites

Although it is possible here to mention only a few, several numismatic organizations maintain excellent Web sites. The American Numismatic Association (ANA) site includes a Resource Center, with lists of available slides and videos, as well as a product catalogue (http://www.money.org). Information about conventions, collector services, conferences, and Young Numismatist awards is included, as is an FTP site where users can download any of the over 1000 scripts for the radio program *Money Talks*. Similarly, press releases, numismatic indexes, project files, and ANA library catalog supplements are readily available. The site doesn't include a lot of specific information about ancients (except the FTP area), but it does provide a good overview of the ANA and its services.

Among the many useful sources of information provided on the American Numismatic Society (ANS) Web site (http://www.amnumsoc.org) are coin, Numismatic Literature and library searches. Accession data and descriptions of coins in the ANS collection are searchable by keyword and a project is underway to add digital images to the online catalogue. The Numismatic Literature resource is an index of numismatic scholarship from various books and periodicals. The information includes author, title, subject, and publication information. In addition, the Numismatic Indexes Project (NIP) sponsored by the Harry Bass Foundation indexes five American Numismatic Society publications: *American Journal of Numismatics, Museum Notes, Coinage of the Americas Conference, Numismatic Notes and Monographs,* and *ANS Proceedings.* Other periodicals in the index are *The Numismatist, Numismatic Scrapbook Magazine, Numismatic Review, Coin Collector's Journal* and *The Celator,* a magazine primarily devoted to ancient numismatics. The extensive library holdings of the ANS are also searchable through the society's Web site.

The Classical and Medieval Numismatic Society (CMNS) Web site (http://home.cogeco.ca/~tczerned/cmns) includes an index to the Anvil, and the Picus, the society's quarterly and annual publications. Also included on this site are links to other sites of interest to collectors of ancient and medieval coins.

Numismatics International is an educational non-profit institution and maintains one of the few lending libraries of numismatic publications in the United States. The NI Web site (http://www.numis.org) includes a searchable master index to the library.

A variety of other numismatic organizations which host their own Web site are listed in tables on the following pages.

Institutional Sites

Virtually every major museum and university has a web site, and many of those with collections of ancient coins have included part or all of their collection online. The British Museum's department of Coins and Medals (http://www.thebritishmuseum.ac.uk/cm/cmhome.html) provides a wealth of information about the holdings and programs of this prestigious museum.

The Hellenic Ministry of Culture includes on its Web site (http://www.culture.gr/2/21/toc/museums.html) an impressive list of all museums and archaeological sites in Greece, along with links to individual Web sites for many of them. Virtual exhibitions of ancient coins may also be found here.

The history of coinage in ancient Judaea is presented through informative online exhibitions of the Israel Museum, Jerusalem (http://www.imj.org.il/eng/archaeology/numismatics/).

A whole series of educational online exhibitions may be seen at the Web site of the National Numismatic Collection (http://americanhistory.si.edu/csr/cadnnc.htm). This division of the

Smithsonian National Museum of American History pays considerable attention to the coinage of antiquity as well as that of the Americas.

Commercial Sites

Other types of Web sites are commercial in nature, and offer ancient coins and related literature for sale either at auction or at fixed prices. Commercial auction sites like Ebay and Yahoo generally have a broad selection of coins posted, but the sellers are often unknown entities and should be checked out carefully before bidding. One section of the Celator Resource Center (http://celator.com/cws/resource.html) lists the advertisers in that publication that have an online presence. Although this may seem like a self-serving list, there is a distinct benefit to the collector who might choose to deal with one of these firms. The publication acts, in a way, like a screening agency. Any dealer who violates prescribed standards will have their advertising rights revoked. This works to the collectors advantage in assuring that "problem" sellers are dealt with expediently.

The Ancient Coin Market (http://ancientcoinmarket.com), brainchild of Thom Bray, hosts distance learning in the form of interactive courses about ancient coins. Promoting this project as the "Ancient Coin University", Bray has assembled a notable team of qualified numismatists to develop and present a growing list of courses, some of which are free and some are tuition based.

Databases

One of the most useful tools provided by modern Internet sites is the searchable database. The number of informational databases is growing at a furious pace and many of the world's major institutions are finding that grant money is available to digitize collection holdings. For example, at the time of this writing, the American Museum of Natural History has 400,000 of its catalogued items online. The Metropolitan Museum of Art has 3,500 works of art online. Of course both of these museums have millions of items in their collections. The fact is, however, that a concerted effort is being made by a wide range of institutions that will eventually provide comprehensive and searchable catalogues, with images, of the holdings of every major museum in the world. The benefits to research, both public and private are incalculable. Numismatic collections are not being left out of this amazing undertaking. The American Numismatic Society has already imaged several thousand coins and is diligently pursuing the goal of providing a complete visual inventory of its holdings. It is only a matter of time until these databases will be linked for concurrent searches across very wide platforms.

Conclusion

In this chapter, we have attempted to introduce the collector to the variety of services and information about ancient numismatics that can be found online. The online chat lists have become virtual communities where one can find the entire gamut of social interaction. It is becoming possible to use online resources for attribution of ancient coins, and the online auction histories provide a fairly good pricing index for certain kinds of coins. A vast amount of historical and biographical information can also be found online with the aid of Web browsers and search engines. The advantages of using the Internet for obtaining information for research should not be underestimated.

Online numismatics and collecting coins of the ancient world seem, at first glance, to have little in common. However, ancient coin enthusiasts are finding that the use of computers and online information systems can generate great results and add a new dimension to their numismatic pursuits. As the industry of online numismatics develops and improves, its benefits can only improve as well. We have seen tremendous advances in the past decade, and yet there can be little doubt that we are only in the crawling stage of this media's evolution.

World Wide Web Resources
Pertaining to Ancient Numismatics

American Numismatic Association .... http://www.money.org

American Numismatic Society .... http://www.amnumsoc.org

Ancient Coins Global Search Engine ... http://www.ancientcoins.net/

Ashmolean Museum ....
..............http://www.ashmol.ox.ac.uk/ash/departments/coin-room/

Asia, History and Coins ....
.... http://www.grifterrec.com/coins/coins.html

Australian Center for Ancient Numismatic Studies ....
....http://www.humanities.mq.edu.au/acans/

Berlin Coin Cabinet ...... http://www.smb.spk-berlin.de/mk/e/s.html

Bibliothèque Nationale .... http://www.bnf.fr/

Bologna Archaeological Museum ....
........http://www.comune.bologna.it/bologna/Musei/Archeologico/

Boston Museum of Fine Arts..
.... http://www.mfa.org/artemis/collections/ancient.htm

British Museum .... http://www.british-museum.ac.uk

Bulgarian National Museum .... http://www.historymuseum.org/

Byzantine Coins................................. http://www.byzantinecoins.com/

Capitoline Museum http://www.museicapitolini.org/index2.htm

Celator .... http://www.celator.com

Celtic Coin Index ....
.... http://www.writer2001.com/cciwriter2001/index.htm

Coriosolites http://www.writer2001.com/exp0002.htm

Chinese Coins .... http://www.charm.ru/index.shtml

Coin Archives .... http://www.coinarchives.com/

Collecting Roman Coins ....
.... http://myron.sjsu.edu/romeweb/rcoins/contents.htm

Dutch National Museum .... http://
www.penningkabinet.nl/collectie/overzicht/collection.html#Coins

Famous People http://members.aol.com/dkaplan888/main.html

Fitzwilliam Museum, Cambridge ....
.... http://www-cm.fitzmuseum.cam.ac.uk/coins/

Gallic Celts .... http://www.kernunnos.com/dlt/home.shtml

Gordian III .... http://mihalkam.ancients.info/gordianiii.html

Greek and Roman Provincial Coin ID ....
.... http://www.ancientcoins.biz/id/

Fitzwilliam Museum . http://www-cm.fitzmuseum.cam.ac.uk/coins/

Hellenic National Numismatic Museum (Athens) ....
.... http://www.culture.gr/2/21/214/21401m/e21401m.html

Hermitage Museum ....
.... http://www.hermitagemuseum.org/html_En/03/hm3_7_1.html

Hunterian .. http://www.hunterian.gla.ac.uk/coins/coins_index.html

Indian C oins .... http://www.med.unc.edu/~nupam/welcome.html

Islamic Coins .... http://users.rcn.com/j-roberts/

Israel Museum, Jerusalem ....
.... http://www.imj.org.il/eng/archaeology/numismatics/

Kernunnos .... http://www.kernunnos.com/Home.shtml

Krause Publications .... http://www.krause.com/

Kunsthistorische Museum .... http://www.khm.at/

Lacus Curtius .... http://
www.ukans.edu/history/index/europe/ancient_rome/E/home.html

Magna Graecia Coins ....
.... http://www.bio.vu.nl/home/vwielink/WWW_MGC/

Macquarie University ....
.... http://www.humanities.mq.edu.au/acans/gale.htm

Money Museum .... http://www.moneymuseum.com

Nickle Art Museum ....
http://www.acs.ucalgary.ca/~nickle/collections.html#numismatics

Numismatica .... http://www.limunltd.com/numismatica/

Odessa Museum of Numismatics ....
.... http://www.museum.com.ua/en/nauch_isled/nauchn_isl.htm

Ottilia Buerger Collection ....
.... http://www.lawrence.edu/dept/art/buerger/index.html

Oslo University .... http://www.dokpro.uio.no/umk/utstill.html

Parion .... http://www.snible.org/coins/parion.html

Parthia .... http://www.parthia.com

Pepperdine University ....
.... http://www.pepperdine.edu/seaver/religion/isar/Coins.htm

Philip I .... http://ettuantiquities.com/Philip_1/

Pontius Pilate .... http://www.pilatecoins.com/

Presveis Project ....
.... http://www.culture.gr/nm/presveis/Pages/Main/About.html

Probus ....
..... http://www.mycoinpage.com/dawsonlewis/Pages/probus.htm

Ptolemaic and Roman Egypt ....
.... http://www.houseofptolemy.org/housenum.htm#ROMCOIN

Roman Egypt .... http://coinsofromanegypt.com/

Roman Empire .... http://www.roman-empire.net/

Roman Republican .... http://www.romanrepublicancoins.com/

Romarch .... http://acad.depauw.edu/romarch/index.html

Royal Ontario Museum .... http://www.rom.on.ca

Sasanian Coins ....
.... http://www.grifterrec.com/coins/sasania/sasanian.html

Severus Alexander .... http://www.severusalexander.com/

Smithsonian .... http://americanhistory.si.edu/csr/cadnnc.htm

Spanish Mint http://www.fnmt.es/esp/museo/emain2.htm

Syracuse, Sicily ....
http://www.mcs.drexel.edu/~crorres/Archimedes/Coins/Arethusa.html

Trajan .... http://www.people.memphis.edu/~tjbuggey/coin.html

Wildwinds database .... http://www.wildwinds.com/

Zoo Coins of Gallienus .... http://www.ruark.org/coins/Zoo/

World Wide Web Resources
Pertaining to Ancient Art, History and Mythology

Ancient Near East (ABZU) .... http://www.etana.org/abzu/

Argos .... http://argos.evansville.edu/

Ancient & Biblical lands - Turkey ....
.... http://geocities.com/~ephesus/index.html

Bulfinch's Mythology .... http://www.bulfinch.org

Cambridge University Gateway ....
.... http://www.classics.cam.ac.uk/everyone/links/links.html

Classics Archive .... http://classics.mit.edu/

Dumbarton Oaks .... http://www.doaks.org/

Electronic Resources for Classicists ....
.... http://www.tlg.uci.edu/~tlg/index/resources.html

Getty Museum .... http://www.getty.edu/museum/

History Sourcebooks http://150.108.2.20/halsall/index.html

Israel Antiquities Authority ....
.... http://www.israntique.org.il/eng/news.html

Kelsey Museum of Archaeology ....
.... http://www.umich.edu/~kelseydb/Exhibits.html

Lands of the Bible .... http://www.
mun.ca/rels/restmov/texts/jwmcgarvey/lob/LOB000A.HTM

Louvre .... http://www.louvre.fr/

Medieval and Classical Library ....
.... http://sunsite.berkeley.edu/OMACL/

Metropolitan Museum of Art .... http://www.metmuseum.org/

Oriental Institute .... http://www-oi.uchicago.edu

Perseus Project .... http://www.perseus.tufts.edu/

Project Gutenberg .... http://promo.net/pg/

Royal Ontario Museum .... http://www.rom.on.ca/

Univ. of Michigan Classics .... http://www.umich.edu/~classics/

Virtual Library for Archaeology .... http://archnet.asu.edu/

THE ANCIENT COIN MARKET
Where Do Ancient Coins Come From?

I t seems strange that ancient coins could have survived for two thousand or more years, and even stranger that today they can be collected by virtually anyone with an interest. Although there are not as many collectors of ancient coins as there are of modern, one would think that the supply would be exhausted quickly. Where do these coins come from?

Ancient coins seem to turn up in the most unlikely places. Believe it or not, ancient coins have been found in North America with a metal detector. No, the Romans didn't sail here to escape the barbarian invasions! Like anything else, ancient coins can be lost. A collector playing flag football, or enjoying a picnic in the country, loses that lucky sestertius of Trajan that has been a pocket charm for years. A house burns, and a collection is scattered with the ashes. At least one hoard has been found in North America. Some years back, a collection of ancient coins—apparently carried to California by Spanish missionaries in the days of the Conquistadors—was found intact near San Diego. Readers of the popular treasure hunting magazines frequently see reports of individual ancient coin finds like this.

Flea markets and antique shops are obvious spots to check for the stray coin or two, but don't expect much. Another source for ancient coins, unpredictable but sometimes lucrative, is the general estate sale. Collectors do not always share their love of the hobby with other family members and a box of old coins is not necessarily of value to one's heirs. Most coin dealers will not bother to track down these sales, which are often held in obscure places and are advertised only in the local newspapers or "shoppers." Consequently, the collector can sometimes gain an edge and buy coins at a bargain—but be careful until you are comfortable with market prices. With ancient coins, age does not necessarily equate to value.

The sources of ancient coins are many. Keep in mind, coins are very durable. They survive quite well, especially if they have been sheltered from direct contact with the sea or soil. Since people in the ancient world often stored their monetary wealth in containers, those that were lost through misfortune (and misfortunes were many) remained intact and protected. These accumulations of coins are called hoards. Hoards may contain the treasury of an army that was annihilated in the field, the change of a merchant's shop, or the grocery money of a household. In addition to hoards, individual finds are not uncommon in the source countries. Depending on the conditions of the soil, coins often survive quite well simply buried under the sands of time. There were millions of people using coinage in those days, and consequently millions of coins were produced. The cumulative effect is staggering. Even though we find only a small percentage of those coins, it adds up to a substantial number.

The modern market for ancient coins dates back to the 14th century, and coins have been enthusiastically sought, accumulated and preserved by collectors since then. Collections of coins are no longer buried in pots, they pass on to heirs and other collectors. Virtually all of the coins that resided in collections of the past 500 years are still around somewhere today. True, some are in museums. But even museums sell their excess coins from time to time. Thus, the coins recirculate every generation or two—usually through the commercial market in the form of auctions or private sales.

In addition to these recirculating coins, new coins are constantly entering the market. In most of the source countries of southern Europe, there are laws prohibiting the export of ancient coins and other antiquities. The laws themselves are controversial, but they do restrict trade to some degree. In some countries, the penalties for violation are severe (see Buying Coins Overseas). Northern European source countries are more liberal (or should we say practical) about the preservation of "cultural property." In recent years, several large coin hoards found in Britain have made their way legally into the market. Inevitably, there are also hoards which "illegally" make their way into the market. In many countries of the world, there are not any prohibitions against buying, selling or collecting antiquities. Therefore, a coin sold in the marketplace is a legal commodity unless it can be proven that the specific coin was illegally exported from a country with prohibitions. This is a very difficult case to prove, since a farmer in Turkey, Greece or Italy is not likely to photograph every coin in a find before taking them to Zurich, Munich or London to sell them.

There have been cases where something like this actually did happen. As a result of the political turmoil in Afghanistan in the 1980s and 90s, the National Museum was looted and many rare and valuable coins were stolen. Fortunately, many coins in the collection had been photographed and published. Over the course of time, some of these coins appeared as offerings in the market. They were identified by conscientious dealers and withdrawn. Eventually, they will probably be repatriated to a stable government in that country.

The most common cause of new material on the market today is the metal detector. Aside from the stray finds mentioned above, there are (legal) clubs in Great Britain that spend their free time searching for artifacts. It is even pos-  sible to take metal detecting excursions to sites where you can do your own exploring for Roman coins and artifacts. The law in Britain regarding found artifacts is quite fair. Most things that are found may, after a hearing, be kept or freely sold. If they are declared property of the state, the finder is fairly compensated. Every year we read an account in the numismatic press about metal detector enthusiasts finding a hoard of ancient coins. These hoards often show up in the market. Metal detectors have made their way to remote corners of the Middle East as well and coins found there seem to find a way to the West.

This brings us to the questions: How many collectors of ancient coins are there? And, how many ancient coins survive? Today, with resources like *The Celator* and the Internet, we do not feel quite so isolated as we were in the past, and the world is for the most part at least aware that coins do survive from antiquity. It is impossible to determine the exact number of collectors because there is no way to conduct a meaningful census. A decade ago, we would have guessed that there were maybe 10,000 active ancient coin collectors in the world. Today, we could speculate that 50,000 is not an unreasonable estimate, and that indeed may be a conservative figure. The operative word here is "active", and that will vary by definition, but for the sake of discussion let us include anyone who makes successive purchases with the intent of preserving ancient coins in their present state (this excludes the buying of coins for jewelry or gifts). How does one arrive at such a conclusion? Not with any precision, for sure. There are more than 200 recognized dealers of ancient coins in the world. The average number of names on a dealer's contact list is typically about 3,000 (this number is derived from personal conversations with various dealers). This gives us a pool of something more than 600,000 names. Assuming a high degree of overlap, say 90%, that still suggests a collector base of 60,000 more or less. Add in a margin of error of another 10,000 or so names and 50,000 becomes a very conservative estimate. In fact, one firm in the trade has accumulated an active list of 16,000+ names, so this estimate does not seem at all unreasonable.

How many ancient coins survive? This is another question that is impossible to answer precisely, but one can surely speculate. There was a time when the number of collectors of classical coins could actually be counted, because they were part of an exclusive club—the intelligentsia of Europe. These princes, clerics and dignitaries amassed huge collections of coins which in many cases became the core of a national collection. The number of coins in a truly major collection often reached into the hundreds of thousands. Several million coins made their way into public collections between the 17th and 20th centuries. This, however, represents only a small percentage of the coins retrieved from mother earth.

The number of coins in private collections undoubtedly exceeds the number residing in public collections. If the average dealer mentioned above carried a stock of 1,000 coins (and that is not a high estimate

considering that we will include coins of all grades and bulk lots) the total number of coins in dealer stocks would exceed 200,000 coins at any given point in time. As a matter of fact, one dealer alone has claimed in media advertisements to have over 100,000 ancient coins in stock. Bulk lots of up to 25,000 coins are commonly seen on the wholesale market and occasionally lots of up to four times that size are offered. It would not be an exaggeration to place the number of coins presently in dealer hands at more than a million coins. Most collectors do not have 1000+ coins in their personal collections, but there are many collectors who have considerably more coins than that. It may be hard to imagine, but yes there really are quite a few people in this position. So, let us argue on the conservative side and say that the average number of coins in a collection is 200. Multiplied by 50,000 collectors, that amounts to 10 million coins residing in private collections.

Now, we have to add to all of the above the number of coins that have been found in archaeological excavations and are stored in pots on basement shelves at institutions all over the world. Thousands of institutions! Millions of coins! Some institutions literally have more coins than they can count..

We have not even touched on the number of coins sitting in bazaar stalls in source countries. Anyone want to guess how many ancient bronzes are floating around the market in Pakistan and India? We hear about 100,000+ Bactrian coins found in a well in Afghanistan or a similar number of denarii found in Bulgaria. Where are all these coins hanging out?

So far, we have talked only in terms of coins from the Western World. A calculation of the number of surviving Chinese Cash from ancient times is mind boggling. Has anyone ever tried to count the number of Abbasid dirhems in the world? Don't try.

The scope of the question begins to take shape when we consider all of the foregoing aspects, and we can see that it is an impossibility to determine, or even to attempt an educated guess about how many ancient coins survive. It is clear that the number reaches into the tens of millions, if not more. So, if you ever thought that maybe there weren't very many coins to choose from—think again.

Most collectors would like to think that their accumulations have some value above and beyond that ethereal benefit of personal satisfaction. But do we really stand a chance, financially, of breaking even or profiting from our effort? Most of us don't think about that too much, perhaps as a defense mechanism to ward off anxiety attacks. But it is a fair question that ought to be considered. Beginning collectors, by nature, tend to lack the sophistication to collect in a way that will maximize their chances of a good return on their investment. Many will be inclined to accumulate a menagerie of inexpensive coins which seem an incredible bargain in comparison to modern issues. Coins like this, which exist in the hundreds of thousands or more, are undeniably worth the price that they bring on today's market. But, will they be worth more tomorrow? My guess is that they will, but only marginally. It is unlikely that a collector who buys a "Heinz" variety of common ancient coins today will be able to resell them anytime in the near future at a profit. As one might expect, the coins that traditionally appreciate most in value are also the most actively sought and competed for in the market. This can be an intimidating environment for fledgling collectors and not everyone is comfortable with it in their formative years. Those who have the financial resources may choose to buy high grade and rare coins right from the start, but they should find a reputable advisor before jumping into the fray. For those who simply want to enjoy collecting and do not have the budget to delve into rare and expensive issues, all is not lost.

There are many areas of ancient coin collecting that are neglected by mainstream collectors. Sometimes, these coins can yield good returns to the collector who bothers to learn about them and to collect them with persistence and purpose.

In coin collecting, like many other pursuits in life, knowledge is power. And, for those who haven't yet figured it out, power = wealth. The best way to turn an inexpensive collection into something of value is to stock it with interesting coins that others have failed to appreciate. So, what are these coins? They can be found in almost any series, but I will mention just a few here to give you an idea of what I am suggesting and then you can figure out for yourself what kinds of coins might suit your taste, budget, and inclination.

Those coins that seem to be found everywhere you look can sometimes hold potential for appreciation, simply because they are so cheap to begin with. What happens when a huge hoard of one type appears is that the market immediately becomes depressed for those issues. Nevermind that there are many rare specimens passing at generic coin prices, the entire market for a given series can suffer from the saturation caused by large hoards. The savvy collector will see this as an opportunity to obtain rarities at common coin prices. But, to do this, one needs to learn the series.

Recent examples of market saturation from large hoards include Severan and Antonine denarii, Roman Provincial coins of the Balkans and silver coins from Greece and Magna Graecia. Huge hoards have made individual coins of these types very cheap in today's market. By the same token, coins of Bactria have appeared in huge numbers and are at an historic low price wise. Keep in mind that hoards come and go. A few years from now, something else will be common and the coins we see today may well be obscure.

We are enjoying a unique bubble in the market today, as there are many more ancient coins available than there are collectors for them. So, rather than chase the high profile coins that everyone will bid dearly for, why not collect the coins that no one pays any attention to? They are cheap, and often they are rare—but at the moment nobody seems to care.

Over time, collections that are assembled with forethought and consistency will outperform those accumulated randomly, regardless of the series which they represent. It can be smart to collect coins that others ignore. At the risk of beating a dead horse, let us say one more time: The way to maximize one's enjoyment and minimize potential loss is to collect with a purpose and don't be afraid to be a bit contrarian. Regardless of your interest, it is better to collect intensely within a managable area than to attempt an accumulation of many diverse and unassociated items. A collector should not think in terms of years, but in decades. It is very difficult to assemble a meaningful collection in a few years. Choose your path carefully and plan to spend a good share of your collecting life following it. If you do, and if you mature as a collector along the way, it is likely that your collection will indeed be worth something to someone when your time with it has come to an end. And, as a bonus, it will bring you a lot more enjoyment in the meantime.

Deciding what and how to collect is important, but knowing how and where to buy is every bit as important for most people. There are a good many ways to buy ancient coins. Some of them are safe, others are not. The following sections will address a variety of the methods commonly employed in the sale of coins, and share some tips about how these vehicles work.

The hardest thing for converts from modern coinage to accept is the loose structure of grading and pricing ancient coins. Whether, as collectors, we like it or not, ancient coins simply do not lend themselves to precise grading and pricing. This makes it all the more important for a collector to understand how the market works. Knowing the difference between coins of strong and weak market value can save money and emotional stress when it comes time to sell. This has nothing to do with a coin's desirability as a collectible. There are many factors that may make a normally unmarketable coin quite desirable to a particular collector. But, if the coin is otherwise unmarketable it should not be bringing a premium just because you happen to want it. Knowing what makes coins more or less valuable will help the buyer gauge whether or not the asking price is appropriate.

As we have said earlier, a major show can be very intimidating to the newcomer. They are usually held in large convention centers, and as many as 1,000 dealers may be set up with tables. Finding your way around can be difficult and it is very easy to become disoriented—not a good way to start a day of collecting enjoyment. How does one act in this foreign environment? Are there rules that everyone seems to know but won't share? Shows aren't the only way to buy ancient coins, and there are some distinct differences between the options for buying by mail. Knowing how an auction works can save you money whether you are bidding by mail or in person. Auctions are not complicated, but they do require a little thought.

Most collectors don't think a great deal about disposing of their collections. The idea of collecting something, after all, is to have and enjoy it. But, interests change and fate deals its cards. There may come a time when it is desirable or necessary to sell a coin or liquidate a collection. Where does one turn in this time of need? All of these are questions that collectors struggle with alone, because they do not know where to turn for help. Keep in mind that there is a sense of fraternalism among ancient coin collectors that is not common to all fields of numismatics— look for those footprints.

All About Caveat Emptor

No, Caveat Emptor was not an obscure Roman emperor—although Didius Julianus might have paid heed to the term. In AD 193, following the murder of Pertinax, the Praetorian Guards held a public auction, offering the position of emperor to the highest bidder. Didius Julianus, a wealthy senator, offered the winning bid of 25,000 sestertii per man. He ruled for 66 days before losing his head, literally. This latin term for "buyer beware" has survived the ages for good reason.

The field of ancient coinage is unquestionably one of those areas where the buyer must be cautious. Due to the very nature of ancient coin production and preservation, the valuing of specimens is subjective. With modern coins, we can precisely determine mintage, extent of wear, and fluctuating market prices. None of this is possible with ancient coins. To some beginners, this is a point of consternation. But, actually it is one of the wonderful things about ancients that attracts collectors from their shiny slabbed cousins. No two ancient coins are alike, and that surely is a part of their charm.

On the following pages, we will discuss some of the elements of consideration in gauging the value of an ancient coin. This information is not going to give the reader a concrete dollar value for any specimen, but it will help the inexperienced learn how certain factors ought to be weighed in deciding which of two specimens might be worth the higher price.

Factors Affecting Coin Value

As hard as it may be to accept, there simply is not a standard and precise guide to the values of ancient coins. Furthermore, there never will be! That may seem like a bold statement, but it is an opinion based on more than a few years of experience. The most useful work of this type that has ever been written is the series by David Sear (see bibliography), and Mr. Sear would be the first to acknowledge that prices published in his works are very tenuous. The Sear catalogues are immensely useful as general attribution guides and relative value guides, but they do not and can not reflect actual market prices for any particular specimen. Some years back, a publication by the name of *Classical Coin Newsletter,* included a section of current market prices based on auction results and dealer observations of prices realized on the bourse floor. It proved to be a very general guide, which required an inordinate amount of effort to update. The publication did not survive.

Given that there are not any guides to follow, what is the beginning collector to do? As one might expect, without any Krause-Mishler catalog or "Redbook" to standardize prices, the asking price for any particular type coin will vary from dealer to dealer. The only practical thing for the collector to do is shop around. Check prices at various dealer tables, check auction estimates and prices realized, read as many fixed price lists and advertisements as you can and develop a sense of what price range a desired type should fall in.

On the facing page is a table of factors to be considered when judging value. Many of the topics have already been introduced in the earlier section about "How Ancient Coins Were Made." Some of these factors influence value in a positive way and are listed in the "POSITIVE" column. Those which tend to influence value in a negative way are listed in the "NEGATIVE" column. A few factors may, depending on the situation, influence value either positively or negatively, these are listed in a neutral column marked + / -. Following this table are some comments about each of the factors listed.

The factors are not listed in any order of priority, and the extent to which each factor plays against the others is a function of personal taste. Some collectors find one detraction very objectionable, while others pay little attention to it. Some may consider a countermark to be a detraction, others may consider it an asset. So, one must keep in mind that this whole process of gauging value is in itself subjective. In any case, the factors are additive, so a preponderance of negatives or positives should skew the value of a particular specimen one way or the other.

FACTORS AFFECTING COIN VALUE

POSITIVE	NEUTRAL	NEGATIVE
+	+ / -	-
Rarity	Surfaces	Die Break
Provenance	Metal	Worn Die
Eye Appeal	Shape	Weak Strike
Toning	Fabric	Flan Cracks
Patina	Centering	Porosity
Authenticity	Overstrike	Crystallinity
Need	Cleaning	Grafitti
Popularity	Fourrée	Smoothing
Importance	Countermark	Corrosion
Size	Grade	Tooling
Relief	Style	Test Cuts
Detail	Striking Errors	Banker's Marks
		Scratches
		Lacquering
		Horn Silver
		Verdigris
		Mounting

+ RARITY: There has never been a complete census of ancient coin types in private collections, and no one really knows how many examples exist of any particular type. The compilers of *Roman Imperial Coinage* (RIC) diligently performed a census of museum holdings to assign rarities in that mammoth 10-volume work. But, experienced collectors and dealers are quick to point out that this census is often misleading. Coins that seldom appear in museum holdings, and are consequently assigned a high degree of rarity in RIC, may be quite common in the commercial market. Conversely, there are certain coins that hardly ever appear in the market, but many museums have specimens due to the good graces of donating collectors. Auction records are sometimes used as a gauge to rarity—the fewer appearances, the greater the rarity. This may work well for very expensive or esoteric coins which generally find their way to auction, but it doesn't help any for the thousands of coins that would only make it to an auction catalogue buried in a large lot. There are some coin types that are universally acknowledged as rare, like Athenian decadrachms and Brutus EID MAR denarii. But some types that are often perceived as rare, like Syracusan decadrachms, are actually more common than one might think. If a coin type or major variety is unpublished in any of the major collections, it can pretty safely be assumed that it is rare. If dealers virtually never see a certain type in circulation, it might also be reasonable to assume that it is rare. If, as a serious collector of a particular series, one has never seen the type offered for sale or catalogued in a collection, it is most certainly a coin of great rarity. The value of a rare coin may easily exceed the value of a common coin of equivalent grade by a multiple of 10 to 100 or more.

+ PROVENANCE: The provenance, or source history, of a coin can sometimes increase the value of a coin. For example, collectors might be willing to pay a slight premium for a coin that can be traced to a well known or published hoard. The gold coins of the Boscoreale Hoard, with their distinctive red toning, always seem to sell quickly and for slightly more than similar non-hoard coins. The recorded provenance to an important collection of the past will generally add something to the value as well. Some collectors perceive a provenance from an important 19th century collection to be a guarantee of authenticity. This is a false sense of security, as forgeries were as much a problem to collectors in those days as they are to us today. In any event, the premium that should be placed on provenance will generally not be great—perhaps in the range of 10% more than for an identical coin without provenance.

+ EYE APPEAL: This factor embodies within it some of the other factors treated singly here and it is not something easily described. However, most readers will know instinctively what it means. Some coins immediately appeal to the viewer as striking examples (no pun intended). Elements of centering, relief, toning, detail and style will combine to produce a positive effect that requires little contemplation or analysis.

+ TONING: Virtually every ancient coin is cleaned at some point in its journey from an underground burial to the tray of a collector. If they were not cleaned, most coins would be totally unattractive. The process of cleaning not only takes away dirt and grime, but often leaves a coin looking shiny and new. This may be acceptable for modern coins, but ancient coins lose much of their emotional appeal if they look new. Coins begin to tone back to a pleasing state immediately after they are cleaned. The process may take several years if left to progress on its own. With the help of chemical agents and the application of heat to accellerate oxidation, that retoning can be achieved very quickly. The gain in time is usually a trade off against quality. The most appealing coins are those that were cleaned 50 to 100 years ago and now have what we refer to as "old cabinet" toning. This term is a reference to the coins having been in a collector's cabinet for some time. Coins with even and natural toning are more desirable, and consequently worth more, than those which have recently been cleaned. Keep in mind that toning is always relative, and time will be your friend, so the premium to attach to nicely toned coins will be a function of one's perception of time and its value.

+ PATINA: According to the American Heritage Dictionary, patina is: "1. A thin layer of corrosion, usually brown or green, that appears on copper or copper alloys, such as bronze, as a result of natural or artificial oxidation. 2. The sheen produced by age and use on any antique surface." Actually, patina is the ultimate conclusion of the toning process described above. Some patina is fragile, and other types can be rock hard. In most cases, patina is desirable. Bronze coins can be covered with beautiful patinas in various shades of red, green, blue, brown or black. Some collectors like mottled patina, where colors are mixed. Regardless of color, a smooth, unbroken patina significantly enhances the value of a bronze coin. Natural patina is always preferred, but artificial toning is sometimes acceptable. In either case, an attractively patinated coin is worth more than one without patina.

A heavily encrusted coin is usually of no value to collectors because the elements of interest are obscured. In severe cases, it may be necessary to strip everything off the surface of a coin in order to remove the encrustation. This is called stripping a coin. It is the position of some numismatists that a stripped coin should be left stripped— that artificially patinating or "toning" the surface is fraudulent. They basically feel that it suggests the coin is something that it isn't. Others feel that helping nature along by chemically oxidizing the coin, saving a few hundred years, is not only acceptable, it is preferable to the alternative.

This can, of course, become an emotional issue and new collectors who witness this debate can become terribly confused—perhaps feeling "cheated" by some dealer who sold them a repatinated coin. This is a sad thing, because it undermines confidence and leaves the new collector grasping for some sense of security.

The truth of the matter is that many ancient coins on the market today, or in past centuries, have been stripped and repatinated. The processes and the extent of the application may vary, but it is not an uncommon practice. And, agree or disagree, it is not normal practice nor is it expected of a dealer to state that a coin has been repatinated. This long established precedent is certainly not a case of fraudulence. Of course it *is* expected that, when asked, a dealer will give his or her honest opinion about whether the patina on a coin is natural or artificial. The broader question of acceptability is really dealt with by the market itself. An undesirable coin, whether it has been repatinated or left encrusted, will not sell. Therefore, any repatination must reflect a certain amount of skill, like any other artistic process. For more on this topic see the section "To Clean, or Not to Clean..." in the subsequent chapter on How to Collect Ancient Coins.

+AUTHENTICITY: It goes without saying that an authentic coin is worth more than one that is not. Sadly, the determination of authenticity is a complicated issue. Without going into that issue here, we should simply point out that an enforceable guarantee of authenticity certainly adds to the value of any coin. How much is that worth? That depends on how willing you are financially and emotionally to suffer any loss yourself.

+ NEED: Theoretically, how badly you need a particular specimen for your collection should not change its market value, but practically speaking it can and does. Most really rare coins find their way to public auctions. All it takes at a public auction to increase the value of a coin is for two potential buyers to need and want it. If a collector sends want lists to several dealers in the search for a needed coin, it can be presumed that the price of that coin, when found, will be at the upper end of its market range. This is only natural considering the time that the dealer needs to expend to locate a specific item.

+ POPULARITY: The more people there are standing in line for the next choice specimen of a popular type, the more expensive it is going to be. In a supply and demand market, popularity is king. Even coins like the Athenian tetradrachms, which are exceedingly common, maintain remarkably high price levels because of their tremendous popularity. Even though they are often found in large hoards, it seems like there just aren't ever enough of them to go around. Another coin of this type is the famous Shekel of Tyre.

+ IMPORTANCE: Rarity and importance are not synonymous. A coin of absolute rarity, being the only known specimen in the world, is still valued to a large degree on its importance. All else being equal, a unique bronze of Constantine the Great will not stand in the same value league with a unique bronze of Cleopatra VII. A Roman Provincial coin that bears a date confirming a previously uncertain event will be priced much higher than a similar undated specimen. The discovery coin for a new denomination in the Roman Imperial series would certainly be more important and more valuable than the discovery coin for a new Nabataean bronze denomination.

+ SIZE: Without a doubt, large coins on average bring higher prices than small coins. Even among coins of the same type, those with large flans bring higher prices than those with small flans. In modern society, bigger is better.

+ RELIEF: Some coin dies are very sculptural, that is, they bear an image with high relief. The high relief causes light and shadow to fall in a way that enhances the beauty of the composition. This is not accidental. A good die-engraver is a talented artist who is sensitive to the medium and creates subjects of superior quality. There is usually a small but predictable premium attached to coins of high relief.

+ / - DETAIL: Wear is of course the enemy of detail, but some coins lacked good detail on the day they were struck. This might come from poor design of the die, or poor execution in the striking process. Flatness is common in some series and low relief is common in others. Surprisingly, coins with low relief tend not to wear as quickly as high relief coins, but they are less appealing artistically. Poorly struck coins will be blurred and lack detail even in the protected areas of the design. Coins with excellent detail always command a premium over those without.

+ / - SURFACES: Wear, abrasions, gouges, encrustation and staining can all detract from the eye appeal of a coin. On the other hand, a coin with smooth and "warm" surfaces deserves some respect when it comes to pricing. The reflectivity and consistency of a coin's surface also have some bearing on how it will look to the human eye. On the whole, it seems that really good surfaces tend to increase the value of a coin more than flawed surfaces detract from one. That is probably because coins with poor surfaces are already considered "bargain coins" in many venues.

+ / - METAL : The term "good metal" is used frequently in numismatics and generally applies to the purity of the planchet upon which a coin is struck. Good silver has a smooth healthy look and a natural color. Often, in a series that extends over several decades or centuries, we see changes in the composition of the metal that are driven by the need for debasement in a failing economy. Some coins of a particular ruler or mint will have higher silver content than others simply because of these changes. What starts off as a coin of high quality silver, for example, may end up as one struck in billon. The metal quality generally has an effect on value even today, as collectors instinctively prefer, and will pay higher prices for, coins of high precious metal content over debased coins.

+ / - SHAPE: Ancient coins are seldom completely uniform in shape, but nice round specimens of even thickness do seem to demand a bit more than the average. Conversely, coins of really irregular shape are generally worth considerably less.

+ / - FABRIC: Like the shape, the fabric of a coin has some bearing on its value. Fabric is a term which loosely describes the nature of the flan and its preparation for striking. Some adjectives that might accompany the word fabric include: thin, thick, crude, dumpy, barbarous or delicate. Generally, a coin of delicate fabric will be more valuable than a coin of crude fabric of the same type. Sometimes, an entire series will typically be found struck on dumpy flans—like the tetradrachms of Athens struck after 300 BC. It is worth paying a premium to find a coin of superior fabric in such a series.

85

+ / - CENTERING: Having been struck individually by hand, ancient coins are not as well centered as machine-made products. They still should be reasonably well centered, however, to command a good price. It is important that the major elements of design are included within the flan. If they are not, an automatic discount is appropriate. Watch for the names of rulers and cities. Are they clear and complete? If the coin *is* off-center, which aspect of the coin is degraded? A portrait, for example, is not terribly degraded if it is off-center in the direction of the back of the head. The same coin with the nose and chin off the flan is seriously flawed. A silver stater of Tarentum may be pleasing enough with the tail of the dolphin off the flan. Chop off the dolphin's nose and you have a coin that will face a lifetime of rejection. This is because the human eye tends to lead the image. We feel comfortable enough when there is extra space in the direction of travel, but put a barrier in that path and we feel stifled. This condition has at least a psychological effect on value in the sense that coins with eye appeal sell better than those without.

+ / - OVERSTRIKE: Overstrikes are an important phenomenon to numismatists but are often underappreciated. An overstrike is the purposeful striking of one coin type over the top of that existing on a previously issued coin. The purpose is to save the time and expense of flan preparation. What is important about overstrikes is that when the undertype is visible they give us unequivocal proof of the order in which the two types were struck. As such, these coins are quite valuable for research. At the same time, the disruptive appearance of the undertype makes such a coin less valuable to the collector who is merely seeking a nice specimen of the overtype. So, the value of an overstrike will depend greatly on the purpose for which it is intended.

+ / - CLEANING: We have discussed the need for and effects of cleaning elsewhere, but the quality of cleaning has just as important an effect on value as whether a coin is cleaned or not. A bronze coin that has been harshly stripped is about as garish as any coin can be. The value of a coin in this condition is minimal. A coin that has been very carefully and professionally cleaned can easily be worth twice as much as it was before cleaning.

+ / - FOURRÉE: Plated contemporary counterfeits are sometimes so normal in appearance that they are difficult to detect. At other times, the plating develops voids where the internal copper core can show through. Most collectors will consider a fourrée as being less valuable than a full silver mint issue. There are, however, collectors who will pay a premium for fourrées and find them very collectable. So, depending on who is buying and who is selling, the price of a fourrée can vary considerably.

+ / - COUNTERMARK: Countermarks can increase the value of a coin if they are clearly recognizable and do not seriously impair the image on the host coin. An historically important countermark, like that of Legion X in Judaea, is of considerable value even if the host coin is obliterated. Conversely, a crude and poorly placed countermark, or worse yet several countermarks, of indescript nature can virtually destroy the value of even a popular coin type.

+ / - GRADE: No single factor has a greater bearing on value than grade. The combination of high grade and high rarity will produce the highest prices possible on a consistent basis. However, grade alone is not enough. A high grade coin, measured in terms of visible detail, may have many of the imperfections discussed in this section. When faced with these limitations, even high grade coins are susceptible to reduced valuations.

+ / - STYLE: We have discussed the aspects of style elsewhere in this volume, and especially in Volume II of this series which deals with Greek coinage. There is no such thing as "good" style and "bad" style. There is only "this" style and "that" style. Many collectors confuse execution and style. The careful rendering of details is, in most periods, a gauge of artistic excellence. Musculature, and features like hair, hands and feet are worth noting. Also watch for realistic proportions in coins of the Classical period and later. Specimens of ancient coinage which faithfully render the style and virtuosity of an important era will ultimately be appreciated by a wider range of sophisticated collectors and the value of these pieces will consequently increase.

+ / - STRIKING ERRORS: Striking errors include double strikes, brockages, clashed dies and all sorts of combinations of the above. To the average collector, these are detractions. However, there are collectors who specialize in error coins and who will pay premiums for nice specimens of a particular error variety. The value of an error coin will depend entirely on the kind of market that it is offered for sale in.

- DIE BREAK: As the pressures of striking take their toll on the structural integrity of a coin die, it starts to fragment and will eventually break up entirely if not pulled from service. Die breaks range from simple dots to thin lines and can result in huge chunks of the image disappearing. Remember that what happens to a die ends up happening in reverse on the coin. So, a dislodged section of the image on a die results in a big blank lump on the coin. The effect that this has on value is directly proportionate to the degree of fragmentation.

-WORN DIE: A worn die exhibits similar characteristics as a worn coin, except that usually only one of the dies suffers from this degradation. There is virtually no redeeming value to a worn die and coins struck from a badly worn die should be avoided if possible.

-WEAK STRIKE: The corollary of a coin struck from a worn die is one poorly struck from a good die. This can result from striking a planchet that is too cool, or from not applying sufficient force. In either event, a weak strike leaves an image that is indistinct and certainly not appealing. Some series, like the antoninianii of the Gallic Empire, are habitually struck weakly and this detraction is not to be avoided if one is to collect the series. But generally speaking, a weak strike is a major detraction and should be appropriately discounted.

- FLAN CRACKS: Like die breaks, flan cracks range from the nearly imperceptible, which are of little concern, to the magnificent. The latter are always a concern, because the coin may literally break in half. Flan cracks are a normal occurrence of striking and should not be judged too harshly, especially in a series like Severan denarii, where they are really prevalent. Value of a coin is not normally affected very much by a flan crack unless it is wide and deep.

- POROSITY: The little pits which cause a sandpaper-like finish on a coin are called porosity. Most coins suffer from some level of porosity, but in minor cases it may only be detectable under a powerful magnifying glass. In advanced cases, the image is literally eaten away by the porous surface. In these cases, the value of a coin is seriously diminished. Some unscrupulous sellers have tried to mask porosity by filling the surface with shoe polish or epoxy resins. This condition is usually detectable because the surface takes on a waxy look. Minor porosity is a minor detraction, major porosity is a major detraction.

- CRYSTALLINITY: Crystallization is one of the major problems encountered with ancient silver. A crystalized coin becomes brittle and can be honeycombed with air pockets. The result is a coin of much lighter weight than normal, a whitish color and the appearance of having been sandblasted. Crystalline coins are worth considerably less than a good metal specimen of the same type. There is always a risk of a crystalline coin breaking, and any coin purchased in this condition should be protected in special holders.

- GRAFFITI: Graffiti is the term used to describe letters or symbols scratched onto a coin's surface, usually in ancient times, by someone who apparently had nothing better to do. Names are often scratched onto a coin as graffiti and can be quite interesting, but they do detract from the coin's value as a collectible item.

- SMOOTHING: The mechanical removal of surface imperfections in the field of a coin is called smoothing. This may lead to a more visually attractive specimen, but most collectors frown upon any alteration to the actual surface metal of a coin. Coins that have been smoothed should be properly described at the time of sale and they are likely to bring lower prices than coins with unaltered surfaces.

- CORROSION: When dissimilar metals are buried together for a long period of time the result can be shocking. Tiny fields of electricity in the soil can cause electrolysis between the metals and lead to a migration of molecules from one to the other. This causes pitting on the surface of the donor coin and accretions on the surface of the receptor coin—not a good thing in either case. Similar pitting or internal corrosion can be caused by natural acids in the soil. A coin corroded internally may be extremely light and quite fragile. Regardless of the cause, serious corrosion severely reduces the value of a coin.

-TOOLING: In the 19th century it was fashionable to take an engravers tool and reincise the hairlines or details of a worn coin. This was especially common with Roman sestertii. In most cases, there was little effort to mask these "improvements" because it was not looked down upon at the time as being deceptive. However, some of the individuals doing this sort of tooling were capable artists. These coins are still around today, and may not be noticed immediately if they were tooled by an expert. Although tooling, like smoothing, is no longer considered ethical, and will be pointed out by most experienced dealers, one should keep an eye out nevertheless.

- TEST CUTS: In order to determine whether a coin was solid silver or plated, chisels and punches were often used to penetrate the outer surfaces of a coin. These ranged from inconspicuous little punches of little affect to the overall image on the coin, to major slashes directly across the highest relief point. In the former case, the coin's value as a collectable is not seriously diminished. But, in the latter case, a badly test cut specimen may bring half or less the price that an uncut specimen will bring.

- BANKER'S MARKS: This may be a misnomer, because we really do not have any solid evidence that these marks were applied by money changers, but the name has stuck anyway. These tiny punch marks are almost too small and too shallow to be tests for a base metal core. Also, the designs seem to have meaning, like the brands on cattle in the American West. Banker's marks do not detract significantly from the value of a coin, and in some cases may even be appealing.

- SCRATCHES: Scratches are never welcome on the surface of a coin, but old scratches that have been patinated over are much less objectionable than modern scratches. Often in the process of retrieving a coin from the ground the surface is scratched. These scratches are called "spade marks". Some coins look like they were heavily scratched in antiquity, with all of the lines running parallel. These are usually a remnant of flan preparation and are a normal condition in certain series like the bronze coins of Pontus. Large gouges or "adjustment marks" on some Roman denarii were done at the mint to adjust the weight of a specified number of coins. Although these adjustment marks are normal, they still detract from the modern collectable value of those marked coins.

- LACQUERING: Coins that have recirculated from old collections sometimes have a coating of lacquer on them as that was a common method of sealing coins against air and moisture in the 19th century. Lacquered coins are artificially shiny and mostly unattractive. They are usually discounted in value.

- HORN SILVER: One problem that is often encountered with silver coins is a thick oxidation called "horn silver." This buildup on the surface of a coin is sometimes difficult to remove, and poorly cleaned coins may have traces of horn silver adhering to crevices or obscuring details of the image. Horn silver is tough to remove and any objectional traces remaining after a coin has been cleaned will probably detract some from the value of the coin, although not as badly as serious corrosion.

- VERDIGRIS: Bronze coins suffer similar problems, but instead of horn silver, they can be afflicted with hard green or red deposits that are difficult to remove without stripping the coin completely down to its surface. A soft powdery green deposit on the surface of a bronze coin is an indicator of bronze disease. This condition is difficult to arrest and should be avoided if possible.

- MOUNTING: The removal of a coin from a jewelry mount almost always leaves traces on the rim. This damage to the coin reduces its value as a collectable by perhaps 20% or more. The other factor associated with coins mounted in jewelry is that they often have been polished or are heavily worn. The combination of these negative factors usually makes ex-jewelry pieces undesirable as collectibles.

One might presume, from the comments above that searching for an acceptable coin could be tough. Ancient coins are seldom perfect—and when they are, they command huge premiums. The average collector, buying the average coin, will certainly tolerate some imperfection. The challenge is finding the best coin, with the fewest imperfections, at the most reasonable price. To do this, one must look at as many coins as possible and develop a sense of value before plunging blindly in the acquisition mode. It sometimes is the case that a whole series of coins suffers, almost uniformly, from the same imperfections. In these cases, one will simply have to accept the norm if one is to collect the series.

As a group, ancient coin dealers are probably among the most conscientious of all coin dealers. Authenticity is guaranteed by virtually all dealers, many allow returns, and some even offer buy-back plans. Still, this is a "caveat emptor" hobby. The buyer is expected to be knowledgeable and aware. If you are not, it is best to tell a dealer right up front and hope that they will show some mercy. It is *never* a good idea to try to convince a dealer that you are the world's expert on a particular series. If you are an expert, you will only be buying the rarest and best coins, right? How much should you pay for the rarest and the best?

The differential between a common low grade coin and the same coin in high grade may be 10 to 1. For example, a slightly pitted Fine AE-3 of Constantine should sell for about $5.00. An EF, well-centered and nicely patinated specimen should sell for about $50, maybe more. This spread is likely to increase for coins of some rarity. A low grade portrait denarius of Julius Caesar is worth four or five hundred dollars, but one choice EF specimen recently brought $15,000.

With pricing as subjective as it is, there can also be significant price spreads between comparable coins. That sounds like a dealer's paradise, but actually it hurts the dealer. Even though a dealer may have paid significantly more than a competitor for a comparable piece, the difference in price will usually be perceived by a collector as "markup." This leads not only to a lost sale, but sometimes to a lost customer—of which there are far too few in this hobby to begin with. Given time, prices tend to stabilize as dealers rotate stock that does not sell. The catalyst that makes this happen is knowledgeable and patient collectors who, in reality, determine the market price themselves.

Having discovered a show within commuting distance, what might the beginner expect? One could probably write a book on the methodology of "working" a coin show. There are some standard approaches and some not so standard. Any veteran dealer who has worked the circuit could offer several stereotypes of collectors and tales that are both shocking and humorous.

One of the first considerations at a show is when to attend. There are those who feel that being first in line on opening day is the only way to obtain any rare specimens that might be available. At the opposite end of the spectrum are collectors who wait until the closing moments of a show because dealers are sometimes willing to give deep discounts on stock that remains unsold. In reality, there is little advantage to either extreme. Really rare coins are often sold during dealer set-up, which is closed to the public. Most dealers have clients waiting for the tough-to-find specimens, and when one appears at a show they buy it for their client and take it back home. This doesn't mean that rare coins are not offered at coin shows, but they are generally as available at mid-show as they are at opening. A show is not simply a selling vehicle for the dealer, it is also a buying opportunity. Coins bought at a show are often sold at the same show, and therefore trying to predict at which moment a rare specimen might appear is like rolling dice at Las Vegas. Conditions are little different for the bargain hunter who sweeps the floor at closing. Dealers who have had a particularly good or bad show have been known to leave a bourse early on the final day. In either case, bargains might be found because the dealer who had a bad show is anxious to cover expenses before leaving and the dealer who had a good show is likely to be more generous than usual. The collector who arrives too late may miss these opportunities. Of course these situations are unpredictable, and this digression is offered only to illustrate that point.

The first thing that a newcomer to shows will notice is that the bourse is typically located in a secure area and the entrance is guarded. The reason for this should be obvious, and one should not take offense at being asked to register and bear a name tag while on the bourse floor. Theft is a serious concern in the bourse environment, and controls are absolutely necessary. We'll get to more on that subject in a moment. At the time of registration, most shows will provide a program or list of dealers in attendance. This is a very useful tool and it will save you a lot of time and aggravation in navigating the bourse floor. It is worthwhile to sit down for a moment and study the floor arrangement, making a note of dealers that you think might have stock that you are interested in. It is easy to get distracted, especially at the larger shows, and one will accomplish a lot more with even a rudimentary plan of attack. Some show organizers group dealers specializing in ancient and foreign coins. This is a great help—look for signs indicating these areas.

There are a few basic courtesies that the collector should observe while on the floor. There are also some that dealers should observe, but this book is not written for them. Many collectors do not fully appreciate the costs associated with setting up a bourse table, and therefore assume that the dealer is just another hobbyist out for a relaxing weekend. A single eight-foot table at a major numismatic convention rents for about $1,000 to $2,000 depending on the spot. Add to this a "special" room rate of $179 per night at the convention hotel and a restaurant tab that would choke a horse. Oh, you flew in? Add a few hundred dollars more. To cover basic expenses, forget about salary, one must realize a profit of about $2,500. Given an average net markup of 20%, this equates to $12,500 volume before the first nickel is made. For most dealers, this represents a substantial risk and a tremendous investment in inventory. Admittedly, a show in Peoria costs something less to do than one in New York City—but the cost versus volume scale is not all that much different. Consequently, dealers are often faced with the harsh reality of doing volume sales.

Getting back to courtesy, it is neither prudent nor courteous for a collector to monopolize the few feet of space available for selling. There are times in every show when a dealer will gladly take the time to chat with collectors, answer questions, offer advice or share "war stories." The collector should be courteous enough to realize when this time is past and other customers require attention. Another consideration is that of parking on prime real estate. Most dealers will group their more expensive stock in one tray. This is done for two reasons: it improves security, and it places those coins where more advanced collectors can view them easily. Beginners who are likely to be looking through boxes of lower priced stock should try to do so without blocking these cases or the main flow of traffic.

Understanding that there are people in this world who collect coins without paying for them, and that they come in all descriptions, the collector should not begrudge a dealer's concern. There are many ways to steal a coin, and this is not a guidebook for the criminally minded, but the most common is slight of hand. A thief might, for example, feign interest by stacking up a pile of coins. At that point the thief employs a distraction by asking for something on a back table which causes the dealer to turn around and lose eye contact. Upon returning, the dealer still sees a stack of coins (less one). To further obscure the theft and to alleviate suspicion, the thief will usually purchase one or two cheaper coins left in the stack. The collector should never feel offended if a dealer watches closely; and, as a courtesy, should try to keep coins in plain view to make the dealer's job easier.

Making a selection is only half of the experience of purchasing a coin. Settling on a price is also important. Every dealer approaches marketing from a slightly different perspective, but in most cases the price indicated on a coin ticket is a reflection of the seller's perceived retail value of the coin. When offered in a fixed price catalogue, this is understood to be the selling price and is not normally a negotiated issue. At a numismatic bourse, however, the price structure is much more flexible. It is unusual to find a dealer in ancient coins that absolutely will not negotiate the price of any item. On better pieces of new stock, which may be destined for a list, the dealer might hold the line. Older stock is usually fair game for discounting. It never hurts to ask a dealer for the best price possible. Sometimes it is an outright revelation.

Buying Coins Overseas

A European vacation, especially to the Mediterranean, is an ancient coin collector's dream, but it can also become a nightmare. The laws of virtually all Mediterranean source countries, i.e. the countries in which ancient coins were originally struck and circulated, prohibit the export of coins or other artifacts which are over 100 years old. In spite of this, the collector vacationing in these countries is tempted constantly by peddlers who have coins to offer. Many of these tourist offerings are blatantly fake, but at the less frequented sites one is likely to be offered authentic pieces. The fact that local officials seem ineffective in controlling these vendors does not negate the law, and to find out how serious the law really is one only needs to encounter a customs official in a foul mood (normal state of mind required for the position). Detention is not unheard of in places like Turkey, Syria and Lebanon, and humane treatment of prisoners is not something that your travel agent will guarantee. The argument for these laws is based on the premise of protecting cultural property. This sounds well and good, but in most cases coins are found randomly and independently. They hold no value as cultural property because they cannot be studied in an archaeologically significant context. Nevertheless, the laws are valid and enforcement can be severe.

Even if a daring tourist were inclined to tempt fate and carry a few coins back as souvenirs, the chances are very good that the price paid in a source country would be higher than one could buy the same coins for in a Northern European or North American market. Although villagers are seldom ancient coin experts, they have seen enough auction catalogs to know that relatively common ancient coins can be worth a lot more money than they are used to earning in a year. They also know that naive tourists often pay extraordinary prices for ancient coins that they know nothing about. If it's 2,000 years old it must be valuable—right? As a result, everything gets priced in an artificial atmosphere. In a situation like this, anyone tempted to break the laws of the country they are a guest in is a fool.

Fortunately, cultural property laws in Northern Europe are less restrictive than in the Mediterranean countries. This may be changing as the European Economic Community moves closer to centralization of monetary and legal processes, but for the moment it is still legal to collect, buy and sell ancient coins in most of these northern-tier countries. The markets which have developed in Europe over several centuries are still very active and well organized. One can find ancient coin dealers, coin shows and auctions in Switzerland, Germany, France, Britain, and virtually all of the former "western block" countries. In some of these countries a formal certification is required before antiquities can be exported, but the dealer can usually arrange this. Some travellers visiting former "iron curtain" countries have described coin shows there as well. The laws about export are ambiguous, so check with customs officials on your way in to see what you can take back out. There are no restrictions in U.S. customs law about individual collectors importing ancient coins or artifacts, and all such items over 100 years old are admitted to the U.S. duty free.

One of the favorite overseas shopping grounds for American collectors is London. The ease of communication and transportation make a coin hunt in London a very enjoyable experience. Being one of the world's largest cities, it should be no surprise that there are ancient coin dealers, and actually quite a few of them, in the London area. In addition to the shows mentioned earlier, a monthly fair is held at the Great Western Hotel at Paddington tube station. The Portobello Road antique market is worth a visit, especially on Saturday, and street vendors will sometimes have ancient coins among their wares. Another spot where coins can be found is the Saturday collector's fair held adjacent to Charing Cross tube station. Metal detector enthusiasts and local collector/dealers usually set up there along with the stamp collectors. These are budget shopping places, that are really fun to explore, but don't expect to see any high powered coins. There are plenty of serious dealers in London for that, including the oldest ancient coin auction firm in the world! A more elegant, and permanent, market is located in a section called the Mews—not too far from Grosvenor Square. Here, one will find higher priced antiques as well as the stray ancient coin. Always ask for coins, because they aren't necessarily on display. Also, look in the yellow pages under Antiquarians.

No visitor to London should miss the opportunity to visit the British Museum. Housed here is one of the world's largest (if not the largest) collections of coins. True, they are stored behind impressive stainless steel doors, but there are more than enough on display to spend a day dreaming. There are also important collections at virtually all of the famous universities of Britain, and with advance notice the keepers of coins are usually congenial as well as enlightening to visit with. Export of typical collector coins from England has not been a problem.

Public Auctions

The public auction is in many ways similar to its mailbid counterpart, and most firms holding public auctions will accept bids by mail. The major difference is that the sale is held in a public place and bidders may execute bids in person from the floor. Unlike a mailbid sale, the lot sold at public auction is offered at an opening bid. This opening bid may be the seller's reserve (lowest price the seller will accept), a percentage of the estimated value, or an amount determined by bids received through the mail and entered into the bidbook. The book, through an agent of the auction firm, may bid against the floor bidders or—if more than one agent of the firm is representing the book—it may bid against itself. Mailbidders generally are allowed the same limit and "increase" provisions available in a typical mailbid sale. Bidding ties are awarded to the book, which takes precedence over the floor. Nonetheless, floor bidders maintain a slight advantage in that they can sense when a lot does not have strong support from mailbidders and may become a bargain. Dealers, who normally attend auctions with the intent of purchasing coins for stock or for their customers, often use this situation to their advantage but any floor bidder enjoys the same opportunity.

Public auctions are much more strict than mailbid auctions when it comes to returns. In a mailbid sale, a lot that is improperly described may, depending on the sale, be declined by the buyer. In a public auction, especially with floor bidders, it is assumed that the lots have been examined and are sold as is. If you raise your paddle and the hammer falls—it's yours! It is sometimes possible, within the discretion of the auctioneer, to reopen a lot that has been bid on in error. This is more the exception than the rule, and it is usually possible only if brought to the auctioneer's attention immediately. Veteran auctioneers can generally call about 250 lots per hour. This leaves little time for pondering, as the lots come and go very quickly. Floor bidders should be prepared, and act boldly or not at all.

Public auctions can be a little intimidating for the beginner, so caution is advisable. It is probably best to attend one or two and quietly observe before bidding seriously. There are many approaches toward bidding at auction, whether it be public or mailbid. Some collectors will carefully examine the auction catalogue and identify coins that they would most like to acquire. They will then set limits that they are prepared to pay, and bid as aggressively as possible. Others will seek out coins that may become bargains, and hope to obtain these at the lowest possible price—sometimes spreading "lowball" bids across a wide spectrum. The floor bidder can watch the action and bid as the circumstance dictates. Each approach commends itself to a different type of collector, but both can be exciting and rewarding. Finding a method that suits one's personality, taste and interests is part of the fun of auctions.

Advanced collectors will certainly want to bid in auctions which are held overseas. Many of the more scarce and nicest coins on the market are sold in European auctions. The cost of catalogues for these auctions is significant, so it helps to have a dealer who knows your area of interest watch for coins that would interest you. If you are a regular buyer in a firm's auctions you will probably get a complementary copy of their sale catalogues, but if you only buy occasionally, be prepared to pay for one.

Bidding in overseas auctions can be done by mail, with bids being executed from the "book," or they may be executed by a commissioned representative. Many dealers who regularly attend overseas auctions will execute your bids on the floor for a fee of about 5%. This may seem like wasted money, but it is really a form of insurance. Mail bids are seldom reduced, so the bidder by mail is really making an offer in the blind. With a floor representative, bids are executed only at the level necessary to obtain a coin. One of the important services that an auction representative provides is lot viewing. If there is a problem with a coin, that does not show up in the catalogue photo, a representative can advise you of it before the sale. Usually, the auction representative can give you an indication of the value of a coin and advise you if the estimate is high or low. This service is not limited to overseas auctions, you may commission a representative to bid in any auction.

The most frequently asked question about auctions is whether coins are cheaper there than they are through other sources. The purpose of an auction is to liquidate coins, but that does not mean that coins will sell cheaply if competition is strong. If a coin is unreserved, and potential buyers are not "tuned in" (for any of a multitude of reasons: poor auction promotion, bad location or weather, dozing on the floor) a coin may sell very cheaply. Usually, this is not the case, and coins tend to bring their actual value at auction—sometimes more. It is sometimes possible, after an auction or mailbid sale, to buy unsold lots at a percentage of the estimate. This is possible only until the lots have been returned to consignors, and certainly does not apply to all unsold lots.

An auction is a competition that is governed by very strict and well published rules. One must adhere to those rules. If one does not adhere to the rules it will usually result in one's bid being rejected and in some cases it could lead to criminal prosecution.

How can it lead to prosecution? Well, in the United States at least, and I suspect in most other countries, it is illegal for bidders to conspire to fix the sale price at an auction—either up or down. For example, it is illegal for Charley to say to John, "If you don't bid on lot 13 I won't bid on lot 17. This seems like a harmless agreement, but it is nevertheless illegal. And, it makes some sense that it should be illegal. After all, auctions are not only for buyers, they are also for sellers. The playing field should be level, and the competition should not be tainted by conspiracy. It is also illegal for an agent to bid up a client's bid. That is, to arrange for another (a shill) to bid against his own bids. Why would someone do that? To increase the agent's commission. Does it ever happen? It has happened, but that doesn't make it legal. And, the repercussions of getting caught at collusion in an auction can be serious.

There are many auction strategies followed by bidders—Bid early, bid late, cut bids (bid less than the full increment increase), bid at the hammer and even sometimes throwing out a jump bid which is a bid of more than the normal increase.. The bottom line is that the person who bids the most for a coin wins it. It does not matter whether that bidder has a particular strategy, as long as it falls within the rules of the auction house and the laws of the state in which the auction is held.

In a public auction, the bidder can sit in the room and watch until the final moment and then place a bid before the hammer falls. The difference between that and a mailbid or online auction is that in the latter a bidder may not have the opportunity to respond. This still does not make it unethical for bidders to place a last minute bid. If a collector is willing to pay X dollars for a coin, then that should be the collector's bid. If the bid is exceeded, it should not matter whether it was exceeded on the first day or the last day of the sale. If that same collector is willing to buy a coin, but only if it goes cheaply enough, then there are strategies to accommodate that also. In the latter case, one should realize that there is a risk of losing the coin to another bidder.

If the collector is really a bottom feeder and only wants to buy coins that are selling at much less than market value, then there are different strategies. In fact, there are a lot of strategies. Some may think it is unethical to bid $10 on a coin that is estimated at $100. It may be impractical, but it is not unethical. If the seller does not want to sell a coin below a certain level, it will not be sold. There are always options for the seller to be safeguarded. It is also very irritating to the auction house to enter a lot of bids that have no chance of winning. A bidder who habitually enters nothing but junk bids will eventually find themselves *persona non grata* at auctions and dealer's tables as well. To protect themselves against this sort of aggravation, some auction houses require minimum bid limits, which are usually a percentage of the estimate—usually ranging from 60% to 80%. In a "no reserve" auction, any bid is ethical.

In conclusion, the auction venue is one of laws and rules, not of ethics. The bidder in an auction has no responsibility to be gentle to his or her fellow bidders. Anything within the rules is fair game and it is truly a case of "winner take all".

How to Read an Auction Catalogue

Finding your way around an auction catalogue can be a little tricky for the newcomer, so we'll spend a few minutes here covering some of the basics. The introductory pages of a sale catalogue give important information that the bidder often overlooks. The auction number, for example, provides some indication of the firm's experience in the auction business. A firm that has already held a fair number of auctions will probably have devised an efficient method to process your bids and execute or record them accurately. The time and place of an auction are not incidental either. It is not unusual for someone to miss a bid because they did not make note of the time and place, loaned their catalogue to a friend, and in a last minute dash could not find the sale. Other items of interest in the introduction are the notices regarding exhibition of the coins for bidder viewing, pertinent abbreviations and conditions. The auction terms are perhaps the most important section of the entire catalogue, next to the coins. If you have a problem, the auction terms may be *more* important than the coins. It is imperative for the bidder to read and understand the terms. If you do not understand the terms, request an explanation in writing.

Ancient coins are usually presented in a sale catalogue according to traditional groupings. If there are a large number of gold coins in the sale, they may be catalogued as a separate group, even though they may be mixed by culture within that group. Lacking a section of gold, Greek coins are the first of the lots to be catalogued, and they are presented by geographical arrangement. Celtic coins and Greek coins from Spain usually lead off the sale and are followed by coins of Italy and Sicily. Coins of northern, central and southern mainland Greece follow, with island coinage and coins of western Turkey catalogued next. Seleucid, Ptolemaic, Baktrian, Parthian, Sasanian and miscellaneous coinage is usually featured at the end of the Greek lots. Judaean coins sometimes form a section of their own between the Greek and Roman sections. If there are not enough Judaean lots for a section of their own, they will be divided between the Greek and Roman sections. City coins generally go with the latter. Roman coins are arranged chronologically, with the Republican coins being listed first. Roman Imperial coins may be separated from Provincial coins, but this is not always the case. If Provincial coins are included in the Roman Imperial section, they are listed chronologically by emperor. If there is a separate section of Provincial coins, they are usually listed geographically by mint. Romaion coins and coins of the Vandals, Ostrogoths, Visigoths, etc. always bring up the end of a sale of ancient coins, unless there are large lots. Large lots are those where several coins to hundreds of coins might be grouped together as a single lot.

118. THESSALY, Larissa. Circa 344-321 BC. AR Drachm (6.12 gm). Head of the nymph Larissa facing slightly left / Horse grazing on plant. Lorber, "Facing Head Drachms of Larissa," 41.2a (this coin). Choice toned EF. Larissa has a wild gaze about her! ($750)

The elements of a catalogue description are fairly standard. The lot number (118) appears first. Next one finds the district **(THESSALY)**, city or ruling authority **(Larissa)** and approximate dates of striking **(Circa 344-321 BC)**. The denomination **(AR Drachm)** and weight **(6.12 gm.)** complete the first line. The obverse and reverse elements are described next. The reference for this particular specimen is an article written by C. Lorber, and the specimen offered is the actual specimen published in that article **(this coin)**. Often, a cataloguer will include two or more references to the variety being offered. If the type is missing from a standard reference (suggesting some level of increased rarity) it may be recorded for example as SG __, meaning that it is absent from Sear, *Greek Coins and Their Values.* Finally, the condition **(Choice toned EF)** and estimated value **($750)** are included (this is CNG's format, others will vary somewhat).

The descriptions will include many adjectives which are unfamiliar. For example, Roman emperors may be described as head (or bust) bare, laureate, radiate or diademed. The glossary in the back of this book should help to define most of those terms.

Any notable imperfections that may not show up in a photo, such as porosity, tooling, cracks or holes are normally described along with the condition. Surface conditions are also noted with some regularity, especially if the condition is appealing. Provenance (place of origin) of a coin is also listed when known. For example, if a coin was formerly in a name collection, such as Bement or Garrett or such, that will be annotated at the end of the listing. Other notations of provenance might include the name of a known hoard from which the coin came. Sometimes previous sale appearances are noted.

Estimates on auction lots are just that. They are the auctioneer's best guess as to what the coin might actually bring at auction. This is a very subjective determination, and it is also influenced sometimes by the reserve that the seller might place on a coin. If, for example, the seller will accept nothing less than $1000 for a coin, the estimate for that coin must at least cover that reserve plus commission. Auctioneers normally will not accept a coin for consignment if they think that the reserve is higher than what the coin might reasonably be expected to fetch. Still, in some cases they may be inclined or pressured to estimate on the high side. The underestimation of value is a more common event. When a coin is underestimated, bargain hunters will actively bid and sometimes the competition drives the coin to an even higher level than if it were estimated at a higher value. The other advantage of underestimating the value of a coin is that the coin will seem to have done very well when it sells—even if the actual sale price is at the normal market price for such a specimen. Be cautious of estimates that seem very high or very low. Bidding is what ultimately determines the price of a coin—not the published estimate.

Another feature of auction catalogues that deserves comment is the photography. Photos can be a wonderful aid or an absolute danger. Depending on the type of lighting used by the photographer, a coin's surface can show every bump and scratch, or it can look like a piece of glass. Some auction firms go to great pains and expense to produce realistic photos. Some don't. The best thing to do is view the lots in person. If that is simply not possible, and you are suspect about some detail of a coin, call the auctioneer and ask about it. You will probably not be very popular if you call often about inexpensive coins, but it is better to be sure beforehand than to attempt to return a coin after the sale.

Following the sale, most firms issue a list of prices realized. This may be mailed separately, or included with the firm's next general mailing. It is important that the prices realized list be kept with the sale catalogue. This is the official record of sale and the prices listed are much more accurate than notes taken on the floor during a sale. The omission of a lot number in the prices realized list means that the lot did not sell. This could be very confusing to someone who attended a public auction and saw a coin hammered down, but it did not appear in the prices realized. The reason for this is straightforward. In most states, it is legal for the consignor of an auction lot to bid against all other bidders up to the reserve price of the lot. If the hammer falls to the consignor, the lot is not sold and therefore the lot is not listed. There is a twist, however. It is often agreed between a consignor and an auction house that the consignor will be allowed to "buy-in" a coin at some agreed upon commission rate which is usually lower than the general public enjoys. If a consignor buys in the coin, it will appear on a prices realized list as a sold lot. Why would anyone pay a commission to buy back their own coin? The psychology of marketing is strange indeed, but an established auction price may provide a base line for the future sale of that coin or another like it. Paying a small commission to set that base line may be advantageous to the consignor at some later date.

Mailbid Sales

The Mailbid Sale is really an auction that is held in absentia. Bidders compete for each lot by submitting a specified limit that they are willing to pay. At the closing of the sale, each bid is tabulated and the lots are awarded to the highest bidders. Mailbid catalogues usually provide an estimated value for each lot and some firms will not accept bids below an established percentage of this estimated value. In many cases the minimum is 60% of estimate. An "unreserved" sale means that the minimum bid does not apply and a bidder can offer any amount. From a practical point of view, however, extremely low bids seldom win because the firm selling a lot will often buy it for stock or protect it against a ridiculously low sale price. Many auction firms "reduce" successful bids. This generally means that the successful bid will be reduced to the next highest increment (normally 10%) above the underbid. For example: Lot #45 receives a bid of $100 and another bid of $150. The second bidder wins the lot at $150, but the bid is reduced to $110 or 10% above the underbid. In some auctions this bid reduction feature applies only to bids above the original estimate. It is the bidder's responsibility to read the terms of auction carefully before bidding. Any questions or concerns should be addressed to the auction director before the sale. It is possible, in most mailbid sales, to bid on more coins than one actually intends to buy, indicating a maximum purchase limit. This allows the bidder to attempt to win a greater number of coins without committing more than a budgeted amount. Another feature of mailbid auctions is that the bidder is often allowed to increase the recorded bid by a set percentage. The utility of this may not seem obvious to the uninitiated, but sometimes there is real value in executing a bid with percentage increases. Assume, for example, that Lot #45 mentioned above is offered in a sale where, as a matter of policy, bids are not reduced below estimate. Let us say that the lot in this case is estimated at $130. With an underbidder at $100, this lot would sell for $130 (estimate) to the bidder of $150 whose bid has been appropriately reduced. If that winning bidder had bid $100, with authority to increase the bid by 50% if necessary to win the lot (still a $150 maximum bid), the lot would have sold for 10% over the underbidder or $110 instead of $130. Over the course of an auction, this subtlety can save the bidder a substantial amount of money without changing the maximum bid on any single coin. The obvious advantage to a mailbid auction is that the buyer has an opportunity to set the purchase price—assuming that competition will allow. One disadvantage is that these sales take time to administer and one may not know immediately if a particular coin has been obtained or not. Another disadvantage from the buyer's perspective is that rare coins which are badly needed for a collection might become very expensive to obtain if competition is stiff.

Buy-or-Bid Sales

The Buy-or-Bid sale is a combination of the fixed price list and the mailbid auction. Coins are listed with a "buy" price in lieu of an estimated value. A collector may purchase the lot outright at the listed buy price, or may bid something less for the coin in the same fashion as a mailbid sale. Occasionally, someone gets terribly confused and bids more than the buy price—a minor embarrassment. This innovation sets a maximum limit for the price of a coin, since the first buy order takes the coin and it is no longer included in the sale. This may be an advantage to the collector seeking a particularly elusive coin, but the buy price set by the seller is likely to be at full retail or even a bit higher in order to offset the potential gains of bidder competition.

One dealer operates something like a "Bid or Buy" sale. A minimum bid is published in the sale catalog (of course you may bid more). Most of those coins that do not sell are carried to the next coin show and sold at a flat percentage of that published minimum bid. Needless to say, the stock rotates quickly.

There are variants to the above methods of mailbid sales, and the collector should always read the seller's terms of sale very carefully to avoid confusion or error. The best place to locate dealers who sell coins by mail is through their advertisements in the commercial publications mentioned earlier.

Mail order—Fixed Price Lists

With collectors widely dispersed throughout the world, mailorder has proven to be a natural and effective marketing vehicle. Many ancient coin collectors have never been to a coin show, and yet have built quite respectable collections—entirely by mail. There are three basic methods of buying coins through the mail: the Fixed Price List; the Mailbid Sale and a combination of the two referred to as the Buy-or-Bid sale. Each has its own advantages and disadvantages. The latter two are really auctions, so we will discuss them a bit later.

The Fixed Price List has been with us for centuries. As its name implies, this is a list of coins which are offered for sale at a specified price. A fixed price list may range from a page or two of offerings with simple line descriptions to a completely illustrated catalogue containing hundreds of specimens. Some dealers issue fixed price lists on a regular schedule, as often as once per month. Others issue lists on a very sporadic basis, as the occasion demands. Most dealers who seriously offer coins by mail in a fixed price list format will produce at least four catalogues per year. The advantage of a fixed price list is that the buyer knows precisely what the sale price will be, and whether or not it is obtainable. It is always prudent to call before ordering coins from a fixed price list, because these are generally one-of-a-kind offerings and are subject to previous sale. One disadvantage of the fixed price list is the possibility of losing a coin to a collector who received his or her catalogue yesterday. Generally, coins offered in this format are priced at something closer to full retail value than one might see as an opening bid or minimum bid in an auction. Of course, there is no element of uncertainty, or potential of competitive bidding, like there is in an auction.

Many dealers will entertain offers on unsold items from their fixed price lists after the list has run its course. This may be in the form of straight discounts or price negotiation. This policy is usually not advertised, but it doesn't hurt to ask. A few dealers actually re-mail their catalogues with sold coins marked out and remainders discounted.

Electronic Auctions

Electronic Auctions work virtually the same way as a live auction. Coins are posted for sale, usually with an illustration and description. The opening price may be set at a pre-established reserve (the lowest accepted bid) or the auction may be opened without reserve, for example at $1.00. Some sort of registration will normally be required to assure that bidders are held accountable for the bids they execute. Most auction software has an automatic bid increase feature that allows bidders to enter a maximum bid, but the actual bid applied is determined by a set increment over the high previous bid. In other words, if you bid $100 for a coin that currently has only a $10 bid on it, your bid will appear as $11. If another party outbids that $11, the software will automatically raise your bid to the next necessary increment until your maximum is reached.

Electronic Auctions have a set closing time, and it is common practice for some bidders to wait until a few seconds before closing to place their bid. The hope is that competition will not have a chance to get in a higher bid. This auction "sniping" actually worked in the early days of Electronic Auctions, but modern software will automatically extend the auction by a few minutes if a last minute bid is placed. Still, to prevent any chance of losing an item at the last minute it is necessary to monitor the sale to the very end.

Electronic Auctions may be conducted by a public auction firm, like Ebay or Yahoo, or by an independent seller. Many ancient coin dealers have web sites of their own, where proprietary auctions are often hosted. In a private auction, the buyer has the advantage of knowing precisely who the seller is and what guarantees may be counted on. In a public auction, the buyer may find coins offered by other collectors who are willing to sell very cheaply. So, either venue may offer an advantage, depending on the needs of the buyer. The serious collector will find that it is necessary to monitor as many auctions as possible. This task can be simplified through the use of auction tracking software which is commercially available or may be included in your Internet browser. Some auction services provide free auction tracking capabilities as well.

Although ancient coin collecting is first and foremost a recreational activity, it is inevitable that changing values will translate at some point into profit or loss. Every collector is thrilled by the prospect of buying a $300 coin for $50. And few collectors could honestly claim that they never give a thought to the resale value of their collections. The difference between a collector and an investor is that the collector seeks coins which fit a different criteria.
A collector, for example, may accept a lower grade or problem coin because of its rarity and difficulty to obtain, whereas the investor focuses only on the resaleability and profit potential of a coin as the criteria for purchase. If Wé should be fortunate enough to realize a profit, one advantage of collectibles is that they fall under the capital gains laws and provide at least some tax relief—depending on the political climate of the day.

Over the years, prices realized for ancient coins have increased in general, and certain coins have increased significantly in price. The question is, have ancient coins increased in value at a faster rate than any other prudent investment? Individuals who purchased the *right coins* at the *right time* and sold them at the *right time* have beyond doubt made a solid and productive investment. The problem has always been, as with almost any investment, finding the right conditions. While overall prices have risen, many ancient coins sell in the market today at prices well below market prices of the 1970s. And many of those that have risen in price have barely kept up with inflation. One unsettling thing about this from an investment point of view is that price histories often cannot be correlated to measurable factors.

The most unpredictable, and from an investment viewpoint disturbing, variable is the supply of certain coins in the marketplace. With modern coins, a finite number of (genuine) coins is known to the collecting world. Therefore, supply can be measured quite easily. Ancient coins were struck in unknown, but often very high, quantities. Even so, the number of any given variety known to exist in the marketplace may be very small. The discovery of a new hoard, or the sale of a major accumulation, can flood the market with types which previously were thought to be rare or even unique. The result, of course, is that the market price for all coins of this type drops.

The average collector is affected little by such discoveries since a collection normally includes such wide variety of coins that a hoard discovery bears minimal impact. In fact, new hoards often provide great opportunities for the collector, as new types appear at generally lowered prices. Perhaps the safest *investment* strategy is for a collector to acquire the coins that he or she loves most; enjoy them to the greatest extent possible; consider their purchase price as an entertainment expense and when it comes time to sell treat the entire sale as theoretical profit (let the tax man deal with any loss).

One other investment consideration is that collectibles, including ancient coins, have always been thought of as a vehicle to store wealth. Since they tend to be recession proof, like gold, ancient coins often are considered as a hedge against monetary collapse. They are also less visible than some other means of accumulating liquid assets. Of course coins are very portable, and lend themselves to conversion in any market. In this respect, they may turn out to be a very good investment if disaster strikes.

If investment is the aim of buying ancient coins, a look at past markets should help the investor to make educated, if not intelligent, choices when it comes to building a portfolio. Historically, market prices have been driven by condition, rarity, and artistic appeal, not necessarily in that order. Markets of 50 years ago placed a premium on artistic appeal, while today's market is condition sensitive. It does not seem unreasonable that the investor who buys rare artistic coins in superb condition will be well placed when it comes time to sell—as long as one is not buying at the height of a bull market. On the other hand, investment in an under-appreciated series can return a significant profit if the popularity of the series increases. The ratio of potential return versus risk is no different for ancient coins than it is for corporate stocks or any other growth investment.

The typical scenario goes like this: a collector discovers ancient coins and is fascinated. The collector buys a coin or two that came with an interesting story (the first thing you learn in ancient coin dealer school is all the good stories—and there are a lot of them!). Not wanting to take too big of a risk, our collector settles for relatively low grade common coins. A few shows come and go and a few more coins are added, but they don't really form a collection. In fact, they probably don't have anything in common at all. As time passed, our collector also did some reading, and looked at some more coins, and began to develop an appreciation of the wonderful possibilities that exist. It is now time to sell those remarkable treasures, with the great stories, and focus on something which appeals at a higher level.

Off to a show, coins in hand, goes our collector. Offering the coins around the floor, the collector begins to feel a sense of rejection as dealer after dealer either passes completely or offers a small percentage of the original purchase price. What happens, all too often, is that the collector is so completely demoralized that interest wanes. Why does this happen? First of all, dealers don't generally need common low grade coins. There are many more of them around than the market can absorb, and dealers are regularly offered such coins in bags at prices far below average retail. Why do dealers sell these coins? Because people buy them! Low grade common coins enjoy the greatest percentage of mark-up in the industry. Trying to sell these coins back to a dealer is not going to be very ego boosting. Sometimes, the dealer that you bought a coin from will take it back in trade just to promote future business, but an outright sale to a dealer could be brutal. This does not mean that the collector should not buy low grade common coins, but think of these purchases as an educational investment. The halls of academia don't give away an education for nothing. What is wrong with investing a few dollars in coins to learn about the ancient world?

The situation changes dramatically once a collector learns to be more discriminating in his or her purchases. A comprehensive collection of almost any series or topical area will tend to do much better on the whole than an equivalent number of unrelated coins. The other advantage of a comprehensive collection is that it normally has time to mature. Over time, coins do tend to appreciate in value, and that appreciation softens the blow of inevitable and necessary dealer markups or commissions.

How to Sell Coins or Liquidate a Collection

Eventually, every collection is sold. Sometimes they stay in the family for several generations, but sooner or later they are all disposed of in some way. More frequently, collectors change their collecting habits and find themselves with coins that no longer suit their objectives. In either case, the coins are going to find a new home.

The key to successful selling is knowing the market for the particular kind of material that you want to sell. If you collect low grade esoteric Roman reverse types from the third century, don't expect to be overwhelmed with offers from big-name dealers. But that does not mean that your coins are unsaleable. After all, you bought them, didn't you? The trick is matching the proper material to the proper audience.

The safest (and perhaps most difficult) way to sell coins is always through a direct sale—sometimes called "private treaty." You locate a buyer (the difficult part), the two of you determine a fair and acceptable price and that's all there is to it. The most popular places for this kind of collector-to-collector dealing have been classified ads in the numismatic publications and club auctions or bourses. The Internet may also be a good place to sell coins to other collectors through e-mail and bulletin boards. The primary advantage of direct sale is that you know how much you are going to receive and the transaction is immediate. However, if you don't really know the value of your coins, this may not be the best route. You can be "cherry-picked" by another collector just as fast as you can by a dealer! A little patience can go a long way toward maximizing your return.

One way to judge the value of a single coin is to offer it for direct sale to a dealer. In fact, offer it to several dealers. Some will decline to make an offer. This does not necessarily mean that they think your coin is worthless. It may simply mean that they don't have any cash reserve for purchases at the moment. Or maybe they don't need it in stock, don't have an immediate buyer in mind, and don't want to offend you with a low offer. Others will make an offer that is for them a "no brainer" good deal. Some, who might need the coin for stock or have a particular customer in mind, may be more generous with their offer. In any event, the offer that you receive from a dealer on the floor of a coin show will probably be a wholesale offer. You can expect that your coin, if sold at this level, will reappear somewhere at a markup of 50% to 100%. Keep in mind, a markup of 50% means that the dealer's cost is really 66% of the sale price (one of those crazy things about math). In most cases the dealer will end up discounting the sale price of that coin by 10% to 30%, depending on whether it's a "retail" or wholesale transaction. So, don't take too much offense at these levels of markup. Some dealers will ask what you expect to receive for the coin. This puts the ball back in your court, and you on the defensive. In this case, if you are not desperate to sell, pitch out a high number (like the price you paid for it) and let the discussion end there. At the end of the exercise you will either have sold the coin or developed a feel for its wholesale value. One other option is for you to place the coin on consignment with a dealer at an agreed upon price. The dealer will either take a commission off this price (typically 20%) or will mark the coin above your agreed price and take any excess as profit. If you really think that your coin is worth more than you paid for it, or more than dealers are willing to pay, offer it to an auction house. They will allow you to reserve the coin if it is, in their opinion, valuable enough. That means, you can set a minimum sale price. If the coin does not sell at this price or higher you get it back and lose nothing. Keep in mind, auction houses are not in the business of cataloguing coins that will not sell. They will not allow you to reserve a coin at a price higher than they conservatively expect it to realize. For their assistance in selling your coin the auction house will charge you between 10% and 15%, and you will have to wait anywhere from four to six months (maybe even longer) between the date of consignment and the settlement date. Sometimes, the dealer's wholesale, cash, on-the-spot offer looks pretty good. The advantage of auction, however, is that your coin may catch the fancy of a couple well-heeled collectors who will bloody each other to own it. Not a chance? Then sell it wholesale.

If you have an entire collection to liquidate, that is usually another matter. With a real collection, i.e., one that was formed over a period of time with some forethought and consistency, the value of the whole is often greater than the sum of its parts. This is even true of collections outside the mainstream of classical numismatics. Three recent examples of this come to mind. Auctions of the Kerry K. Wetterstrom Collection of coins from Roman Egypt, the Spengler/Sayles Collections of Turkoman coins, and the Fred B. Shore Collection of Parthian coins, all broke previous market records for coins from a narrowly focussed area. Accumulations, on the other hand, seldom bring much above wholesale at auction. Aside from a private treaty offer from some institution, or serious collector of your specialty, auction is usually the best venue for entire collections.

If you really don't trust the market at all, or don't particularly need the money, you can always donate coins or collections to one of the non-profit institutions and take the tax write-off. Several years back, a tax window was opened which allowed gifts to non-profit institutions to be deducted at current market (appraised) value rather than cost. This is a wonderful provision. It actually encourages giving, as it allows the collector to see some appreciation in value. If you are really lucky, and have had the coins for a while, the deduction may be sufficient to cover your original cost. These provisions of the tax rules change constantly, so check with your tax advisor before launching into a giving spree.

Universities, unfortunately, are seldom equipped to deal with a coin collection, and some wonderful collections have become even more ancient in the basements of academia. In spite of their promises and good intentions, the lack of a numismatic staff will generally relegate donated coins to a dusty vault. The museums of the American Numismatic Association and the American Numismatic Society (see Groups and Societies) are in a better position to utilize a gift of coins. The National Collection, housed at the Smithsonian Institute in Washington, also accepts numismatic donations. All of these institutions have full-time numismatic curators. Some public museums also have displays of ancient coins, but it would be prudent to visit the museum yourself and see what might become of your donation—unless, you just don't care!

There are youth education programs that appreciate donations of coins, but this is not a reasonable outlet for serious collections. Two of the most well-known programs are the Young Numismatists program conducted in association with the New York International Numismatic Convention, and the David Cervin Roman Coins program sponsored by the American Numismatic Association in Colorado Springs. Many elementary and high school teachers use ancient coins in their history programs. It may be more difficult to claim donations to such individuals as a tax write-off, but the coins will generally be put to good use. Churches often use ancient coins in biblical studies classes, and might be welcome recipients of a donation. Most members of the clergy have been exposed to ancient coins in their education, and are very grateful to have coins for teaching purposes.

E very collector new to ancient coins asks for a single book that covers all of the different coins. This is like asking for a map that shows every named street in the U.S.A. It simply is not possible. Of course the collector does not realize this, and usually becomes disgruntled that no one will produce such a useful book. There are basically two kinds of books that the collector will find helpful. The first is historical, the second is technical. Learning about ancient history is an important part of becoming an ancient coin collector. If you do not have an interest in ancient history, you will probably not enjoy collecting ancient coins. Given an interest in the history of any particular period, the collector will usually want to find coins which relate to that period. Interpreting and recording the details of a coin's legends and symbols, and placing it in the proper context, is called attribution. If you plan to attribute coins on your own, you will need a library of reference works. If you have narrowed down the series that you wish to collect and attribute, your library may be relatively small. If, on the other hand, you are buying random lots of unidentified coins, your library may need to be very large. Books are always a good investment, but a little focus on collecting interests will save you needless effort and expense.

The adage "Buy the book before the coin" has been around for a long time, and it is sound advice. For the average collector, a reasonable budget for numismatic literature might be 10% or more of that set aside for coins. Knowledge of the subject is extremely important in this field. But, how broad is the subject, and how much knowledge is required? Used books about ancient coins are seldom inexpensive, but they are still a sound investment. The print run of a typical reference work is usually 1,000 or less. Considering that these books are seldom reprinted, they often become scarce and therefore more valuable. Remarkably, individuals selling their collections have often found that their libraries appreciated in value more than their coins. No wonder—the books are generally in shorter supply than the coins they describe.

When buying books it helps to know a little about the language of the trade. Therefore, we have included here a section dealing with technical information and a glossary of book terms.

If you can't afford to build a good library, you *can* compile a good bibliography and use the inter-library loan system of a major public library to borrow references. Some numismatic societies and associations, like the American Numismatic Association and Numismatics International, maintain libraries which are available for loan to their members. Local ancient coin clubs often maintain a reference library for their members' use as well. A specialized bibliography is the key to effective research, and no serious scholar can begin to attempt a study of ancient coins without being able to consult the prevailing view on the subject. There are literally thousands of sources, and only a good bibliography can lead the reader to them. We have listed the primary ones in this section.

We also have included here some recommendations of useful works for the beginning and more advanced collector. This section includes works that are readily available in the trade, are relatively up-to-date, and form a nucleus around which a more detailed and specialized library can eventually be formed. In other words, these are the books that we would recommend as some of a collector's first purchases.

There are several dealers in the United States who specialize in numismatic literature, both new and used. They can be found through their advertisements in the commercial publications and society journals listed in the previous chapter. Some of these dealers are also on the Internet and can be located through search engines or links on other dealer pages. For really obscure or out of print books, there are some useful Internet sites. Alibris (http://alibris.com), Abe Books (http://abebooks.com) and Bibliofind (http://bibliofind.com) all offer very large inventories of rare and used books with excellent search capabilities. Other online book resources are included in a table near the end of this section.

The collecting of books is a serious pursuit in itself, and many coin collectors also are bibliophiles. Antiquarian books are especially desirable as collectibles, and it is not impossible to obtain a library of original works dating back to the 16th century. Because of the difficulty of transporting books to a show, most books are sold by mail. A few book dealers set up displays at shows near their businesses, and a few tote books to shows that they can drive to, but mailorder is by far the most common method of buying books. Like coins, books are sold through fixed prices lists and through Mailbid auctions. Occasionally, books are sold at Public Auction. The New York International in December hosts a combined public auction by two major booksellers. The ANA summer convention sometimes has an associated book auction as well. In addition to the dealers and booksellers who carry a regular stock, many auction houses routinely include a section of numismatic literature in their sales.

Books are generally listed in alphabetical order by author, with titles sometimes being divided into topical sections. Following are a few things to watch for when considering the purchase of a book:

• Binding— Bindings may vary from expensive leather to very inexpensive laminated card stock. The method of attaching the pages together (sewn or glued) will determine the useful life of the book.

• Size — Good things often come in small packages, but very small books, and oversize books may create storage problems. See the chart on the facing page. Also, an impressive title can obscure the superficiality of a 20-page monograph. Very thin or very thick books are difficult to bind and use as the pages do not want to lay flat. Therefore, two moderate sized volumes are usually better than one very large one.

• Condition — Book binding is a disappearing art, if a book needs serious repair, the cost of repair may exceed the cost of the book. See the grading chart for a list of terms and their meanings.

• Date — Is the work fairly current, or is it outdated? Some standard works are getting up in years, but obscure titles from ages past should be investigated before purchase.

• Publisher — Oxford, or Friendly Fred's Book Club, which do you think attracts authors of substance? Respected publishers seldom issue inferior works.

• Illustrations — Nothing is more boring than a book without illustrations. If it is unavoidable, at least be prepared for the worst.

• Language — Is the text written in a language that you can decipher? Reference books are not bad, because you can generally understand the basics, but the useful introductions and analyses will be lost.

Bidding on books at auction is just like bidding on coins. See the section on buying coins at auction. Don't forget, though, shipping costs are the responsibility of the buyer. Shipping a coin is inexpensive, but shipping a set of BMC Greek or a run of auction catalogues from some venerable firm, may be quite expensive. This is especially true of books that are purchased from foreign sales.

While numismatic books are seldom found in used book stores, they do occasionally appear, almost by accident. Sometimes this presents a great opportunity for numismatists, because the market for numismatic books is not well understood by the average bookseller. It is possible to find rare works at a fraction of the price that they normally bring.

Another source for numismatic publications is the academic press. Many university presses, as well as art museums, have issued works on ancient numismatics that are unfamiliar to the general collecting fraternity. This is unfortunate, but it is a reflection of the chasm between academics and hobbyists. Reviewing *Books in Print* at the reference section of your local library, may turn up some real treasures. Academic periodicals often include articles about ancient coins, and these are something that can be monitored at your local library as well. Books and journals subsidized by educational institutions tend to be much less expensive than those produced only for the collector fraternity.

Books are an important part of every collector's cabinet. They are necessary tools of the trade, and pay for themselves over and over again. Building a library, even a very specialized one, is an integral part of building a collection. It can also be a very enjoyable aspect of the hobby which returns significant rewards.

BOOK SIZES

F⁰ (folio) .... over 13"
4to (quarto) .... 12 "
8vo (octavo) .... 9"
12mo (duodecimo) .... 7-8"
16mo (sextodecimo) .... 6-7"
24mo (vigesimoquarto) .... 5-6"
32mo (trigesimosecundo) .... 4-5"

CONDITION

As New / Mint: No signs of wear or defects.

Very Fine: Near new, mini–mal signs of use.

Fine: Nice clean copy, slight signs of use.

Very Good: Some wear, no serious defects.

Good: Average used and worn book, complete.

Reading Copy: Poor but readable.

Ex-Library: With library iden–tification marks.

Glossary of Book Terms

Bead: A thread crossing horizontally on the spine, to create a raised effect.

Binding: A bookcover, in any style.

Blinding: Making an impression in leather or cloth with a heated finishing tool.

Buckram: Strong and expensive covering material, made of woven linen or a mixture of linen and cotton.

Case bound: An economical form of binding where the front and back boards, and their covering, form a wrap for the sewn sections which are pasted inside.

Colophon: An inscription at the beginning or end of a book, usually including the printer's name and details of production.

Cover: The cloth, leather, vellum or other material forming the surface of a binding.

Edge gilding: The application of gold leaf to the edges of the pages of a book.

Embossed: Impressed with a pattern.

Endpapers: The sheets of paper (two or more) which come between the cover and the sewn sections.

Foxing: The brown stain that comes with age and contamination.

Frontispiece: The illustration facing the title page of a book.

Half binding: An economical covering where the spine and corners, or spine and foredge strips, are covered with a good material and the remainder with a cheaper one.

Linings: Pieces of strong paper pasted to the inside of boards to counteract warping by the covering material.

Marbled paper: Paper with a decorative, marble-like appearance.

Morocco: Goatskin tanned with oak bark or sumach.

Perfect bound: Card cover binding where the pages are glued directly to the cover.

Plates: Diagrams or illustrations, at the end of the text or separately.

Recto: Right-hand page of a book, usually with an odd page number.

Saddle stitching: Connecting the leaves of a section by sewing with thread or stapling through the back fold.

Sewn binding: A binding made up of sections sewn together.

Title page: The page containing the complete title of the book, author, volume number, date, patron, publisher's name, and place and date of publication.

Verso: A left-hand page of a book, usually with an even page number.

Numismatic Bibliographies are a wonderful source of information about past scholarship. The bibliography is simply a listing, either by author or subject, of books and/or articles which pertain to a particular field. Books will usually include a limited bibliography, toward the back, with further reading on the subject at hand. A comprehensive bibliography may require a book in itself, and in the field of numismatics there are several.

One of the earliest works of this type (AD 1644) was *Bibliotheca nummaria*, in two parts, by the French scholar Philippe Labbé. Others appeared in the succeeding years, but the most accessible of these early bibliographies is that of Johann Gottfried Lipsius, from Leipzig, which covers numismatic books printed before 1800. It lists most of the early attempts at numismatic cataloguing and gives us a record of research and collector interest in the post Renaissance period. The Lipsius bibliography was supplemented to 1866 by his successor J. Leitzmann, and the combined work was reprinted in 1977. The bibliographic opus of Christian Dekesel, currently a work in progress, will clearly replace the venerable Lipsius.

Many bibliographies reflect a particular approach; these are referred to as select bibliographies. In 1984, Elvira Clain-Stefanelli produced the monumental *Numismatic Bibliography*, which in one volume presents 1,850 pages of references to numismatic books and articles of the 20th century. Most select bibliographies are much less ambitious, but they can be indispensable to the researcher or serious collector.

The American Numismatic Society in New York City publishes an online listing of recent articles and books under the title *Numismatic Literature*. Although not bibliographies in the true sense, the library catalogues of the American Numismatic Association, the American Numismatic Society, and the numismatic related titles in the New York Public Library, are very good bibliographical references. Articles about ancient and medieval coins and antiquities which have been published in *The Celator* over the past eight years (some 500 in number) are listed in a cardcover index, as well as on the Internet. See the sections titled Commercial Periodicals and Ancient Coins on the Internet, for contact information.

Dennis J. Kroh, a professional numismatist from Florida, has compiled a series of short and insightful reviews which provide subjective ratings of most ancient coin reference works available to the general collecting public. *Ancient Coin Reference Reviews* is particularly useful to the new collector because it groups these reviews by collecting category. Any collector interested in forming a library, no matter how specialized, should begin by reading Mr. Kroh's book.

Bibliographies
relating to ancient history and numismatics

Caron, Pierre and Jaryc, M. World list of historical periodicals and bibliographies. Oxford, 1939.

Carson, Robert A.G. "A report on research in Roman numisma–tics, 1936-1952," *Congrès international de numismatique,* Vol. I, Pp. 31-54. Paris 1953.

Clain-Stefanelli, Elvira E. *Numismatic Bibliography,* Batterburg-Verlag, München, 1985.

Clain-Stefanelli, Elvira E. *Select Numismatic Bibliography,* Stack's, 1965.

Daehn, William E. *Ancient Greek Numismatics, a guide to reading and research,* Cold Spring, MN 2001.

Dekesel, Christian. *Bibliotheca Nummaria* (Vol. I, 16th century; Vol. II, 17th century; Vol. III, 18h century in progress), Crestline, CA 1997, 2003.

Grierson, Philip R. *Bibliography Numismatique,* Brussels, 1966.

Grierson, Philip R. *Coins and Medals: A select bibliography,* London 1954.

International bibliography of historical sciences, 16 vols., Paris and Oxford, 1926.

Jenkins, G.K and Carson R.A.G. "Greek and Roman Numisma–tics 1940-1950," *Historia* 1953, Vol. II, part 2, pp. 214-234.

Jones, J.R. *A numismatic index to the "Journal of Hellenic Studies" 1880-1969,* Cambridge, 1971.

Kumpikevikius, Gordon C. and Tooth, Mark E. A *Bibliography of Classical Numismatics in Canada,* Toronto, 1994.

Lipsius, J.G. and Leitzmann JJ. *Bibliotheca Numaria,* (reprint) Colchester, 1977.

Mattingly, Harold, and Harold B. "The Republic and the early Empire," *Congresso internazionale di numismatica,* pp. 147-157, Rome, 1961.

Miles, George C. "Islamic and Sasanian numismatics: Retrospect and prospect, *Congrès international de numismatique,* Vol. I, pp. 129-144, Paris 1953.

Numismatic Literature, American Numismatic Soc., New York, 1947 +.

Survey of numismatic research, 1960-1965 (Copenhagen, 1967), *1966-1971* (New York, 1973), *1972-1977* (Bern, 1979).

Vermeule, Cornelius C. *A Bibliography of Applied Numismatics, in the Fields of Greek and Roman Archaeology and the Fine Arts,* London, 1956.

Recommended Ancient Coin References

For the Individual:

A good classical dictionary is very helpful for both the novice and experienced collector. It is one book that will be consulted over and over, and will certainly earn its keep. Used book stores are a good place to look for Lempriere's Bibliotheca Classica or Smith's Classical Dictionary of Biography, Mythology and Geography. For general information about the ancient world we recommend the one volume Oxford History of the Classical World. The titles listed below are introductory works or consolidated references of value to the collector who wishes to maintain a limited library.

Greek—

Head, Barclay V. *Historia Numorum*, 1911 (reprints available).
Hurter, S. & Mildenberg, L. *The Arthur Dewing Collection of Greek Coins*, Published by the A.N.S., 1985.
Icard, S. *Dictionary of Greek Coin Inscriptions*, (reprint, 1968).
Jones, J.M. *A Dictionary of Ancient Greek Coins*, 1986.
Lindgren, H.C. (with F. Kovacs on vol. I). *Ancient Greek Bronze Coins:...*, three volumes (titles vary). 1985 and later.
Plant, R.J. *Greek Coin Types and Their Identification*, 1979.
Sayles, Wayne G. *Ancient Coin Collecting II, Numismatic Art of the Greek World*, Iola, WI 1997.
Sear, David R. *Greek Coins and Their Values*, 2 vols., London, 1978-9.
___. *Greek Imperial Coins and Their Values*, London, 1982.

Roman—

Failmezger, Victor. *Roman Bronze Coins, from Paganism to Christianity 294-364 AD*, forthcoming.
Foss, Clive. *Roman Historical Coins*, 1990.
Jones, J.M. *A Dictionary of Ancient Roman Coins*, 1990.
Klawans, Z. *Reading and Dating Roman Imperial Coins*, Racine, 1959. (Reprint: combined with *An Outline of Ancient Greek Coins*, in *Handbook of Ancient Greek and Roman Coins*, K. Bressett, ed., Racine, 1995.)
Sayles, Wayne G. *Ancient Coin Collecting III, Politics and Propaganda in the Roman World*, Iola, WI 1997.
___. *Ancient Coin Collecting IV, Roman Provincial Coins*, Iola, WI 1998.
Seaby, H.A. *Roman Silver Coins*, Vol. I, (Republic to Augustus), 1978.
Sear, David R. *Roman Coins and Their Values*, 2 vols. Millennium Edition, London, 2000-2002.

Sear, David R. *Greek Imperial Coins and Their Values*, London, 1982.
Vagi, David L. *Coinage and History of the Roman Empire*, 2 vols.,
    Sidney OH, 1999.
Westdal, Stewart J. *Dictionary of Roman Coin Inscriptions*, New
    York, 1982.

Romaion (Byzantine)—

Berk, Harlan J. *Eastern Roman Successors to the Sestertius*,
    Chicago, 1988.

Sayles, Wayne G. *Ancient Coin Collecting V, The Romaion/Byzantine
    Culture*, Iola, WI 1998.

Sear, David R. *Byzantine Coins and Their Values*, 1987.

Non-Classical—

Broome, M. *A Handbook of Islamic Coins*, London. 1985.

Sayles, Wayne G. *Ancient Coin Collecting VI, Non-Classical Cultures*,
    Iola, WI 1999.

Forgeries and Reproductions—

Hill, G.F. *Becker the Counterfeiter*, London 1924-5 (reprint: London,
    1955).
Lawrence, R.H. *Medals by Giovanni Cavino, the "Paduan."* New York.
    1883 (reprinted).
Sayles, Wayne G. *Classical Deception, Counterfeits, Forgeries and
    Reproductions of Ancient Coins*, Iola, WI 2001.
Klawans, Z. *Imitations and Inventions of Roman Coins: Renaissance Medals of
    Julius Caesar and the Roman Empire*, Santa Monica, 1977.

Note: All of the above works were in print
or obtainable in used condition at the time of this writing.

Recommendations for the Numismatic Library:
(of the advanced collector)

Greek—

BMC. *A Catalogue of Greek Coins in the British Museum,* 29 volumes.
(Forni reprints available, some volumes still in print.)
Calciati, R. *Corpus Nummorum Siculorum,* three volumes
(complete coverage of the bronze coinage of Sicily).
Jenkins, Kenneth. *Ancient Greek Coins,* 1990 (revision).
Price, M. *The Coinage in the Name of Alexander the Great and Philip
Arrhidaeus, a British Museum Catalog,* two volumes, 1991.
SNG Copenhagen. *Sylloge Nummorum Graecorum,* 43 volumes
(reprinted in 1982 in eight hardbound volumes).
SNG Von Aulock. *Sylloge Nummorum Graecorum,* 18 volumes
(reprinted in 1987 in four hardbound volumes).

Roman—

BMC. *A Catalogue of Roman Coins in the British Museum,* six vol–
umes, 1923-1962 (out of print).
Breglia, L. Roman Imperial Coins, *Their Art and Technique,* 1968.
Carson, R.A.G. *Principal Coins of the Romans* (3 vols.), London, 1978-81.
*Catalogue of The Late Roman Coins in the Dumbarton Oaks Collection
and in the Whittemore Collection from Arcadius and Honorius to
the Accession of Anastasius,* 1992.
Crawford, M.H. *Roman Republican Coinage,* two volumes, 1974.
RIC. *Roman Imperial Coinage,* ten volumes, London, 1923-1994.
Stevenson, Seth M. *Dictionary of Roman Coins, Republican and
Imperial,* 1889.

Romaion(Byzantine)—

DOC. *Collection of the Byzantine Coinage in the Dumbarton Oaks and
Whittemore Collections,* five volumes, 1966-1999.
Grierson, Philip. *Byzantine Coins,* 1982.
Whitting, Philip D. *Byzantine Coins,* 1973.
Wroth, Warwick. *The Catalogue of the Imperial Byzantine Coins in the
British Museum,* two volumes, 1908 (reprinted in 1966).

Online Books, E-texts, Reviews and Bibliographies pertaining to the ancient world

Alibris .... http://www.alibris.com

ANS Online Publications ....
.... http://www.numismatics.org/publications/

Ancient Culture .... http://westernculture.com

Bibliofind .... http://www.bibliofind.com

Bryn Mawr Classical Review ....
.... http://ccat.sas.upenn.edu/bmcr/2002/2002-10-40.html

Byzantine Books ....
.... http://storesonline.com/members/byzantinebooks

CGB .... http://www.i-numis.com

Classical Numismatic Group ....
.... http://www.cngcoins.com/book_list.asp

Dumbarton Oaks Electronic Texts ....
.... http://www.doaks.org/etexts.html

George Frederick Kolbe .... http://www.numislit.com/

Gnomon Online ....
http://www.gnomon.ku-eichstaett.de/Gnomon/Gnomon.html

KIRKE .... http://
www.phil.uni-erlangen.de/~p2latein/ressourc/ressourc.html#bibl

Mevius Numisbooks International .... http://mevius.nl/

Numismatic Bibliomania Society .... http://www.coinbooks.org/

Online Books .... http://digital.library.upenn.edu/books/

Papyrus Books .... http://papyrusbooks.com/

Questia .... http://questia.com/

Svoronos, Ptolemaic Coinage (online translation) ....
.... http://www.coin.com/images/dr/svoronos_book2.html

University of Adelaide .... http://
library.adelaide.edu.au/guide/hum/classics/subject/numis.html

Wayne G. Sayles, Antiquarian ....
http://ancientcoins.ac/wgs/books.html

Trying to use a modern atlas to study ancient history is a futile exercise. The boundaries and names of nations have changed so many times over the millennia that, with only a few exceptions, it is impossible to relate modern names and places to their ancient sites. Furthermore, the modern spelling of ancient place-names is often confusing. Depending on whether the name comes from a French, German or English source, it will sometimes be spelled quite differently. For Example, coins of the *Roman Empire* appear in some French catalogues as *Romaines Impérial* or *Empire Romain,* and in some German catalogues as *Römischen Kaiserzeit* or *Romische Kaiserreich.* Place names beginning with the letters C and K are particularly troublesome, as they interchange among languages. This will all become clear after a time, but it takes some getting used to.

Individual maps of the ancient world are often available from used book stores, and dealers who specialize in maps. If they are more than a hundred years old, the place-names are likely to be recorded in Latin. Unlike numismatic titles, atlases hold a more universal appeal and there are several good atlases available in the general book trade. Listed below are a few atlases that will help to define the ancient world:

Cooke, Kramer & Rowland-Entwistle. *History's Timeline,* Crescent Books, 1981.

Cribb, Cook & Carradice. *The Coin Atlas,* Facts on File, 1990.

Finley, M.I. *Atlas of Classical Archaeology,* McGraw-Hill, 1977.

Grant, Michael. *Atlas of Ancient History,* Dorset Press, 1971.

McEvedy, Colin. *The Penguin Atlas of Ancient History,* Penguin Books, 1967.

Nebenzahl, Kenneth. *Maps of the Holy Land,* Abbeville Press, 1986.

Pagani, Lelio. (intro.) *Cosmography: Maps from Ptolemy's Geography,* Magna Books, 1990.

Maps Online

A tremendous amount of information about the history of cartography, and detailed images of maps from the earliest times, can be found on the Internet. Just browsing through the online collections is a joy, but the researcher who needs contemporary maps is often able to find that special resource much more quickly online than through a visit to the map room of a major library. Listed below are some Web sites that provide searchable databases and images of their map collections.

Maps of the Roman Empire ....
.... http://www.dalton.org/groups/rome/RMAPS.html

University of Melbourne ....
.... http://www.lib.unimelb.edu.au/collections/maps/

Cartographic Images .... http://www.henry-davis.com/MAPS/

Interactive Ancient Mediterranean Project ....
.... http://iam.classics.unc.edu/

University of Texas ....
.... http://www.lib.utexas.edu/maps/map_sites/hist_sites.html

Lacus Curtius .... http://www.ku.edu/history/index/europe/
ancient_rome/E/Gazetteer/Maps/Periods/Roman/home.html

WWW-Virtual Library ....
.... http://www.ihrinfo.ac.uk/maps/webimages.html

Library of Congress ....
.... http://memory.loc.gov/ammem/gmdhtml/gmdhome.html

Kelsey Museum .... http://www.umich.edu/~kelseydb/Maps.html

Oriental Institute ....
.... http://www-oi.uchicago.edu/OI/INFO/MAP/ANE_Maps.html

AncientGreece.com ....
.... http://www.ancientgreece.com/geography/geography.htm

IDENTIFYING ANCIENT COINS
Learning the Skills of Attribution

A ttribution is unnecessary if one buys only packaged coins from commercial sources, but few in the hobby are satisfied to distance themselves from the coins in this way. Learning to attribute ancient coins is one of the most enjoyable aspects of the hobby, even though it may be intimidating to the beginner. It is possible to attribute a coin to ruler, mint, or perhaps even date, without using any references at all. However, this takes a very good understanding of the coin itself. Most dealers and collectors attribute coins by comparing them to examples published in a handbook or in a major collection. Therefore coins will generally be identified by a catalogue number like "Sear 1422" or "RIC 29a." Sometimes a coin will be annotated with a small "v." after the catalogue number. This means that the coin is a variety of that type, but not exactly identical. This is very often the case with coins attributed to a Sear number, because the Sear handbooks are just that—a handbook, not a comprehensive reference. They are very useful, but they do not come close to listing every variety. The absence of a particular type or variety in Sear, or any other handbook, does not necessarily mean that it is rare.

Even if you use a handbook or collection catalogue to attribute coins, it is inevitable that you will have to read the inscriptions on the coin and accurately identify the images on it. This takes a bit of practice. As we point out in the following chapter, many beginning collectors choose to focus on Roman coins, because the legends are readable. Although written in Latin, the letters are at least recognizable because they are common to most western languages. Greek, Aramaic, Phoenician or some of the other scripts that appear on coins may be very difficult for the untrained mind to decipher. We will deal here with basic attribution of coins with Latin and Greek legends. This covers the majority of coins found in the market and will at least get the collector started toward self-sufficiency in this aspect of the hobby. Specialized references will deal with the attribution of Non-Classical coins.

The first task in selecting one from a pile of mixed ancient coins is to distinguish it by basic type. Then, a determination of the ruler or mint is necessary. With Roman and Romaion coins, determining the denomination is relatively easy, as is the approximate date, once the ruler has been identified. Greek coins are more difficult to distinguish by denomination, and a scale may be needed to get a precise weight. A description of the images on the coin's obverse and reverse are important to the attribution as well. For a specific attribution to a standard reference, the coin will need to be compared very carefully against the various listings and matched against one.

Greek tetradrachm of Rhodes

Early Greek coins are often irregular in shape, relatively thick, and are usually struck in high relief. Later they become more uniform and are struck in lower relief. Although portraits appear in Hellenistic issues, Greek coins usually depict gods, goddesses, animals or inanimate objects, rather than individuals. The most identifiable feature, however, is the legend or letters found on the coin. The Greek alphabet contains many letters that are identical to those used by the Romans, but notable differences are Γ rather than C; Δ rather than D, Σ rather than S, etc. (see table).

By way of contrast, coins of the Roman Empire are fairly uniform in appearance. They are relatively round, and designs are struck in low relief. In other words, the image does not stand very high on the surface of the coin. They look more like modern coins in size and shape. The edges may be irregular, but overall they seem more uniform in production. Roman coins usually depict the issuing emperor, or members of the imperial family. Note that in Latin legends the "V" is read by us as a "U." The English "J" does not appear in Latin, and is rendered as "I" in Latin inscriptions.

Roman denarius of Septimius Severus

Romaion coinage is very low in relief compared to either Greek or Roman. The emperor is often depicted, but portraits are very spiritual. They de-emphasize the details of mortal flesh, and through the eyes open a window to the soul. During the seventh century, and later in the empire, they are often very crudely struck and irregular. Sometimes they are even struck on broken flans and cut down coins of earlier reigns. The features are eventually abstracted to the point that they look like line drawings. Many of the bronze Romaion coins bear large denomination marks on the reverse. For example, M, K and I stand for 40, 20 and 10 nummia respectively. Alternately, some issues used Roman numerals to mark the denomination.

The cup-shaped scyphate coins of the later empire are distinctive and easily recognizable.

Romaion AE 40 nummia of Justinian I

Ancient Alphabets

Early Greek		Later Greek	Latin	
α	ΛꓯꓩꓥΛ	Α Λ	a	ΛꓥꓦΡΛ
β	ΒΒ⟨ᴄꓩ𝕾ꓢꓨ𝖵	Β Β	b	Β
γ	⟨ᴄΛΓΓ	Γ	c g	⟨ᴄᴄ G
δ	ᗡᗡΔ	Δ	d	D
ε	ꓱꓱꓱꓱ⟆ꓱꓱ	Ε Ε	e	Ε Ε Ⲥ ‖
ϝ	⟨ᴄꓱꓽꓽΛꓥ		w.f	ꓳꓳⵏ
ᙆ	ꓞꓲ	Ⲓ Ζ	z	Ζ
η,h	ꓥꓧꓜꓨꓨθꓧⵏ	Η	h	Η
θ	⊞⊠⬦⬦⊕⊗▢⬦	⊙θ⬦⊟	th	
ι	ꓢꓢꓢꓱⲤⵏ	Ⲓ	i	Ⲓ
κ	Κ	Κ	k	Κ
λ	ⵏꓩ∧ΓΛ	Λ	l	ⵏⵏ⌊
μ	⩘⩘⩘⩘⩘	Ϻ Ϻ	m	⩘⩘⩘
ν	⩘ꓦꓠ∧∧Ν	Ν	n	Ν
ξ	ⵏ⨯ⵎⵑⵣⵤⵥ	ⵣⵥⵤⵦ	x	Χ
ο	▢⬦⊙Ⲟ⍉Ⲥ	Ⲟ	o	⬦Ⲟ⬦⍉
π	ΓꓩⲤ	ΓⲠⲠ	p	Γ ΡΡ
ϙ	ϙϙϙⲨ		q	ꓢ ϙ
ρ	ꓣꓣᗡᗡꓩꓩ	Ρ	r	ᗡ ꓣ
σ	ꓢꓢⵣⵤⵥϺ	ꓢⲤⲤ	s	ꓢⵦꓢ S
σσ	ⵏⵜ			
τ	�X⊤	⊤	t	⊤
υ	ⵎꓦꓦ	Ꙟ	u	Ꙟ
φ	⊟ⵌⵁⵀφⲞᴦᴮ	φⵀⵀ		
χ	ⵎⵚⵎⵜⵎⵡⵡⵡ⨯	Χ		
ψ	ⵡⵜꓦ	Ψ		
ω	⊙Ⲟ Ω	ΩꓪⲰꓪ		

After Barclay V. Head
Historia Numorum

Attributing Greek Coins

Once coins are sorted by type, we can attempt to read the legends and identify the rulers or issuing cities. With Greek coins, this takes some research. First of all, the legend must be fairly complete. Often, they aren't. If the name of the city is not abbreviated, it will surely be struck off the flan or completely covered by rock-hard verdigris. Trying to figure out the name of a city from obscure legends is nightmarish. Fortunately, Dr. Icard has given us the remedy. The *Dictionary of Greek Coin Inscriptions* is a *must* for anyone wishing to attribute Greek or Roman Provincial coins. This ingenious work lists inscriptions in fragmentary form. That is, you can start anywhere in the legend and read the letters in sequence. Then turn to Icard, and Eureka! Once the city is identified, it is usually only a matter of checking reference catalogues for a precise attribution. The handiest reference for this purpose is David Sear's *Greek Coins and Their Values* in two volumes. As we stated before, Sear does not list every variation by any means, but no single volume does. What Sear's book provides is a general guide to get you in the ball park. If you are really a die-hard and want to find exactly the same coin, you will probably have to turn to the larger references like the SNG series or the British Museum Catalogues (29 volumes).

Many Greek coins are dated. Of course the dates do not conform to our dating system. They are calculated either from the foundation of the city, or from the beginning of a ruling dynasty. The Seleukid era, which is named after Seleukos, the founder of the dynasty, dates from the year 312 BC and was used by some cities well into Roman times. The Greeks indicated numerals with the corresponding letter of the alphabet, therefore reading dates is fairly easy. Regnal dates, although written the same way, are slightly more difficult to interpret. They begin and end with a particular ruler, whose identity may not be apparent on some coins. Issue dates can often be used to identify the ruler.

GREEK DATES

1	A	20	K	100	P
2	B	30	Λ	200	Σ
3	Γ	40	M	300	T
4	Δ	50	N	400	Y
5	E	60	Ξ	500	Φ
6	S	70	O	600	X
7	Z	80	Π	700	Ψ
8	H	90	Q	800	Ω
9	Θ				
10	I				

Greek dates are written in letters, and are read either from right to left or left to right. For example, the year 123 is written ΓΚΡ or ΡΚΓ, depending on the time and place. Since their calendar year did not start on January 1, as ours does, a Greek year will be expressed in overlapping AD dates like 148/9.

In addition to the Ruler's name or the name of an issuing city, Greek coins often bear the name of a magistrate who was authorized to strike coins. There were so many of these magistrates that their names are often unknown to us. In fact, it is not too unusual in certain issues to discover a type with an unpublished magistrate. Sometimes the magistrates placed their monograms on these coins instead of their names. A monogram is a device composed of one to several letters combined in creative ways to produce a compact but identifiable stamp. Magistrates were not the only ones to use monograms, some mints, kings and emperors used them as well.

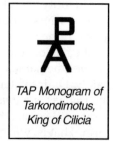

TAP Monogram of Tarkondimotus, King of Cilicia

Artists sometimes placed their names on the dies that they designed and engraved. These may be spelled out in their entirety or sometimes placed inconspicuously in the field as an initial or two. It is often impossible to tell whether the letters in a Greek coin's field are mint control marks, magistrate's initials, or artist's signatures. The silver tetradrachms of Alexander the Great and his successors have many such devices in the fields, as do some of the issues from Athens, Corinth and from southern Italy. Part of the fun of collecting Greek coins is to try to identify the purpose of each element of the coin's motif.

The main aid to attribution of Greek coins is the primary element of the design. Most Greek cities used the same emblematic devices over a long period of time and they became well associated with the city so that coins from that city were immediately recognizable. Richard Plant's Book, *Greek Coin Types and Their Identification,* groups coins by their motif and helps make identification easier. It is quite useful.

Emblematic Devices on Greek Coins

City	Device	City	Device
Aigina	Turtle	Kyzikos	Tunny fish
Akragos	Crab	Leontini	Lion
Alexandria	Eagle	Messana	Rabbit
Amphipolis	Tripod	Metaponton	Wheat
Antioch	Tyche	Phoenicia	Galley
Athens	Owl	Rhodos	Rose
Boeotia	Shield	Sicyon	Dove
Corinth	Pegasos	Sidon	Europa
Carthage	Horse	Seleukeia	Anchor
Chios	Sphinx	Tarentum	Dolphin
Crete	Labyrinth	Thorion	Bull
Ephesos	Bee		
Judaea	Palm		
Kyrene	Silphium		

These devices also appear as generic images on coinage of many other cities, but they tend to predominate in the cities listed.

Major Divisions and Dynasties of the Greek World

(For subdivisions see *Greek Coins and Their Values*)

Geographical Divisions

1. Spain
2. Gaul
3. Britain
4. Celts
5. Italy
6. Sicily
7. Northern Greece
8. Illyria
9. Central Greece
10. Peloponessos
11. Cyclades
12. Crete
13. Asia Minor
14. The East
15. Egypt
16. North Africa

Political Dynasties

Macedonian Kingdom
Kingdom of Thrace
Seleukid Kingdom
Pergamene Kingdom
Pontic Kingdom
Bithynian Kingdom
Cappadocian Kingdom
Kings of Armenia*
Parthian Kingdom*
Baktrian Kingdom*
Ptolemaic Kingdom

* Although we treat these dynasties as Non-Classical, they often are arranged under Greek coinage for cataloguing purposes.

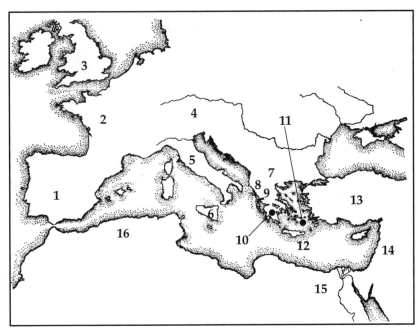

Greek Denominations (Attic Standard)

Athens,
AU - Stater,
297-296 BC,
8.57 gm

Athens,
AR - Decadrachm
480-449 BC,
43 gm

Athens,
AR - Tetradrachm
449 BC,
17.2 gm

Athens,
AR - Drachm
449 BC,
4.3 gm

Athens,
AR - Obol
449 BC,
.72 gm

Athens,
AR - Hemiobol
449 BC,
.36 gm

Athens,
AE - 18mm
87/86 BC,
7.65 gm

Corinth,
AR - Stater
400-350 BC,
8.6 gm

Corinth,
AR - Drachm
400-333 BC,
2.9 gm

Corinth,
AR - Diobol
4th c. BC,
.9 5gm

Table of Greek Weight Standards

Standard	Major Unit	Weight
Achaean	Stater	8.0 gm
Aiginetan	Stater	12.2 gm
Attic	Tetradrachm	17.2 gm
Campanian	Stater	7.5 gm
Corinthian	Stater	8.6 gm
Euboic	Stater	17.2 gm
Lycian	Stater	10 gm
Persian	Siglos	8.55 gm
Phoenician	Shekel	7.0 gm
Rhodian	Tetradrachm	15.2 gm
Sicilian	Litra	.86 gm

The denominations shown in the accompanying photos are not inclusive. For example, the Attic system consists of no less than 14 silver denominations. Many of these denominations were infrequently used. Bronze denominations can be determined by markings on some issues, especially from Sicily, but most are simply identified and catalogued by their diameter in millimeters.

Alexander the Great

The coinage of Alexander the Great has been a favorite attraction of ancient coin collectors for centuries, and probably was represented in the first collection of ancient coins ever assembled. The historical and emotional appeal of this great figure is truly monumental. Fortunately, the silver coins of Alexander are not rare. These coins, which were struck in the millions, circulated throughout the Greek world—and far beyond. There are more than 1,300 different varieties of the tetradrachms alone (some of these being struck in the name of Alexander's half-brother Philip Arrhidaeus). The standard type bears the head of Herakles, wearing a lion's scalp, on its obverse and Zeus enthroned and holding an eagle on the reverse. Although Alexander only ruled from 336 to 323 BC, coins of this standard type and bearing the name of Alexander were still being issued by some mints two centuries after his death.

The issues struck between 336 and 323 are referred to as "lifetime" issues and those struck after 323 are referred to as "posthumous" issues. For many years, it was believed that the lifetime issues were characterized by a parallel arrangement of the legs of Zeus. The issues on which

Lifetime issue of
Alexander III
Memphis mint
332-323 BC

Posthumous issue of
Alexander III
Aspendus mint
194/193 BC

Zeus has his legs crossed were thought to be posthumous. The definitive study of this series by the late Dr. Martin Price of the British Museum has shed much light on this issue. Although the appearance of crossed legs represents a 99% chance that an issue is posthumous, one cannot conversely assume that a coin with parallel legs is a lifetime issue. Price has identified upwards of 50 types with parallel legs that were struck after Alexander's death. Another 50 or so varieties of this type are listed by Price as uncertain. Another rule of thumb that collectors erroneously followed in the past was that the title ΒΑΣΙΛΕΩΣ did not appear on Alexander's coins during his lifetime. Although rare, some lifetime specimens do bear the title.

Following the trail of Alexander's conquests is a popular pastime of many people who do not even collect ancient coins, but tracing the route numismatically is even more fascinating. As Alexander's army marched across Asia Minor, the Levant, Egypt, Mesopotamia, Central Asia and even to parts of India, it required huge amounts of coinage for payment of the troops. The mint marks of coins from these various places provide graphic testimony of Alexander's presence. It is also interesting to compare the styles of representation from geographical place to place. In some places, Alexander retained local coin types with only slight modifications.

During the third century BC, Hellenistic coinage changed in fabric to a wider and thinner flan. Although their imagery remained the same, the Alexander type tetradrachms followed this pattern. Consequently, large and thin flan tetradrachms of the Alexander type are always posthumous.

There is substantial controversy on the issue of whether the figure wearing a lion's scalp on the obverse of Alexander's tetradrachms and drachms was intended to represent the king himself. Some commentators believe that all of the Alexander type coins were intended to be portrait coins, some believe that none of the types were, and others believe that some might have been. The latter position seems most defensible, and there are certainly dies, like that at the head of this section, that present a portrait-like image. For more on Alexander portraits see the section by that name in a later chapter.

Alexander had married Roxanne, the daughter of a Sogdian chieftain, and she was pregnant with a son who was born after Alexander's death. The boy was taken under security guard to Macedon, where he and his mother took up residence with Olympia, the mother of Alexander and surviving wife of Philip II. The succeeding years were marked by bitter dispute over the regency of the child and the partitioning of Alexander's empire. The child of Alexander was eventually murdered by Cassander. There is considerable reason to suspect that some of the posthumous Alexander type silver and bronze coins, and maybe the gold as well, were issues in the name of Alexander's son, just as some of the issues formerly thought to have been coins of Philip II are now assigned to Philip III.

The luster of Alexander's name and the perceived benefit of mere association with it has always been strong. In addition to the long run of Hellenistic coins of Alexander type, several Roman Provincial coins bear his portrait. Epic tales of his exploits were still being published in the Middle Ages everywhere from Persia to Northern Europe. Naturally, the glorification of Alexander was a popular theme during the Renaissance, and one could fill a library with modern works detailing every known shred of evidence about his life. Alexander's body was literally hijacked by his general Ptolemy and taken to Egypt for burial. The modern discovery of the tomb of Philip II at Vergina in northern Greece, filled with precious artifacts of the Macedonian Kingdom, has kindled a new round of speculation and hope that the sands of Egypt will eventually give up the final resting place of Alexander.

Alexander IV?

Hyla Troxell, in Studies in the Macedonian Coinage of Alexander the Great (ANS, NY, 1997, pp. 96-98) argues that the Tetradrachms from Amphipolis with Royal title on reverse actually were struck in the name of Alexander IV, the surviving son of Alexander the Great. Note that on this issue (Price 108), struck after 323 BC, the figure of Zeus is depicted with legs parallel, not crossed.

Baktrian Coins

As a result of the wars between the successors of Alexander the Great, Seleukos gained control of the easternmost lands of Alexander's empire. The province of Baktro-Sogdiana was ruled by the Seleukid Kings until 256 BC when Diodotus, the Satrap of Antiochos II, declared himself independent and ruler of his own kingdom. Diodotus was able to defend his claim, and a succession of Baktrian kings emerged. Coins of the Baktrians retain the Greek flavor, although they incorporate bilingual Greek and Karosthi legends. The Baktrians expanded south and maintained their dominance until about 130 BC when the dynasty was overrun by Scythian invaders and was split into two branches. The end came with the Kushan defeat of Hermaios in 1 BC . Baktrian coins have appeared on the market in great numbers in recent years, and it is possible to find exceptional specimens at historically low prices.

Menander
AR Drachm
ca. 155-130 BC
2.46 gm

Demetrios I
AE 24mm
200-190 BC
8.37 gm

Euthydemos I
AR Tetradrachm
230-190 BC
16.16 gm

Antimachos
AR Tetradrachm
ca. 185-170 BC
16.64 gm

Many beginners attempt to attribute Roman coins by portrait recognition. This is something that we do every day of our lives and which doesn't require any special training. In some cases it is possible, especially with coins struck in the early days of the empire, but eventually the collector will have to read a coin's legends to properly attribute it.

Claudius
AE - As, AD 41-54

Most legends on Roman coins read clockwise, but a few read counterclockwise No, we don't know why they occasionally did it backwards! Regardless of the direction, the legends will contain essentially the same information. David Sear's *Roman Coins and Their Values* and Stewart Westdal's *Roman Coin Inscriptions,* are useful aids to deciphering the inscriptions.

The Romans loved honors and titles and had to abbreviate words in their legends to make everything fit. This is the only really confusing thing about them. Once the collector learns to recognize these abbreviations, the reading becomes simple. Listed below are some of the more common abbreviations found on Roman coins:

Abbreviated titles on Roman coins

AVG: Augustus (the title bestowed on an emperor/empress)
ARM: Armeniacus (conqueror of Armenia)
CAES: Caesar (designated heir)
CENS: Censor (magistrate who determined the size of the Senate)
COS: Consul (one of two chief magistrates)
DAC: Dacicus (conqueror of Dacia)
DIVI: Divine (acclaimed a deity)
DN: Dominus Noster (Our Lord)
FIL: Filius/Filia (son or daughter of ...)
GERM: Germanicus (conqueror of Germany)
IMP: Imperator (title reserved for victorious leaders/emperors)
NOB: Nobilissimus or [-ma=feminine] (noble)
OPTIMO: Optimo Principi (the best prince)
PART: Parthicus (conqueror of Parthia)
PERP: Perpetuatae (for life)
PF: Pius Felix (pious, happy)
PM: Pontifex Maximus (high priest)
PP: Pater Patriae (father of his country)
SC: Senatus Consultus (with the permission of the Senate)
TR P: Tribunicia Potestate (the tribunician power)

Let us take, for example, a typical coin of Constantine the Great as Caesar, and decipher its legends:

On the obverse, we find the inscription:
FLVALCONSTANTINVSNOBC This may seem like alphabet goulash, but it really is quite logical. Spelled out, the legend reads:
FL(avius) VAL(erius) CONSTANTINVS NOB(ilissimus) C(aesar)

The name Constantine (CONSTANTINUS) may be separated from the rest of the legend without too much difficulty. Once the ruler's name is isolated, the rest of the abbreviations in a Roman legend are simply forenames, titles and accolades. Flavius and Valerius are parts of Constantine's name, Nobilissimus and Caesar are explained on the preceding page. A list of emperors' names appears on the following pages.

Some of the common forename abbreviations are:
A(ulus), AEL(ius), AUR(elius), D(ecimus), C(aius or Gaius), CN(aeus), FL(avius), L(ucius), M(arcus), N(umerius), P(ublius), Q(uintus), SER(gius), SEX(tus), SP(urius), TI(berius), T(itus), AP(pius), V(ibius). For an extensive list of these abbreviated names, see the *Dictionary of Roman Coin Inscriptions* by Stewart Westdal.

On the reverse, we find the inscription:
GENIOPOPVLIROMANI PTR S F This inscription consists of the three words Genio Populi Romani, or loosely translated, "to the genius of the Roman people." In the exergue (base) of the coin is a mint mark, PTR, from the mint of Treveri (Trier) in Germany. S and F in the right and left fields are mint control marks. Standing left is a personification of Genius. The mints were very highly organized, and mint officials could tell from certain letters or symbols on a coin (stars, dots, etc.) exactly when, where and perhaps by whom the coin was struck.

Roman legends, especially on the reverse of a coin, are typically laced with propaganda. Many beseech the assistance of the gods, for one need or another, others announce a particular success through personal intervention of the gods. It never hurt to have them on your side! As well as representing gods on the reverse of their coins (remember, as polytheists they worshipped more than one), Romans also personified (represented as people) a variety of virtues and elements. Honor and virtue, fidelity, peace, happiness, security, good health and prosperity were only a few. Genius, on the coin described above, is a personification of one of the proclaimed virtues of the Roman people.

The obverse generally heralded the emperor's authority, while the reverse propagandized his strengths, compassion, kindness, and personal association with the gods—all those admirable things that often led to assassination. Occasionally, the obverse of a coin bears only a portrait, with no legend at all. These coins are called "anepigraphic," which is simply a fancy word for "no inscription." Anepigraphic coins were usually struck as a way of commemorating some special event. For example, an important visit by Constantine the Great to the city of Antioch led to the issuing of a complete series of anepigraphic bronze coins. Featured on these special issues are portraits of Constantine, his mother, wife, and four sons. Portrait collectors find anepigraphic coins very appealing, because the artist employed to engrave dies for a commemorative series were usually the most talented available.

A typical catalogue attribution for the coin inset here would be:

CONSTANTINE I, AD 307-337. AE Follis (2.04 gm). Struck AD 324-325. Antioch mint. Anepigraphic, laureate head right/CONSTAN/TINUS/AVG in three lines below wreath / SMANTE. RIC VII 52. EF, R4, chocolate brown patina.

Anepigraphic bronze of Constantine the Great

In order of appearance we find the emperor's name; dates of his reign; denomination of this coin; weight in grams; actual date struck; mint; obverse description; reverse legend and description; pertinent reference; and additional notes. RIC VII 52 means that this coin type is published in *Roman Imperial Coins*, vol. VII, under Constantine I, Antioch mint, as catalogue number 52. The R4 refers to a rarity condition assigned in RIC. Rarities in this reference are listed as Common, Scarce and R1-R5 with R5 being the highest degree of rarity. The slash marks in the described legends show where the legend breaks on the coin. Weights are not always provided, but are very useful in some situations, such as studying economic conditions or determining authenticity of a coin. Bronze coins tend to vary in weight much more than silver and gold coins. A good digital scale will be accurate to .01 grams, and can be purchased for about $175.

140

THE ROMAN EMPERORS

AUGUSTUS	(27 BC - AD 14)	
TIBERIUS	(AD 14-37)	
CALIGULA	(37-41)	**JULIO-CLAUDIANS**
CLAUDIUS	(41-54)	
NERO	(54-68)	
CLODIUS MACER	(68)	
GALBA	(68-69)	
OTHO	(69)	
VITELLIUS	(69)	
VESPASIAN	(69-79)	
TITUS	(79-81)	**FLAVIANS**
DOMITIAN	(81-96)	
NERVA	(96-98)	
TRAJAN	(98-117)	
HADRIAN	(117-138)	
AELIUS (CAESAR)	(136-138)	**ADOPTED EMPERORS**
ANTONINUS PIUS	(138-161)	
MARCUS AURELIUS	(161-180)	
LUCIUS VERUS	(161-169)	
COMMODUS	(180-192)	
PERTINAX	(193)	
DIDIUS JULIANUS	(193)	
PESCENNIUS NIGER	(193-194)	
CLODIUS ALBINUS	(195-197)	
SEPTIMIUS SEVERUS	(193-211)	
CARACALLA	(198-217)	
GETA	(209-212)	
MACRINUS	(217-218)	**SEVERANS**
DIADUMENIAN	(218)	
ELAGABALUS	(218-222)	
SEVERUS ALEXANDER	(222-235)	
MAXIMINUS	(235-238)	
MAXIMUS (CAESAR)	(235-238)	
GORDIAN I	(238)	
GORDIAN II	(238)	
BALBINUS	(238)	**GORDIANI**
PUPIENUS	(238)	
GORDIAN III	(238-244)	
PHILIP I	(244-249)	
PHILIP II	(247-249)	
PACATIAN	(CA. 248)	
JOTAPIAN	(CA. 248)	
TRAJAN DECIUS	(249-251)	
HERENNIUS ETRUSCUS	(251)	
HOSTILIAN	(251)	
TREBONIANUS GALLUS	(251-253)	

VOLUSIAN	(251-253)	
AEMILIAN	(253)	
URANIUS ANTONINUS	(CA. 253-254)	
VALERIAN	(AD 253-260)	
GALLIENUS	(253-268)	**VALERIANI**
VALERIAN II (CAESAR)	(253-255)	
SALONINUS	(259)	
MACRIANUS	(260-261)	
QUIETUS	(260-261)	
REGALIANUS	(CA. 260)	
POSTUMUS	(259-268)	
LAELIANUS	(268)	
MARIUS	(268)	
DOMITIANUS?	(268?)	**GALLO-ROMANS**
VICTORINUS	(268-270)	
TETRICUS I	(270-273)	
TETRICUS II	(270-273)	
CLAUDIUS II	(268-270)	
QUINTILLUS	(270)	
AURELIAN	(270-275)	
VABALATHUS	(271-272)	
TACITUS	(275-276)	
FLORIANUS	(276)	
PROBUS	(276-282)	
BONOSUS	(CA. 280)	
SATURNINUS	(CA. 280)	
CARUS	(282-283)	
NUMERIAN	(283-284)	
CARINUS	(283-285)	
JULIAN OF PANNONIA	(284-285)	
DIOCLETIAN	(284-305)	
AMANDUS	(285-286)	
CARAUSIUS	(287-293)	
ALLECTUS	(293-296)	**THE TETRARCHY**
DOMITIUS DOMITIANUS	(296-297)	
MAXIMIANUS	(286-310)	
CONSTANTIUS I	(305-306)	
GALERIUS	(305-311)	
SEVERUS II	(306-307)	
MAXENTIUS	(306-312)	
MAXIMINUS II	(309-313)	
ALEXANDER OF CARTHAGE	(308-311)	
LICINIUS I	(308-324)	

LICINIUS II (CAESAR)	(317-324)	
VALENS	(314)	
MARTINIAN	(324)	
CONSTANTINE I	(AD 307-337)	
CRISPUS (CAESAR)	(317-326)	
DELMATIUS (CAESAR)	(335-337)	
HANNIBALLIANUS (REX)	(335-337)	
CONSTANTINE II	(337-340)	
CONSTANS	(337-350)	
CONSTANTIUS II	(337-361)	**FAMILY OF CONSTANTINE**
MAGNENTIUS	(350-353)	
DECENTIUS	(351-353)	
VETRANIO	(350)	
NEPOTIAN	(350)	
CONSTANTIUS GALLUS	(351-354)	
JULIAN II	(360-363)	
JOVIAN	(363-364)	
VALENTINIAN I	(364-375)	
VALENS	(364-378)	
PROCOPIUS	(365-366)	
GRATIAN	(367-383)	
VALENTINIAN II	(375-392)	
THEODOSIUS I	(379-395)	
MAGNUS MAXIMUS	(383-388)	
FLAVIUS VICTOR	(387-388)	
EUGENIUS	(392-394)	
ARCADIUS	(383-408)	
HONORIUS	(393-423)	
CONSTANTINE III	(407-411)	
CONSTANS	(408-411)	**FAMILY OF THEODOSIUS**
MAXIMUS	(409-411)	
PRISCUS ATTALUS	(409-10; 414-15)	
JOVINUS	(411-413)	
SEBASTIANUS	(412-413)	
CONSTANTIUS III	(421)	
JOHANNES	(423-425)	
THEODOSIUS II	(402-450)	
VALENTINIAN III	(425-455)	
MARCIAN	(450-457)	
PETRONIUS MAXIMUS	(455)	
AVITUS	(455-456)	
MAJORIAN	(457-461)	
LEO I	(457-474)	

SEVERUS III	(461-465)
ANTHEMIUS	(467-472)
OLYBRIUS	(472)
GLYCERIUS	(473-474)
LEO II	(473-474)
JULIUS NEPOS	(474-475) (to 480 in exile)
ROMULUS AUGUSTUS	(475-476)

* The year 476 historically marks the end of the Western Roman Empire, but some Romans in the West were at least nominally under the rule of Eastern emperors for a short time. Zeno was regarded as the sole ruler of East and West, but most of the provinces of the West were already lost to Germanic kings. Coinage struck during this period rests in a numismatic nether land. Strangely enough, gold coins of Zeno are often treated by dealers and cataloguers as "Byzantine," while the small bronze coins of this emperor are treated as late Roman.

ZENO	(474-491)
BASILISCUS	(475-476)
LEONTIUS	(484-488)
ANASTASIUS	(491-518)

Reading about the Romans

It is not difficult to find books about the Romans or the individual personalities and their lives. Any bookstore, specializing in either new or used books, will have a wide selection. It is not necessary to list recommendations here, but it may be worth pointing out that there are different kinds of books on the subject. As general histories, there are of course the original works by Julius Caesar, Cicero, Cassius Dio, Livy, Ammianus Marcellinus, Marcus Aurelius, Petronius, Polybius, Pliny, Plutarch, Seneca, Suetonius, Tacitus, Virgil and others. Inexpensive paperback translations of these are readily available. Older copies cost only a dollar or two at used bookstores.

Another source of information is college text books, which also are inexpensive in non-current editions. The best historical source that the author has encountered is Victor Duruy's *History of Rome and of the Roman People,* published in eight two-part volumes, Boston, 1894. Purchased at a used bookstore for $75, the set has been a faithful and dependable companion for many years.

Finally, there are the monographs about individual Romans that stem from PhD dissertations as well as the popular press. These are usually relaxing and enjoyable to read, because they are generally written in a narrative rather than documentary style.

Dating Roman Coins

Roman coins can usually be dated to within a few years simply by identifying the emperor who issued the coin. The list of emperors on the preceding pages includes the beginning and ending dates of their reigns. It may be useful, though, to identify the date of a coin more precisely. This is particularly true for the student of history who is studying coins related to a specific dated event.

Fortunately, in addition to knowing the dates during which Roman emperors ruled, we also know the years in which they were awarded various titles of honor. This information comes from preserved or copied manuscripts, inscriptions in stone, and a variety of sources. It is lucky for us that the Romans kept very detailed records, and left monuments (many in stone) to practically everything.

The most common titles recorded on coins are IMP (Imperator), COS (Consul) and TR P (Tribunicia Potestate). These titles were placed on a coin (either obverse or reverse) during the year of their conferment by the Roman Senate. Don't get the idea that this was always a sign of regard, no ambitious senator would dare object to an emperor assuming any title he desired. Many emperors renewed their Tribunician Powers annually. A thorough accounting of these titles and their dates is found in *Roman Imperial Coinage* (RIC). Attribution by specific year is not normally something that a beginner would attempt, but we have included the titles and dates pertaining to the first emperor, Augustus, in order to illustrate its practicality.

Dating coins of the emperor Augustus	
23 BC .... TR P I; COS XI	4 BC .... TR P XX
22 BC .... TR P II	3 BC .... TR P XXI
21 BC .... TR P III	2 BC .... TR P XXII; COS XIII
20 BC .... TR P IV; IMP VIIII	1 BC .... TR P XXIII
19 BC .... TR P V	AD 1 .... TR P XXIV
18 BC .... TR P VI	AD 2 .... TR P XXV; IMP XV
17 BC .... TR P VII	AD 3 .... TR P XXVI
16 BC .... TR P VIII	AD 4 .... TR P XXVII
15 BC .... TR P VIIII; IMP X	AD 5 .... TR P XXVIII
14 BC .... TR P X	AD 6 .... TR P XXVIIII; IMP XVII
13 BC .... TR P XI	AD 7 .... TR P XXX
12 BC .... TR P XII; IMP XI	AD 8 .... TR P XXXI
11 BC .... TR P XIII; IMP XII	AD 9 .... TR P XXXII; IMP XIX
10 BC .... TR P XIV	AD 10 .... TR P XXXIII
9 BC .... TR P XV; IMP XIII	AD 11 .... TR P XXXIV; IMP XX
8 BC .... TR P XVI; IMP XIIII	AD 12 .... TR P XXXV
7 BC .... TR P XVII	AD 13 .... TR P XXXVI
6 BC .... TR P XVIII	AD 14 .... TR P XXXVII; IMP XXI
5 BC .... TR P XVIIII; COS XII	

Having identified the emperor by name and dates of rule, we next are faced with determining the denomination of a coin. Roman coins were struck in four metals, gold, silver, billon and bronze. Each metal was struck in several denominations over time. Therefore, the denomination may be determined partly by the period of issue, and vice versa. See the chart and illustrations below for a comparison. AV=gold; AR=silver and AE=bronze. Some rare denominations are not listed.

Denominations of the Roman Empire		
Early	Middle	Late
AV Aureus	AV Aureus	AV Solidus
AV Quinarius	AV Quinarius	AV Semissis
		AV Tremissis
AR Cistophorus	AR Antoninianus	
	Billon Antoninianus	AR Miliarense
AR Denarius	AR Argenteus	AR Siliqua
AR Quinarius	AR 1/2 Argenteus	AR 1/2 Siliqua
AE Sestertius	AE Sestertius	
AE Dupondius	AE Denarius	AE Follis/AE 1
AE As	AE Semis	Centenionalis (AE2)
AE Semis		AE 3/4
AE Quadrans		

There are a few identifying characteristics that help to determine the denomination of otherwise confusing issues. For example, the middle-sized bronze of the early empire was struck in copper and also in orichalcum (brass). On the copper As, the emperor is usually crowned with a laurel wreath, on the orichalcum Dupondius he wears a radiate crown. Although the color of the two metals is different, the As being reddish and the Dupondius being yellow, patina can sometimes obscure the metal completely. In this case the two could be, and are, confused in cases where the radiate crown is missing. On the Dupondii after the reign of Caracalla, females are usually depicted with a crescent moon beneath their shoulders.

Philip I
AR-Ant.

A parallel may be seen between the Denarius, Rome's standard silver coin, and the Antoninianus (double denarius). These coins can be virtually the same size. The Antoninianus, however, features a radiate crown or a crescent to mark its value.

The bronze Follis decreased in size from 30mm to as little as 17mm as inflation took its toll. The terms AE-1 through AE-4 are arbitrary references to diameter, and have nothing to do with original denominations, which are uncertain. AE-1 = 25mm or greater; AE-2 = 24-21mm; AE-3 = 20-17mm and AE-4 = 16mm or under.

Roman Denominations (Early Empire)

Weights indicated are approximate

AV - Aureus
27 BC - AD 14 (7.8 gm)
Augustus

AR - Denarius
AD 14-37
Tiberius (3.7 gm)

AE - Sestertius
AD 37-41
Caligula (28 gm)

AE - Dupondius
(distinguished by
   radiate crown)
AD 117-138,
Hadrian (12 gm)

AE - As
AD 138-161 (11 gm)
Antoninus Pius

AE - Quadrans
AD 100-150 (2.5 gm)
Anonymous

147

Roman Denominations (Later Empire)

Weights indicated are approximate

AV - Solidus
AD 375-392 (4.4 gm)
Valentinian II

AV - Semissis
AD 383-408
Arcadius (2.2 gm)

AV - Tremissis
AD 379-395 (1.5 gm)
Theodosius I

AR - Siliqua
AD 392-394 (2.5 gm)
Eugenius

AE - 1
AD 361-363 (9 gm)
Julian II

AE - 2
AD 379-395 (5 gm)
Theodosius I

AE - 3
AD 365-366 (3 gm)
Procopius

AE - 4
AD 450-457 (1 gm)
Marcian

Mint Marks on Roman Coins

The next step to proper attribution is to identify the mint at which a coin was struck. Sometimes this is relatively easy, as the mint is indicated in the exergue (bottom reverse). There may be only a single letter, or there may be six or seven letters. This means that you may have to find the mint abbreviation among other abbreviations, as with the obverse legend. Usually, the mint name comes first, or is preceded by the letters P (Pecunia=money) SM (Sacra Moneta=Imperial money) or M (Moneta). The letter or letters following the mint abbreviation generally refer to the specific officina (workshop) at which the coin was struck. Therefore, a typical abbreviation might be SMANTE — denoting the fifth workshop at Antioch. In some cases, a mint is not indicated on the coin. The best source for identifying mints on these issues is *Roman Imperial Coins* (RIC), a ten-volume specialized reference. Following is a list of common abbreviations.

Common Mint Abbreviations	
AL, ALE	Alexandria
AMB	Ambianum
AN, ANT	Antiochia
AQ	Aquileia
AR, ARL, CON, KON	Arelatum (also named Constantina for a period)
BA	Barcino
C	Camulodunum
CL	Clausentum
K, PK, KART	Carthago
C, CON, CONS	Constantinople
CVZ, K	Cyzicus
H, HT	Heraclea
M, MLN, PLN	Londinium
LG, LVG, PLG	Lugdunum
MD, MDPS	Mediolanum
N, NIC, NIK	Nicomedia
MOST	Ostia
RV, RAV	Ravenna
R, RM, ROMOB	Roma
SD, SER	Serdica
SM, SIRM	Sirmium
SIS	Siscia
TS, TES, THS	Thessalonica
T	Ticinum
TR, TRE, TRPS	Treveri

The Confusing Constantina Mint

In AD 328, the city of Arles (Arelate) was renamed Constantina in honor of Constantine II. After his death, the city returned to its original name for a time and then resumed the name Constantina during the reign of Constantius II. During this period, coins struck at Constantina were mintmarked CONS just like the coins struck at Constantinople.

Constantine II, AE-3, Constantina Mint
Above: Workshop 2 (S=secunda before CONS)
Below: Workshop 1 (P=prima before CONS)

The workshops at Arles identified themselves with the latin ordinals prima, secunda, tertia, and quatra for 1st, 2nd, 3rd and 4th. The abbreviations for these ordinals were placed before the mint name as (P), (S), (T) and (Q).

Constans, AE-centenionalis, Constantinople Mint
Workshop 3 (Γ=gamma after CONS)

Individual workshops at the Constantinople mint numbered themselves with Greek letters A, B, Γ, Δ. These letters were placed after the mint name. Therefore, the mints of Constantina and Constantinople, even though the both used the abbreviation CONS, can be distinguished by the type and position of their officinae designations.

Attributing Roman Provincial coins is not really as hard as it looks. The obverse is usually quite similar to Roman Imperial coins in that it bears the portrait and titles of the emperor. The names are normally written in Greek, but that is not a difficulty once one learns the alphabet, which has been provided in an earlier chapter. The inscriptions sometimes include unfamiliar letters—for example, the lunate sigma "C" like the c in cedar is often substituted for a normal Greek sigma (Σ) and "O" sometimes takes the place of omega (Ω), and a lunate episilon (Note in

Syedra, Cilicia
AE-33mm
AD 253-268
"Judgement of Ares"

the inset here that Syedra is spelled CYEΔPEΩN with a lunate sigma and lunate episilons). Likewise, the cursive omega (ω) is frequently encountered. The emperor's titles may be in Latin or in Greek, therefore the obverse words and abbreviations change slightly. The abbreviation for Augustus, for example may be rendered AVG or AYΓ, or the title might be translated to Sebastos. The variations are numerous. Dates are recorded in Greek numerals, A=1, B=2, Γ=3, etc. Most provincial mints in the West used Latin legends, as did Eastern cities which had been accepted as a Roman colony.

Collectors of provincial coins tend to collect either by topical area or by mint city. Many of the provincial cities produced a prolific series of coins with interesting motifs, yet very little is known about them. This is the real beauty of the Roman Provincial series. Collectors can do very productive research in an area that scholars never seem to find time for.

This series is filled with narrative reverse types, that is, themes that tell a story. Recognizing the mythological story depicted on the reverse of a large provincial bronze is really an adventure. There are so many different stories, and coin types, that it can be addictive—like working crossword puzzles. Sometimes the themes are very simple, like a pair of clasped hands representing an alliance or marriage. Sometimes they are more complex and individual figures must be identified by whatever distinguishing attributes the celator has provided.

The collector has lacked a comprehensive catalogue of the Roman Provincial series, but the ongoing publication of *Roman Provincial Coins* (RPC) promises to fill that void. With two volumes in print and others expected shortly, the work already has established itself as the most authoritative work on this series that has ever been written.

151

Reading Reverse Legends

within the wreath:
ΠΡΟΤΑ• ΚΟΙΝΑ
ΑCΙΑC CΜVΡΝΑΙΩΝ

=

First Council of Asia, Smyrna

around the outer edge:
ΕΠΙCΤΡΑΚΛΡΟVΦΙΝΟVCΟΦΙ
(ΕΠΙ. CΤΡΑ. ΚΛ.
ΡΟVΦΙΝΟV CΟΦΙ)

=

*Eponymous Strategos
Claudius Rufinus, Sophist*

The key to attribution of a Roman Provincial coin is generally found in its reverse legends. The obverses are normally straightforward imperial types with portraits and legends bearing the ruler's name. In addition to the name of the mint city on the reverse, one often finds titles of honor bestowed upon the city.

Roman Imperial Titles in Greek Translation

Augustus	= Sebastos	as: CEB, ΣΕΒ
Consul	= Ypatos	as: ΥΠΑΤΟC
Council	= Koinon	as: ΚΟ, ΚΟΙ, ΚΟΙΝΟΝ
Divo	= Theos (Deus)	as: ΘΕΟΣ, ΘΕΟC
Felix	= Eutyces	as: ΕΥΤΥ
First	= Protes	as: ΠΡΟΤΕ
Illustrious	= Endoxos	as: ΕΝΔΟΞΟΣ
Imperator	= Autocrator	as: ΑVΤ, ΑVΤΚ
Inviolable	= Asylia	as: ΑΣΥΛΟΥ
Of (named for)	= Eponymous	as: ΕΠΙ
Nobilissimus	= Epiphanes	as: ΕΠΙΦ
Optimus	= Aristos	as: ΑΡ, ΑΡΙ, ΑΡΙΣ
Pius	= Eusebes	as: ΕΥC
Proconsul	= Anthepatos	as: ΑΝΘΥΠΑΤΟΣ
Educator	= Sophist	as: CΟΦΙ, ΣΟΦΙΣΤΗΣ
TR P	= Demarc. Ex.	as: ΔΗΜΑΡΧ ΕΞ

Roman Provincial Mints

There are literally hundreds of mints that struck provincial coinage under the Romans. It is not possible to list them here, but the collector who wishes to specialize in this series can refer to David Sear's *Greek Imperial Coins and Their Values,* or Icard's *Dictionary of Greek Coin Inscriptions,* for the names of mint cities. Some of these cities issued a very prolific run of types. The city of Anazarbus, in Cilicia, is a good example. Although this relatively small city issued coins only from 19 BC until AD 253, there are over 850 known dies. Sometimes eight to ten different types were issued in the same year. The reason for this is that the coins were serving as tools of propaganda, and newly bestowed titles were quickly announced in the coinage of the city. Since it is not unusual to find several cities with the same name, coins of the Roman Provincial series are usually identified by city and district or province to avoid confusion. Following is a list of a few active provincial mints that dated coins, the era they date from, and their names as they are spelled on the coins. This list is illustrative of the diversity of dating systems and is intended only to introduce the subject. Specialized references should be consulted for detailed listings.

City and Province	Date	Spelling
Aegeae, Cilicia	47 BC	ΑΙΓΕΑΙΩΝ
Amasia, Pontus	2 BC	ΑΜΑϹΙΑϹ
Anazarbus, Cilicia	19 BC	ΑΝΑΖΑΡΒΕΩΝ
Bostra, Arabia	AD 105	ΒΟϹΤΡΑ
Cibyra, Phrygia	84 BC	ΚΙΒΥΡΑΤΩΝ
Damascus, Coele Syria	312 BC	ΔΑΜΑϹΚΗΝωΝ
Emisa, Syria	312 BC	ΕΜΙϹΗΝΩΝ
Flaviopolis, Cilicia	AD 73	ΦΛΑΥΙΟΠΟΛΕΙΤΩΝ
Laodiceia ad Mare, Syria	48 BC	ΛΑΟΔΙΚΕΩΝ
Neapolis, Samaria	AD 72	ΝΕΑΠΟΛ. ϹΑΜΑΡΕ.
Samosata, Commagene	AD 71	ϹΑΜΟϹΑΤΕΩΝ
Seleucia Pieria, Syria	109 BC	ϹΕΛΕΥΚΕΩΝ ΠΙΕΡΙΑϹ
Sidon, Phoenicia	111 BC	ΣΙΔΩΝΟΣ
Soli-Pompeiopolis, Cilicia	66 BC	ΠΟΜΠΗΙΟΠΟΛΕΙΤΩΝ
Tiberias, Galilaea	AD 20	ΤΙΒΕΡΙΕΩΝ
Tyre, Phoenicia	126 BC	ΤΥΡΟΥ ΙΕΡΑΣ ΚΑΙ ΑΣΥΛΟΥ
Viminacium, Moesia Superior	AD 239	P M S COL VIM

The Coins of Roman Egypt

Cleopatra
Queen of Egypt

In 31 B.C., Octavian's armies defeated the combined forces of Marc Antony and Cleopatra at Actium in western Greece. This marked the end of the long struggle for supremacy in the Roman world. Antony fled, along with Cleopatra, to Egypt where they both committed suicide a year later. This brought to a close the long reign of the Ptolemaic Dynasty in Egypt and Octavian inherited the rich lands of Egypt as his own personal province.

The coinage of Roman Egypt is well published, and is a popular collecting specialty. It is a dated series, and spans over 300 years of Roman history. The most current and complete reference in this field is Keith Emmett's *Alexandrian Coins,* Lodi, WI, 2001.

The main mint in Egypt was at Alexandria, and the series is often referred to as "Alexandrian" coinage. The main denomination in Egypt during this period was the tetradrachm, which started as a debased silver successor to the Ptolemaic tetradrachms. Over the course of years, this denomination became more and more debased and eventually became a small bronze coin. One of the most impressive denominations from Roman Egypt was the bronze drachm. This large diameter coin (over 30mm) is remarkable for its imagery, with many mythological and astrological allusions. The drachm was struck on a cast flan, and its tapered edge is quite distinctive. These coins are usually well worn, indicating that they served their purpose well. Smaller denominations in

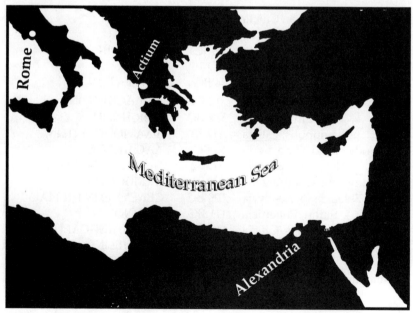

bronze also circulated, but are less ambitious in their themes. In fact, the coins of Roman Egypt form one of the most artistically appealing groups in the whole Roman series. The coins were also struck with superior technical skill. All denominations are usually very well struck, although the shape of the flan caused rapid wear, especially on the obverse. Portraits on coins of this series are often as well executed as those on the large imperial bronzes. The soil conditions in Egypt lend themselves to preservation of antiquities, and most of the coins in this series enjoy lovely patinated surfaces, even when highly worn.

The date of issue is generally engraved into the right or left reverse field. The letter "L" meaning "year" is followed by a Greek letter date. For example, the letters LIZ stand for year 17 of the reigning emperor. Reverse motifs typically portray Egyptian gods like Sarapis, Nilus and Isis, or personifications like Agathodaemon (fertility), Elpis (hope), and Tyche (fortune). Tetradrachms are fairly common in high grade, drachms are rather scarce, even in lower grades. Mythological and Astrological reverse types are very scarce.

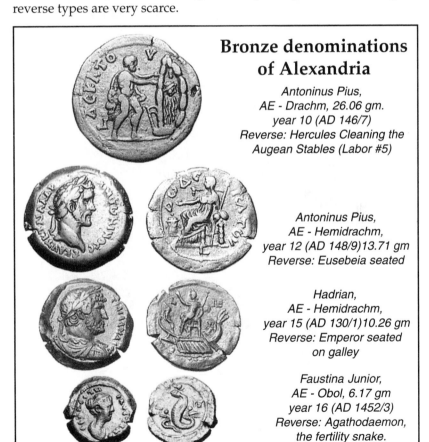

Bronze denominations of Alexandria

Antoninus Pius,
AE - Drachm, 26.06 gm.
year 10 (AD 146/7)
Reverse: Hercules Cleaning the Augean Stables (Labor #5)

Antoninus Pius,
AE - Hemidrachm,
year 12 (AD 148/9)13.71 gm
Reverse: Eusebeia seated

Hadrian,
AE - Hemidrachm,
year 15 (AD 130/1)10.26 gm
Reverse: Emperor seated on galley

Faustina Junior,
AE - Obol, 6.17 gm
year 16 (AD 1452/3)
Reverse: Agathodaemon, the fertility snake.

155

The Pharos of Alexandria

Construction of a lighthouse on Pharos Island at Alexandria was started during the reign of Ptolemy I and finished during the reign of his son Ptolemy II in 279 BC. Estimated to have been as much as 300 feet high, it is considered today as one of the Seven Wonders of the Ancient World. The edifice appears on several coins of the Roman period struck at Alexandria.

Trajan, year 11
AE hemidrachm

Hadrian, year 19
AE hemidrachm

Marcus Aurelius
year 18 (as Caesar)
AE hemidrachm

Commodus, year 29
BN tetradrachm

Hadrian, year 18
AE drachm

Antoninus Pius, year 5
AE hemidrachm

Alexandrian Reverse Types

Although the obverses of Alexandrian coins are generally occupied by an imperial portrait, the reverses offer a remarkable diversity of types. The mythology of Egypt and Greece are frequent subjects.

Trajan, AE drachm, year 17
Agathodaemon Serpents
with modius on column

Hadrian, AE drachm, year 19
Harpokrates on Lotus

Antoninus Pius, AE drachm, year 29
Nike with trophy and wreath

Trajan, AE drachm, year 16
Dionysos in Panther Biga

Hadrian, AE drachm, year 18
Sphinx

Hadrian, AE drachm, year 18
Androsphinx

Client Kings

The Romans found that it was often easier to allow a suppliant local ruler to remain on the throne than to administer a new province themselves. These "client kings" derived their power from Rome, and served at the will of the emperor, but they often were left pretty much alone to take care of internal matters. They held the Roman title *Rex*, and were allowed to place their own portraits on coinage issued in their domain. These form an interesting group of personalities to study, because they had to be remarkable people to survive under Roman rule. The subject deserves a book unto itself, but we have yet to see such a work. From the Kings of the Bosphorus, to the Kings of Edessa, and Arabia to Mauretania, names like Abgar and Polemo are recorded in the pages of history alongside the names of their Roman patrons. Juba II of Mauretania is one whose story is intriguing.

Juba's father, the king of Numidia, had lost his throne during the battle of Thapsus in 46 BC. The elder Juba (I) had supported the Pompeians, and Caesar's victory left him exiled from his own cities. He died voluntarily at the hand of his own slave. His son, only an infant, was taken to Rome, where he grew up under the protection of the family of Caesar. During childhood, Juba and Octavian became close friends and Juba was very well educated in Roman culture. He was a patron of the arts and every bit a Roman. In 25 BC, two years after Octavian had been proclaimed emperor, Juba was given the Kingdom of Mauretania. Within a few years, Juba married the surviving daughter of Cleopatra and Marc Antony and she bore a son who was named Ptolemy. Juba enjoyed a very long reign, 48 years, and was succeeded by his son in AD 23. Ptolemy was assassinated in AD 40, ending the Ptolemaic bloodline some seventy years after the suicide of his famous grandmother.

Juba II ca. 20 BC
with Cleopatra Selene

Another client king of interest is Tarkondimotus, King of Cilicia. The son of a local king, Tarkondimotus took to piracy in his youth and ravaged the Cilician shores laying waste to Roman shipping. Having been subdued by Pompey, he managed to retain the kingdom by pledging allegiance to Rome. He became a supporter of Marc Antony, honoring Antony on his coins, and fought for Antony at Actium where he was killed. After a period of about ten years, Octavian restored the kingdom of Cilicia to a son of Tarkondimotus who retained it for about 40 years.

There are many other interesting political figures that ruled during the time of the Romans, but were not really Roman themselves. As a group their coins make an interesting collectable area.

Our knowledge of the ancient world is greatly enhanced by the images seen on ancient coins. Nowhere is the saying that "a picture is worth a thousand words" more appropriate. The artists of antiquity were masters of allegorical expression and symbolism. Modern art is supposedly notable for its abstraction, but the Greeks and Romans were far advanced in this respect two millennia ago. They took the abstract and presented it in a three-dimensional world through complex symbols and personifications. Richard Brilliant's study of *Rank and Gesture in Roman Art* and Margarete Bieber's *History of the Greek and Roman Theater* demonstrate how deeply rooted certain conventions of expression were to the general populace. The fine arts and the performing arts share a common language and complemented each other in ways that we would not imagine in the 21st century.

Because we do not always understand what we see, we tend to characterize the images on coins as being something like generic representations of relatively incidental things. That is virtually never the case. There was little mileage to be gained from incidental representation, and coins were the most important device of communication that ancient authorities possessed. It is a pretty safe bet that images which still seem unexplained to us are only so because of our own ignorance, not because of capriciousness at the mint.

The personifications seen on ancient coins cover the spectrum of human needs, emotions, fears, achievements, endeavors and relationships with the universe. Everything from beauty to the weather was personified. Deities were given recognizable traits and faces. The spirit of a river was captured in human form. In this edition, we have significantly expanded the sections dealing with images on coins in the hope that doing so will help develop an awareness of the scope of this phenomenon and stimulate reader interest in the further study of images from the ancient world. The bibliography of works on this subject is extensive in itself, and would take us too far afield for the purposes of this book, but for those readers with Internet access, we recommend a very useful article, "A Gallery of Reverse Images and What They Symbolize", which may be found at http://myron.sjsu.edu/romeweb/rcoins/sub1/contents.htm

MYTHOLOGY

Mythological subjects are very common both on Greek and Roman coins, however, much of the fascination of these coins is lost without a basic understanding of mythology itself. Any bookstore will have a wide selection of books about Greek and Roman mythology, and we recommend that the reader choose one from the many that are well illustrated. Roman mythology is modeled partly on that of the Greeks. Therefore, reading Greek mythology gives the collector an edge on understanding that of the Romans. The names change in some cases, for example Zeus was known to the Romans as Jupiter, and Artemis as Diana, but the stories are basically the same. The incomplete list offered here is intended only to acquaint the reader with the breadth of mythological subjects that will be found on classical coinage. It should be noted that most deities were worshipped in several different variations depending on time and place.

ACHELOUS: Greek river god with the body of a bull and head of a man. Suitor of Deianeira in competition with Herakles. On a bronze coin of Akarnania, 300-167 BC.	
AENEAS: Son of Anchises and Venus, ancestor of the founders of Rome. Carrying his father and the Palladium on a denarius of Julius Caesar, 47-46 BC.	
AJAX THE LESSER: Son of Oileus. Lokrian hero who defiled the prophetess Cassandra during the sack of Troy. On a stater of Locris, ca. 360 BC.	
AJAX THE TELAMONIAN: Greek hero of the Trojan War who committed suicide when he failed to win the armor of Achilles. On a bronze of Caracalla struck at Prusa ad Olympum, AD 198-217.	

AMAZON: Asian tribe of female warriors. Normally dressed in a short chiton, often depicted with a bow. On a bronze of Amisos, wearing a wolf's scalp, ca. 85-65 BC.

AMPHITRITE: Sea goddess and wife of Neptune (Greek Poseidon). On Roman Republican denarius of Q. Crepereius M.f. Rocus, 69 BC.

AMPHILOCHUS: Seer and Trojan War hero who founded several cities and especially the oracle at Mallus. On a Roman Provincial bronze of Mallus.

APHRODITE: Roman Venus, Phoenician Astarte, goddess of beauty and love. Attributes: Cupid, apple and dove. On a denarius of Julius Caesar, 48-47 BC.

APOLLO: The Sun god, patron of music and poetry. Embodies the civilized characteristics of man. Attributes: Lyre and tripod. On a tetradrachm of Antiochos I, 280-261 BC.

ARES: Roman Mars, god of war. Attributes: spear, armor and trophy. On a bronze sestertius of Titus as Caesar, AD 73.

ARETHUSA: Nymph who was turned into an underground river. On a silver tetradrachm of Syracuse, 317-289 BC.

ARTEMIS: Roman Diana, goddess of the hunt, the moon goddess. Attributes: bow and arrows, stag. On a Republican silver denarius.

ASKLEPIOS: Roman Aesculapius, the god of medicine and healing. Attribute: staff with entwined serpent. On a tetradrachm of Roman Egypt.

ATHENA: Roman Minerva, goddess of wisdom and war. City goddess of Athens. Attributes: helmet, Nike (victory) and owl. On a tetradrachm of Side in Pamphylia, ca. 2nd - 1st c. BC.

BAAL: A Semitic deity with similarities to the Greek Zeus . At Tarsus he is often referred to as Baaltars. On a silver stater of Tarsus, 361-334 BC.

CALYDONIAN BOAR: Wild boar killed by a band of heroes led by Meleager. On a silver hemidrachm of The Aetolian League, 279-168 BC.

CENTAUR: Head and torso of a man, body of a horse. Base and brutal creatures which symbolized the victory of civilization over barbarism. On a denarius of M. Aurelius Cotta, 139 BC.	
CHIMAERA: Monster with the body of a lion, head of a goat growing out of its back, and tail of a serpent. On a silver stater of Sicyon, 431-400 BC.	
DEA CAELESTIS: Carthaginian deity regarded by the Romans as the Celestial Goddess. On a bronze as of Septimius Severus, AD 193-211.	
DEMETER: Roman Ceres, goddess of agriculture or harvest. Attributes: grain, ears of corn and torch, sometimes veiled. On a silver nomos of Metapontion, ca. 280 BC.	
DIDO: Daughter of a Tyrian king and foundress of Carthage. On a Siculo-Punic tetradrachm, ca. 320-315 BC.	
DIONYSOS: Roman Bacchus and Liber, god of wine. Attributes: panther, grapes, thyrsus. On a tetradrachm of Maroneia, ca. 146 BC.	

DIONE: Goddess worshipped at Dodone as a consort of Zeus. On a silver didrachm of the Epirote Republic, ca. 234-168 BC.	
DIOSKOURI: Roman Dioscuri, the twins Castor and Pollux (Gemini). On a follis of Maxentius, AD 306-312.	
EUROPA: Daughter of the King of Sidon, ravished by Zeus in the guise of a bull. On a Republican denarius of L. Volteius L.f. Strabo, 81 BC.	
GORGON: Monster with protruding tongues and snakes for hair. Their gaze turned men to stone. Medusa was a Gorgon. On a 20 as silver coin of Populonia in Etruria, ca. 211-206 BC.	
GRIFFIN: Monster, half lion, half eagle. On a silver drachm of Teos.	
HELIOS: (Roman Sol) the Sun god. Attribute: radiate crown. On a silver drachm of Rhodes, ca. 304-167 BC.	

HEPHAESTOS: (Roman Vulcan) god of fire and the forge, made the armor of the gods. On a Roman Republican denarius of Lucius Aurelius Cotta, 105 BC.	
HERA: Roman Juno. Consort of Zeus. Attribute is the peacock, often wears a polos. On a silver drachm of The Bretti, 215-205 BC.	
HERAKLES: Roman Hercules, god of strength and virtue. Attributes: club and lion skin. On a tetradrachm of Alexander III, 336-323 BC.	
HERMES: Roman Mercury, messenger of the gods. Attributes: winged cap or petasos and caduceus. On a Republican bronze semiuncia, 211-210 BC.	
INO: Daughter of Cadmus and Homonia who loaned a magic veil to Ulysses. On a bronze of Domitian struck at Cibyra, AD 81-96.	
ISIS: Egyptian deity adopted by the Greeks and Romans. Wife of Osiris. Attributes: Lotus head-dress and sistrum. On a bronze of Cossura, ca. 3rd-2nd c. BC.	

JANUS: Roman god of beginnings. Attribute: double heads back to back. On a Republican didrachm, ca. 225-212 BC.

KABIROS: A deity of Asia Minor associated with the earth and fertility. On a bronze of Birytis, ca. 4th century BC.

KORE: A maiden. The kore Soteira on a silver tetradrachm of Kyzikos, ca. 350-300 BC.

KRONOS: Roman Saturn. God of agriculture and the easy and happy life. Attribute: sickle. On a Republican denarius of L. memmius Galeria, 106 BC.

KYBELE: Roman Magna Mater. The Great Mother goddess of Asia Minor. Attributes: turreted crown and pair of lions. On a tetradrachm of Smyrna, ca. 165 BC.

LEUKIPPOS: Hero/founder of Metapontion (Roman Metapontum) in Lucania. On a silver nomos of Metapontion, ca. 320-325 BC.

MAENAD: Female companion of Dionysos and the satyrs. Being carried off by a satyr on a stater of Thasos, ca. 500 BC.	
MELKART: Phoenician equivalent of Herakles. On a silver half shekel of Tyre.	
MEN: (Roman Lunus) An eastern male moon god. Attributes are a Phrygian cap and a crescent. On a Roman Provincial bronze of Antinoüs struck at Ancyra in Galatia, before AD 130.	
NIKE: Roman Victory, winged goddess of victory. Holds laurel wreath. Often held as a tiny figure in the hand of a god or seen flying above a victor. On a gold stater of Philip III of Macedon, 323-317 BC.	
PAN: Roman Faunus. God of woods, fields and shepherded animals. Attributes: legs of a goat, pointed ears and horns. On a gold stater of Panticapeum.	

PARIS: Son of King Priam, whose judgement of the most beautiful goddess led to the Trojan War. On a bronze of Maximinus I struck at Tarsus, AD 235-238.

PEGASOS: Winged horse born from the blood of Medusa. On a denarius of Domitian, dated AD 76.

PENATES: Roman state and household gods of good fortune. On a denarius of C. Sulpicius C.f. Galba, 106 BC.

PERSEPHONE: Roman Proserpine. Daughter of Demeter stolen by Hades and taken to the underworld. On a silver hemidrachm of Lokris (x2).

PERSEUS: Son of Zeus and Danae, was the hero who beheaded Medusa. Attributes: harpa, winged sandals and winged helmet or cap.

POSEIDON: Roman Neptune, god of the sea. Attributes: dolphin and trident. On a Macedonian tetradrachm of Demetrius Poliorcetes, 306-285 BC.

ROMULUS & REMUS: Twin brothers suckled by a she-wolf. Romulus was the legendary founder of Rome. On a silver denarius of Carausius, AD 287-293.

SELENE: Roman Luna, the moon goddess (associated with Artemis/Diana) Attribute: crescent moon. On an antoninianus of Julia Domna struck in AD 215.

SILENOS: A drunken and cowardly companion of Dionysos with horse's ears and tail. He and his offspring (seleni) are not to be confused with satyrs, which they resemble in some ways. On a silver tetradrachm of Naxos in Sicily, ca. 460 BC.

SERAPIS: Egyptian god of sun and life. Attributes: Modius and Cerberus. On a tetradrachm of Roman Egypt.

SPHINX: Winged lion with the face and breasts of a woman; devoured travellers. On a tetradrachm of Chios, 412-350 BC.

TALON: (Roman Talus) Defender of the island of Crete. On a silver stater of Phaestos, ca. 300-270 BC.	
TANIT: Principal goddess of Carthage, similar in many ways to the Greek goddess Demeter. On a billon 1.5 shekel of Carthage, ca. 264-241 BC.	
TARAS: Son of Poseidon, founder of Tarentum. Usually riding on a dolphin. On a silver nomos from Tarentum, ca. 334-330 BC.	
THETIS: A Nereid, the mother of Achilles. Often depicted with a hippocamp. On a silver drachm of The Bretti, ca. 215-205 BC.	
TRIPTOLEMOS: Gave the gift of grain and its cultivation to man. Attribute: chariot drawn by serpents. On a bronze coin of Caracalla struck at Hadrianopolis, AD 198-217.	
TYCHE: Roman Fortuna. Goddess of good fortune. Attributes: turreted crown and veil. On a tetradrachm of Seleukeia in Syria, ca. 100 BC.	

VESTA: Roman goddess of family life. Attributes: veiled, patera and scepter. On a Republican denarius of P. Galba, 69 BC.

ZEUS: (Roman Jupiter) Most powerful of the Olympian gods. Attributes: scepter, eagle, thunderbolt. On a tetradrachm of Philip II, 359-336 BC.

ZEUS, HERA, POSEIDON AND HERMES

ABSTRACT PERSONIFICATIONS

Artists of antiquity personified a variety of virtues, strengths, human needs and ideals, but the trend is especially noted in the coinage of the Romans. Some personifications are clearly recognizable by the attributes that accompany them, others may be identified by the accompanying inscriptions. Personifications are not gods or goddesses, they are intangible concepts that the artist has presented in human form.

Pax

There was a standard "language" in the use of these personifications, and they are often recognizable by their pose and gestures alone. The following table lists the personified subject, followed by its Roman and Greek names (as applicable), and the personification's most commonly seen attributes. Just as the Romans adopted many of the Greek deities, the Greek population of lands conquered by the Romans (especially Roman Egypt) adopted many of the Roman personifications.

ABUNDANCE: **Abundantia** (Greek Euthenia). Cornucopia, corn ears. On a gold aureus of Trajan Decius, AD 249-251.	
AFFECTION: Caritas. The abstract idea of concord between two parties, embodied in the image of clasped hands. On a silver antoninianus of Pupienus, AD 238.	
AUTUMN: Veiled head of young boy, crowned with reeds. On a bronze quadrans of Marcus Aurelius, AD 161-180.	

CLEMENCY: Clementia. Holds branch and scepter, sometimes leaning on column. On an antoninianus of Florian, AD 276.

CORN HARVEST: Annona / Corn ears and modius or prow of ship. On a sestertius of Philip I, AD 244-249.

COURAGE: Constantia. Armor and spear. On a bronze as of Claudius, AD 41-54.

EQUITY: Aequitas (Greek Dikaiosyne). Scales and cornucopiae. On a gold aureus of Pertinax, AD 193.

ETERNITY: Aeternitas. Holding globe, torch, phoenix or rudder resting on globe. On a gold aureus of Faustina I, after AD 141.

FERTILITY: Fecunditas. Female figure seated, holding flower and scepter, children playing. On a denarius of Julia Maesa, AD 218-222.

FIDELITY: Fides. Cornucopia or fruit basket, military standards. On a denarius of Macrinus, AD 217-218.

FORTUNE: Fortuna (Greek Tyche). Rudder and cornucopia. On a bronze as of Trajan, AD 98-117.

FRUITFULNESS: Uberitas. Female figure holding an object that is sometimes described as a purse or a cow's udder. On a gold aureus of Trajan Decius, AD 249-251.

GOOD LUCK: Bonus Eventus. Figure holding basket of fruit and grain ears. On a denarius of Septimius Severus, AD 193-211.

HAPPINESS: Felicitas (Greek Eutycheia). Caduceus and cornucopia. On a bronze sestertius of Trajan Decius, AD 249-251

HARMONY: Concordia — **Homonoia** / Patera and cornucopia, also as figures with clasped hands, or clasped hands alone. On a silver denarius of Pupienus, AD 238.	
HEALTH: Hygieia (Roman Salus). Patera and serpent. On a silver denarius of Macrinus, AD 217-218.	
HONOR: Honos. Laurel wreath, olive branch and cornucopiae. On a sestertius of Marcus Aurelius, AD 161-180.	
HOPE: Elpis (Roman Spes). Holds flower and lifts skirt. On a silver denarius of Diadumenian, AD 217-218.	
JOY: Laetitia. Wreath and scepter or anchor. On a gold aureus of Gordian III, AD 238-244.	
JUSTICE: Justitia. Female figure holding Olive branch and patera or scales and cornucopiae. On a denarius of Pescennius Niger, AD 193-194.	

LIBERALITY: Liberalitas. Counting tablet (abacus) and cornucopiae. On a sestertius of Balbinus, AD 238.

LIBERTY: Libertas (Greek Eleutheria). Female figure holding scepter and pileus (the pointed cap of liberty). On a bronze sestertius of Galba, AD 68-69.

MERCY: Indulgentia. Female figure holding patera and scepter. On a sestertius of Hadrian, AD 117-138.

MERRIMENT: Hilaritas. Palm and cornucopia. On a gold aureus of Marcus Aurelius, AD 145.

MODESTY: Pudicitia. Veiled female figure, holding scepter. On an antoninianus of Herennia Etruscilla, AD 249-251.

MONEY: Moneta. Scales and cornucopiae. On a bronze as of Domitian, AD 81-96.

NATURE (trees, springs, etc.): Nymph. Female. Often a semi-divinity because of parentage involving a god and a human. Frequently depicted as a personification of a particular place. Usually with hair ties, fillets or similar head adornment. On a silver nomos of Velia, ca. 400-365 BC.

NOBILITY: Nobilitas. Veiled and draped figure holding Palladium and scepter. On a silver denarius of Geta as Caesar, struck in AD 199.

PEACE: Pax (Greek Eirene). Olive branch and scepter. On a gold aureus of Severus Alexander, AD 222-235.

PIETY: Pietas (Greek Eusebeia). Veiled female figure with patera and scepter, usually sacrificing over altar. On a denarius of Julia Mamaea, AD 222-235.

PROVIDENCE: **Providentia** (Greek Pronoia). Baton, globe or star. On a denarius of Pertinax, AD 193.

REST: Quies. Female figure holding laurel branch and hasta pura (staff without a head). With Providentia on a follis of Diocletian, struck in AD 305-306 to herald the abdication of Diocletian and Maximian.

RETRIBUTION: Nemesis. Female holding scales, with wheel beside. On a Roman Provincial bronze of Macrinus, struck at Marcianopolis, AD 217-218.

RIVERS: River god. Young male semi-divinity, usually with horns, sometimes with flowing hair, sometimes shown swimming. On a bronze trias of Gela in Sicily, 420-405 BC.

SECURITY: Securitas / Female figure holding branch, patera and/or scepter. On a silver denarius of Gordian I, AD 238.

SPIRIT: Genius / Patera and cornucopia, sacrificing above altar. On a denarius of Septimius Severus, AD 193-211.

STRENGTH: Virtus. Helmeted, with armor and spear or scepter and parazonium. Sometimes holding Victory. On a gold aureus of Septimius Severus, AD 193-211.	
SUMMER: Small boy crowned with grape vines and garland of grape leaves around his neck. On an anonymous bronze quadrans of AD 160-180.	
VICTORY: Victoria (Greek Nike). Winged, wreath and palm. Also worshipped as a goddess at Rome. On a denarius of C. Valerius Flaccus.	

GEOGRAPHICAL PERSONIFICATIONS

Aside from the personification of abstract ideas, the Romans often represented particular places in human form. Among the subjects presented on coinage in this way are various cities, rivers, provinces, lands of allies and enemies and especially lands over which the Romans claimed military victories. In many cases, these subjects lacked the standard and clearly recognizable attributes that characterized other personifications. Therefore, the accompanying inscription often cited the referenced subject.

ACHAIA: (Greece) Draped female figure beside vase and palm. On a sestertius of Hadrian, AD 117-138.	
AEGYPTOS : (Egypt) Female figure holding sistrum. Accompanied by ibis. On a gold aureus of Hadrian, AD 117-138.	
AFRICA: Elephant headdress. On a gold aureus of L. Cestius and C. Norbanus, 43 BC.	
ALAMANNIA: Tribes of the upper and lower Rhine which invaded Italy several times in the 3rd and 4th centuries AD. Depicted as a mourning female figure beneath trophy. On a gold aureus of Constantine the Great, AD 307-337.	

ALEXANDRIA: Turreted female figure holding scepter, palm branch. On a bronze coin of Julia Mamaea, struck in AD 230/231.

ARABIA: Standing figure holding branch and bunch of cinnamon sticks, camel at feet to left. On a sestertius of Trajan, AD 98-117.

ARMENIA: Seated figure, bound, wearing royal tiara, accompanied by river gods Tigris and Euphrates. On a sestertius of Trajan, AD 98-117.

BRITANNIA: (Britain) Female figure seated on rocks among discarded armor and standard. On a bronze as of Antoninus Pius, AD 138-161.

CAPPADOCIA: Province in central Asia Minor—holds a model of Mt. Argaeus a local holy mountain, and a legionary standard. On a bronze sestertius of Hadrian, AD 117-138.

CARTHAGE: (North Africa) Female figure standing left, holding tusk and standard, lion at feet. On a bronze follis of Maximianus, AD 286-305.

CONSTANTINOPLE: (the city): Constantinopolis. Turreted or helmeted, holding scepter and globe, usually enthroned. On a gold solidus of Valentinian II, AD 375-392.

DACIA: Draped female figure holding Aquila, accompanied by small children holding grapes and grain. On a dupondius of Trajan, AD 98-117.

DANUBE: River god reclining left on rocks, before prow of ship. On a denarius of Trajan, AD 98-117.

GALLIA: (Gaul) Veiled female head with carnyx behind. On a Roman Republican denarius of L. Hostilius Saserna, 48 BC.

GERMANIA: (Germany) Bare breasted female barbarian, sometimes with dishevelled hair and leggings. On a gold aureus of Domitian, AD 81-96.

HISPANIA: (Spain) Veiled or wreathed female figure, sometimes with olive branch. On a silver denarius of A. Postumius A.f. Sp.n. Albinus, 81 BC.

ITALIA: (Italy) Turreted and draped figure seated on globe, holding cornucopiae and scepter. On a denarius of Antoninus Pius, AD 138-161.

JUDAEA: Veiled female figure, sometimes with palm tree. On a gold aureus of Vespasian, AD 69-79.

MAURETANIA: (North Africa). Horseman holding javelin. On a dupondius of Hadrian, AD 117-138.

NILE: River god Nilus, reclining, with cornucopiae and sometimes with hippopotamus. On a bronze sestertius of Hadrian, AD 117-138.	
PANNONIA: Roman Province of Eastern Europe, divided into Upper and Lower Pannonia, covering the region from Austria and Hungary to Bulgaria and Serbia. Female figure holding standard, wearing a cap of the region, on a bronze sestertius of Aelius, Caesar.	
PARTHIA: Bound captive with quiver, bow and shield in front. On a silver denarius of Lucius Verus, AD 161-169.	
RHINE: River god with horns, reclining before river boat. On an antoninianus of Postumus, AD 259-268.	
ROME: Roma. Helmet (sometimes winged), shield and spear. Often enthroned. On an anonymous Republican denarius, 194-190 BC. Sometimes confused with Minerva, the Roman equivalent of Athena.	
SISCIA: Seated female figure holding open diadem, between river gods Savus and Colapis. On an antoninianus of Probus, AD 276-282.	

Romaion gold and silver coins basically continued in the denominations of late Roman coinage for several centuries. It was the bronze coinage that changed dramatically with the reform of Anastasius. The only bronze coins circulating in the empire up until that point were tiny minima, which must have been nearly valueless. The steps to attributing Romaion coins are quite similar to those for Roman

Justinian II (2nd reign)
struck AD 705-711
AU Solidus (4.42 gm)
with Tiberius

and Roman Provincial coins, and need no further clarification here, except to say that reading the inscriptions takes a little practice. A mixture of upper and lower case Greek letters can be confusing for a bit until the collector understands what is happening. Legends are arranged in the

same manner as on earlier Roman coins. Many of the coins are dated with Roman numerals by regnal year, and mint marks in the exergue are standard. Romaion coinage was imitated by practically all of their neighbors, and the collecting of these imitations, especially those referred to as "Arab-Byzantine," is a field in itself.

Theodora
AD 1055-1056
AU Tetarteron (4.01 gm)
Empress as sole ruler

Joint reigns are very common in this series, and the list of emperors which follows will indicate many overlapping dates. Sometimes four or five family members ruled jointly. This is also a series where women appear on the coins as independent rulers of an empire rather than simply as spouse or regent. The Latin sacking of Constantinople in AD 1204 led to a government in exile, called the Nicaean empire. The legitimate heirs of the throne ruled from Nicaea until 1261 when the city of Constantinople was restored to

Nicaea, AD 1222-1254
John III Ducas-Vatatzes
AE Tetarteron (2.16 gm)
bust of St. George (x 2)

them. This interregnum is indicated in the list of emperors.

Some Romaion gold is very common and very inexpensive. It is perhaps the easiest ancient gold to collect, since EF solidi of common rulers are obtainable in the $300 range. Smaller denominations of gold sell for even less. Silver coins are much more scarce and are seldom offered. The only thing more scarce than Romaion silver is *collectors* for Romaion silver. This is unexplainable, and anyone looking for an underappreciated collecting area should take note! Bronze coins are very common, and can be purchased out of junk boxes for a few dollars each. There are some

Constantine IV
struck AD 668-669
AR Hexagram (6.56 gm)
an extremely rare silver coin

Constantine XI
ca. 1453 AD
AR Stavraton (6.46 gm)
the last Romaion emperor

great rarities in the series and, because few people pay attention, they often are obtainable at junk box prices.

Sear's *Byzantine Coins and Their Values* is highly recommended for the collector of this series. It contains a tremendous amount of information for one volume, and is a very handy reference. A useful addition in the revised work was the inclusion of plates picturing known counterfeits. A particularly useful guide to attribution of Romaion bronze coins is Dan Clark's *Speedy Identification of Denominationally Marked Byzantine Bronzes*. Unlike most books, which list coins chronologically by emperor, this heavily illustrated work arranges the coins by reverse type. It is especially handy for attributing piles of low grade Byzantine bronzes while learning the series, and best of all, it sells for under $20.

The Romaion Emperors

ANASTASIUS I	(491-518)
JUSTIN I	(518-527)
JUSTINIAN I	(527-565)
JUSTIN II	(565-578)
TIBERIUS II	(578-582)
MAURICE TIBERIUS	(582-602)
PHOCAS	(602-610)
HERACLIUS	(610-641)
HERACLIUS CONSTANTINE	(613-641)
HERACLONAS	(638-641)
CONSTANS II	(641-668)
CONSTANTINE IV	(654-685)
TIBERIUS	(668-681)
JUSTINIAN II	(685-695)
LEONTIUS	(695-698)
TIBERIUS III	(698-711)
JUSTINIAN II AND TIBERIUS	(705-711)
PHILIPPICUS	(711-713)
ANASTASIUS II	(713-715)
THEODOSIUS III	(715-717)
LEO III	(717-741)
CONSTANTINE V	(720-775)
LEO IV	(751-780)
CONSTANTINE VI	(776-797)
IRENE	(780-802)
NICEPHORUS I	(802-811)
STAURACIUS	(803-811)
MICHAEL I AND THEOPHYLACTUS	(811-813)
LEO V AND CONSTANTINE	(813-820)
MICHAEL II	(820-829)
THEOPHILUS	(821-842)
CONSTANTINE	(830-835)
MICHAEL III	(840-867)
BASIL I	(866-886)
CONSTANTINE	(868-879)
LEO VI	(870-912)
BASIL I	(879-886)
ALEXANDER	(879-914)
CONSTANTINE VII	(908-959)
ZOE	(914-919)
ROMANUS I	(920-944)
CHRISTOPHER	(921-931)
STEPHEN AND CONSTANTINE	(924-945)
ROMANUS II	(945-963)
BASIL II	(960-1025)
CONSTANTINE VIII	(961-1028) →

THEOPHANO	(963)
NICEPHORUS II	(963-969)
JOHN I	(969-976)
ROMANUS III	(1028-1034)
MICHAEL IV	(1034-1041)
MICHAEL V	(1041-1042)
ZOE AND THEODORA	(1042)
CONSTANTINE IX	(1042-1055)
THEODORA	(1055-1056)
MICHAEL VI	(1056-1057)
ISAAC I	(1057-1059)
CONSTANTINE X	(1059-1067)
EUDOCIA	(1067)
CONSTANTINE	(1067-1071)
MICHAEL VII	(1067-1078)
ROMANUS IV	(1067-1071)
ANDRONICUS	(1067-1071)
NICEPHORUS III	(1078-1081)
NICEPHORUS MELISSENUS	(1080-1081)
ALEXIUS I	(1081-1118)
JOHN II	(1092-1143)
MANUEL I	(1143-1180)
ALEXIUS II	(1180-1184)
ANDRONICUS I	(1183-1185)
ISAAC II	(1185-1195)
ALEXIUS III	(1195-1203)
ISAAC II AND ALEXIUS IV	(1203-1204)
ALEXIUS V	(1204)

AT NICAEA:

THEODORE I (AT NICAEA)	(1204-1222)
JOHN III (AT NICAEA)	(1222-1254)
THEODORE II (AT NICAEA)	(1254-1258)
JOHN IV (AT NICAEA)	(1258-1261)
MICHAEL VIII (AT NICAEA)	(1258-1261)

EMPIRE RESTORED:

JOHN IV	(1261)
MICHAEL VIII	(1261-1282)
ANDRONICUS II	(1273-1328)
MICHAEL IX	(1295-1320)
ANDRONICUS III	(1325-1341)
JOHN V	(1341-1376)
JOHN VI	(1347-1354)
MATTHEW	(1353-1354)
MANUEL II	(1373-1376; 1379-1423)
ANDRONICUS IV	(1376-1379)
JOHN VII	(1399-1402)
JOHN VIII	(1421-1448)
CONSTANTINE XI	(1448-1453)

Romaion Denominations (bronze)

*Anastasius, AE40 Nummia (large follis) struck in AD 512-17
Constantinople mint, Officina B*

*Tiberius II Constantine, AE 30 Nummia
AD 578-582
Constantinople mint, Officina A*

*Phocas,
AE 5 Nummia,
AD 602-610
Antioch mint*

*Justinian I, AE 20 Nummia (half follis)
struck in AD 532-37
Antioch mint, Officina Γ*

*Maurice Tiberius,
AE 10 Nummia, year 10,
struck in AD 582/3
Catania mint*

*Phocas, AE 20 Nummia (half follis)
dated year 2, struck in AD 603/4
Nicomedia mint, Officina B*

*Revolt of Heraclius,
AE 10 Nummia
struck in AD 608-10
Carthage mint*

Imitations of Romaion (Byzantine) Coins

Visigoths in Spain
AD 507-18
AU Tremissis 1.40 gm
portrait of Anastasius / Victory

Danishmendid AE fals
Nasir al-Din Muhammad,
Malatya
557-65/1162-70
Virgin crowning emperor

Arab Imitation
AH 50-66 / AD 670-85
AE fals, Emesa
Standing Caliph/
transformed cross on steps.

Artuqid AE fals
Fakhr al-Din Qara Arslan
539-70/1144-1174
Hisn Kayfa
imitation of anonymous follis

Zengid AE fals
Nur al-Din Mahmud,
Halab (Aleppo)
541-69/1146-74
imitation of follis of Constantine X

Bulgarian AE Trachy
Constantine Tikh Asen
AD 1255-1277
imitation of Romaion
scyphate trachy

Learning to attribute coins of the cultures listed here is an adventure to say the least. Not only must one learn the history of a people who are virtually neglected in Western histories, but one must learn their language as well. That is, one must learn their alphabet, and learn to find the key elements on coins that make attribution possible. This is not an impossible undertaking, many neophytes have become self-taught specialists, if not experts. It will take some time and persistence, however.

We have presented here only a visual glance at the coinage of these cultures, so that the reader can see how they differ and more or less distinguish between them. Standard references for each have been listed in chapter II (see page 32). Each of these cultures developed its own art and images, and the coinage has its own "look" about it. Learning to recognize the differences only requires observation on the part of the collector.

Practically every sale catalog has some of these coins offered. The tendency for many collectors is to focus on a single series and ignore the remainder of a catalogue. This is really throwing away free education. Why not examine the whole catalogue closely, and learn whatever may be gleaned from the descriptions of coins from non-classical cultures? One does not have to collect these coins to understand and appreciate them. A vast area of untouched ground exists in the non-classical arena, and any collector who makes the effort to learn a series well will reap substantial rewards.

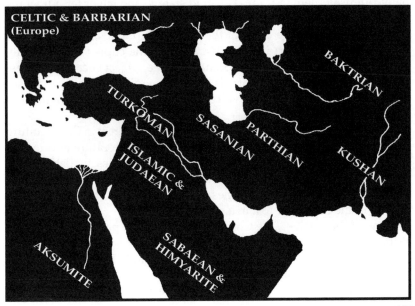

Celtic Coins

The Celts originated in northern Europe (present Germany and France) and, over a period of about seven centuries, migrated in every direction. They were formidable warriors who served as mercenaries, and reached their highpoint during the second century BC. At that time Celts controlled lands from Ireland to Spain and nearly to the borders of Greece. As a people, they did not leave monuments or detailed histories about themselves. The only evidence of their existence is their art, which is found on utilitarian objects of all sorts, the coins which they struck in vast numbers, and the stories

The Ambiani
2nd-1st c. BC
AV hemistater
Reverse imitating a gold stater
of Philip II of Macedon

about them which were written by their literate foes. Their coinage, which exists in gold, silver and bronze, often copies the designs of their neighbors. This is probably due to the fact that they did not need coins internally, but used them in trade. The gold staters and silver tetradrachms of Philip II and Alexander III of Macedon were copied frequently, as were silver and bronze coins of the Roman Republic and Roman Empire. Original Celtic art is very abstract, and the copied coins usually reflect this abstract disposition. Sometimes the subject becomes increasingly abstract to the point that it is barely recognizable. The warrior society of the Celts finally was overcome by Roman expansion in the first century AD.

There has been a tremendous blossoming of interest in Celtic culture during the past several decades, not only in art, literature and music, but in coins as well. Practically all of the major studies available today were written in the past fifty years. The most recent focus seems to be on establishing distinct identities for individual Celtic tribes which tended in the past to be lost in a sort of generic fog.

One of those tribes, the Coriosolites, inhabited part of what is now Brittany. They were one of the tribes called "Armoricans" meaning "from the country by the sea". An extensive study by John Hooker of the coinage of this tribe, culminating ten years' effort, is now in preparation for publication in the series of British Archaeological Reports (B.A.R.). The entire contents of the report are provided free of charge online (http://www.writer2001.com/improvisations.htm) with maps, charts and exceptional line drawings which trace the development of images in art historical fashion. Also on the award winning Hooker and Perron site is a remarkable animation through morphing technology of the change from a Philip II gold stater to a Celtic imitation. Just click on the image and watch it transform before your very eyes.

Just as interest has increased in recent years, so has the availability of Celtic coins. At one time, it was difficult to find Celtic coins at anything less than a major coin show in the United States. The market was broader in Britain and Northern Europe, but still was obscure in comparison to the broader market for classical coins. That situation is changing as a number of dealers now specialize in Celtic coins and many dealers carry at least a few examples because of their growing popularity.

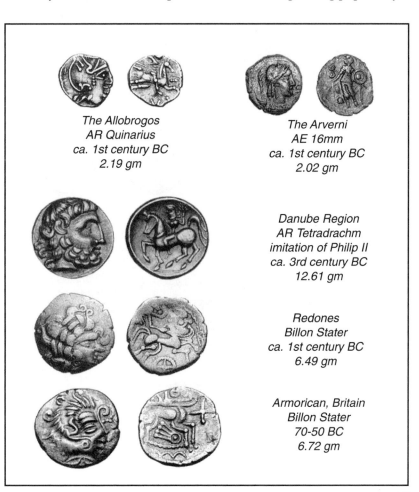

The Allobrogos
AR Quinarius
ca. 1st century BC
2.19 gm

The Arverni
AE 16mm
ca. 1st century BC
2.02 gm

Danube Region
AR Tetradrachm
imitation of Philip II
ca. 3rd century BC
12.61 gm

Redones
Billon Stater
ca. 1st century BC
6.49 gm

Armorican, Britain
Billon Stater
70-50 BC
6.72 gm

Parthian Coins

The Parthian dynasty began in 238 BC with the expulsion by Arsaces of the Seleukid Satrap of the province of Parthia. Arsaces was the leader of a nomad tribe which was to create one of the most formidable empires of the ancient world—nearly as powerful as Rome. The coinage of the Parthians, like that of the Baktrians, retained a semblance of Hellenistic style, and used Greek inscriptions until very late in the dynasty. The clashes between the Parthian dynasty and Rome have filled many history books, and the outcome of famous battles caused their fortunes to shift back and forth across Mesopotamia. Parthian coins are abundant in lower grades, but exceptional examples tend to stimulate strong competition at auction. All coins illustrated here are from the Shore Collection, which brought record prices at auction in December 1995.

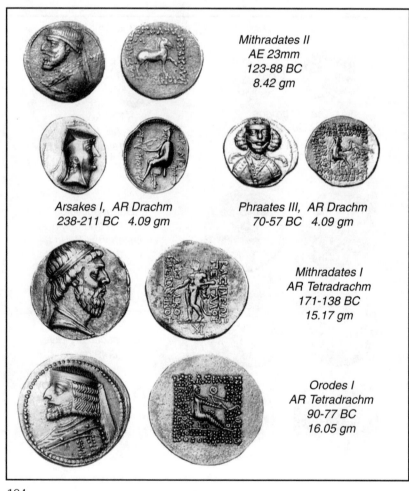

Mithradates II
AE 23mm
123-88 BC
8.42 gm

Arsakes I, AR Drachm
238-211 BC   4.09 gm

Phraates III, AR Drachm
70-57 BC   4.09 gm

Mithradates I
AR Tetradrachm
171-138 BC
15.17 gm

Orodes I
AR Tetradrachm
90-77 BC
16.05 gm

Sasanian Coins

In AD 224, the Sasanians supplanted the Parthians in Persia. Ardashir, who had captured the Parthian Vologases VI in 222, defeated the sole remaining Parthian Artabanos IV and established the Sasanian Dynasty.

Coins of the Sasanians are notably different from those of the Baktrians and Parthians. Not only are they struck in a completely different fabric, being large and thin, the images are radically different. As Zoroastrians, the Sasanians were fire-worshippers. The reverse of their silver dirham typically portrays two attendants standing beside a fire altar. Portraits of the ruler are very stylized and ornamentation is distinctively Eastern. The last Sasanian ruler to hold out against the Arabs was Yazdgard III, who fell in AD 651. Sasanian coins are less popular than Baktrian and Parthian, but serious collectors do compete for the rarities in this series.

Shapur I
AR Dirham
241-270 AD 3.26 gm

Piroz
AR Dirham
457-483 AD 4.13 gm

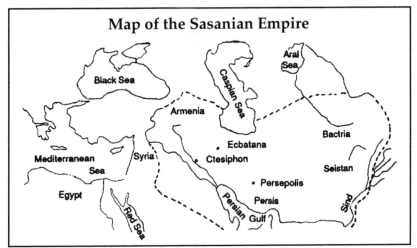

Map of the Sasanian Empire

Aral Sea
Black Sea
Caspian Sea
Armenia
Bactria
Ecbatana
Mediterranean Sea
Syria
Ctesiphon
Seistan
Egypt
Persepolis
Persis
Red Sea
Persian Gulf
Sind

Sabaean and Himyarite Coins

The coins of Saba and Himyar are steeped in romance, but there is very little information published about them. These cities were important centers of trade on the Arabian Peninsula, and are best known for their supply of gold, spices and two important incenses called frankincense and myrrh. These aromatics were used in religious and burial ceremonies. The land of the Sabaeans was also the home of the biblical Queen of Sheba. An excellent introduction to the coinage is provided through two articles, both of which appeared in *The Celator*. The first, by Joel Hettger, was published in February 1992; the second, by Marvin Tameanko, was published in May 1994. Michael Mitchiner's *Oriental Coins and Their Values: The Ancient and Classical World* (MACW) is the most useful guide for attribution.

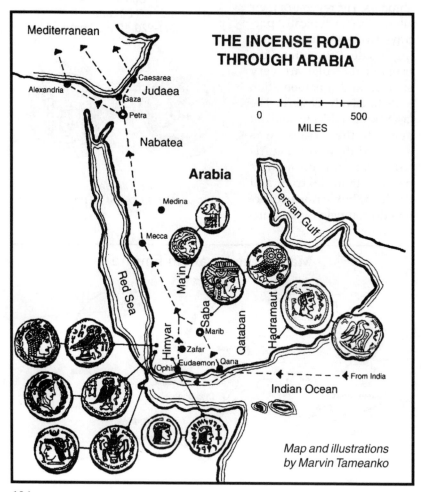

Map and illustrations
by Marvin Tameanko

Aksumite Coins

The Aksumite Kingdom, in the east African highlands, was the only region of Northern Africa independent of Roman or Persian control. They also dominated southern Arabia during much of this time, which opened to them the resources and trade routes of the former Himyarite dynasty. From their seat in Ethiopia, the Aksumite kings issued gold, silver and bronze coins for a period of about 400 years, beginning in the third century AD. Legends on the coins appear in Greek and Ethiopic.

The dynasty itself arose about the time of the birth of Christ and lasted until the rise of Islam. Aksum was a trading culture and their position on the Red Sea gave them access to both Persian and Roman markets, as well as connections with India and Ceylon. The Aksumite king Ezanas converted to Christianity early in the fourth century and it became a state religion. The coins of Aksum (sometimes spelled Axum) are among the earliest known with Christian symbols. The city of Axum was abandoned by the Ethiopian kings in the 7th century, due to a general decline in trade opportunities. Aksumite coins seldom appear on the market in quantity, and there is little historical information about the kingdom. Fortunately, the coins are published in a good introductory work, *Aksumite Coinage* by Stuart Munro-Hay and Bent Juel-Jensen.

King Endubis
AU Quinarius
ca. 270 AD 2.72 gm

King Ezanas
AR Unit
ca. 330 AD .71 gm

King Khaleb
AU Tremissis
ca. 525 AD 1.31 gm

King Armah
AE 22mm
ca. 6th-7th c. AD
3.10 gm

Kushan Coins

The Kushans were a branch of the Yueh-Chi from China who moved into Northwest India (Ghandara) in the 2nd century BC. The first coins of this tribe in India were issued by Kujula Kadphises in about AD 10. These coins retained the Greek influence of the Baktrian prototypes, but soon thereafter the legends and images became distinctly Kushan. Kushan coins were issued in gold and copper, but silver is very rare if it exists at all. The influence of Roman coins, which made their way to India in commerce, is seen in the portraiture, and images on Kushan bronzes. The Kushans finally succumbed to the advancing Sasanians in the 3rd century AD. For a time, a series of Kushano-Sasanian coins were struck for use in the conquered lands. Kushan bronze coins are usually inexpensive. Kushan gold coins are fairly easy to find in excellent states of preservation and also at reasonable prices.

King Wima Kadphises
AU Quarter Dinar
ca. 166-230 AD 1.96 gm
Head of King/ Trident

King Kanishka I
AU Dinar
ca. 232-260 AD 7.89 gm
King/ Goddess Nana

King Huvishka
AU Dinar
ca. 260-292 AD 7.81 gm
Bust of King/ Sun God Mithra

King Vasudeva II
AU Dinar
ca. 312-350 AD 7.59 gm
King stg / Siva and Bull

Soter Megas
AE Tetradrachm
ca. 55-105 AD
Bust of King / King on Horseback

Islamic Coins

The rise of Islam in the 7th century AD is unparalleled and the coinage that has been issued by Islamic dynasties is immeasurable. Westerners have had a tendency to ignore the Islamic world because it is a closed society, and because the language and culture are so much different than our own. This is unfortunate, because the history of Islam is every bit as fascinating as that of the Greeks and the Romans.

One would think that in order to collect Islamic coins it would be necessary to read Arabic script. This is not the case. There are many areas of collecting in which a knowledge of Arabic is not necessary. However, reading dates and mint names is not an unrealistic goal even for the amateur. The place to start is Richard Plant's classic little book, *Arabic Coins and How to Read Them*. Next, pick up a copy of Stephen Album's *Checklist of Popular Islamic Coins*. Finally, find a copy of Marsden's *Numismata Orientalia Illustrata* (reprinted and revised). Armed with these three tools, and some effort, anyone could learn the basics of collecting Islamic coins.

There have been so many different dynasties in the Islamic world that it is impossible even to list them here. As a sampler, however, we will illustrate coins of some of the more important dynasties and those of some dynasties whose coins regularly appear in the market.

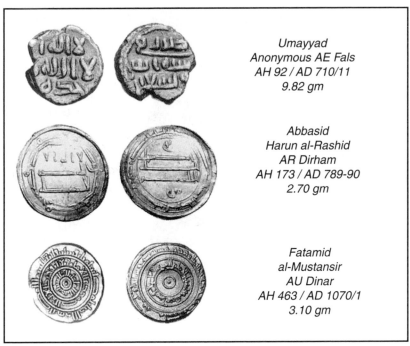

Umayyad
Anonymous AE Fals
AH 92 / AD 710/11
9.82 gm

Abbasid
Harun al-Rashid
AR Dirham
AH 173 / AD 789-90
2.70 gm

Fatamid
al-Mustansir
AU Dinar
AH 463 / AD 1070/1
3.10 gm

Turkoman Coins

The Turkic tribes made their way from Central Asia into the Near East in the 10th to 11th centuries and acquired lands through military service to the Islamic Caliph. Two tribes in particular settled in the lands between the Tigris and Euphrates rivers known as Mesopotamia, (in Arabic, the Jazira). The Artuqids settled at Hisn Kayfa and Mardin, and the Zengids, settled in Mosul, Sinjar and Aleppo. The history of these tribes is fascinating, but their coinage is even more fascinating. For a period of about 100 years they produced coins with distinctive classical motifs. These coins are published, along with historical and art historical narratives, in *Turkoman Figural Bronze Coins and Their Iconography* (Spengler/Sayles). Many of the coins depict specific astrological events, while others bear motifs taken directly from ancient coins.

Seljuq of Rum
Ghiyath al-Din Kai Khusru
AH 588-98 / AD 1192-1201
AE Fals, 3.29 gm

Artuqid
Nur al-Din Muhammad
AE Dirham, Hisn Kayfa
AH 571-81 / AD 1175-85
Angel Gabriel

Zengid
Saif al-Din Ghazi II
AE Dirham, Mosul
565-76 / 1170-80
copy of a
Greek tetradrachm

Artuqid
Husam al-Din Yuluq Arslan
AE Dirham, Mardin
580-97 / 1184-1201
Roman Emperor Nero
with crowned figure:
depicts an occultation
of Jupiter

Judaean and Biblical Reference Coins

There are basically three types of coins that fall into this category. First, there are Jewish coins that date back to the Persian period. Secondly, there are coins of the Romans that were struck in Judaea and the surrounding provinces. And thirdly, there are coins that were not struck by or for the Jewish populace, but nevertheless circulated in Judaea or are mentioned in the Bible.

As one might expect, this is a very popular collecting area and the series is intently studied. David Hendin provides an excellent introduction in his *Guide to Biblical Coins*. The market for the coinage of Judaea is highly developed and rarities can be relatively expensive. It is unusual to find well-preserved Judaean bronzes, or city-coins of the Roman occupation, so condition warrants a substantial premium.

Several dealers specialize in Judaean coins, and most dealers will have at least a few in stock. Check the ads in the periodicals listed earlier. Practically every auction will have at least a few Judaean coins, and there have been auctions dedicated entirely to the Judaean issues.

AR Shekel of Tyre
13/12 BCE 14.15 gm
Jerusalem Mint
Considered to be the coin
(of 30 pieces)
used to pay Judas for
the betrayal of Christ

Herod the Great,
40 BC E - 4 CE
AE 8 Prutot 6.95 gm
Tripod / Incense burner

Tiberius, 14 - 37 CE
AR Denarius 3.74 gm
"Tribute Penny"

First Revolt
Year 1, 66 CE
AR Shekel, 13.87 gm
Chalice / Pomegranates

Titus, 79-81 CE
AE As 8.39 gm
"Judaea Capta"
commemorating the
subjugation of Judaea

Bar Kochba Revolt
CE 133/4
AE 26mm, 9.21 gm
Grape cluster / Palm Tree

Marcus Aurelius, 161-180 CE
AE 25mm, 10.50 gm
Caesarea mint
Aurelius / Sarapis

China and the Far East

China, Han Dynasty
202 BC - AD 220

Some would argue that the invention of coinage in China predates that of the Greeks. The comparison is difficult because the earliest currency in China did not resemble coins as we think of them today. Tools were used for barter from a very early period, and later these were replaced by small bronze replicas of hoes and knives. The knife coins, called *tao*, were about six inches long and sometimes bore inscriptions with the issuing authority and value. Similar "coins" were made in the shape of a hoe.

Round coins with a hole in the center were introduced by the emperor Shih Huang-ti during the final quarter of the 3rd century BC and underwent many changes of size, shape and metal over the years, evolving into the standard type called *cash* with a square hole in the center. The "Kai-yuan" type of the T'ang dynasty, introduced by the emperor Kao-tsu in AD 621, became a standard of Far Eastern currencies to almost the Twentieth Century. These coins are dated, sometimes including a mint name, and are quite collectable. Their popularity in the West has increased significantly with the recent publication of catalogues in English.

The circle and square recall familiar Chinese religious symbols called the bi and zong or heaven and earth respectively. On the coins, they represent the balance of nature and spirit. One collector and student of Chinese art and culture has suggested to me that this combination of forms was possibly a form of imperial propaganda which promoted the emperor as the "son of heaven" and the earthly force which maintained that balance.

Early in the eighth century AD, Japan began to issue coins on the model of the Chinese. However, in the tenth century coinage was abandoned and the country returned to an official monetary system based on commodities. Unofficially, Chinese coins were imported and imitated locally. Japan was without an official coinage until 1624 when the copper *kwan-ei* was first issued. In Korea, copies of contemporary Chinese *Kai-yuan* coins were made during the ninth and tenth centuries. By the twelfth century, the Koreans were issuing coins with local inscriptions, but they still followed the Chinese model. The early coinage of Southeast Asia also imitated Chinese bronzes, with Viet Nam developing its own coinage in the tenth century. Cambodia did not have its own coinage until the fifteenth century. The earliest coinage of Thailand and Burma was modeled after Indian prototypes.

HOW TO COLLECT ANCIENT COINS
The Yellow Brick Road

E ven before you have really digested the term "ancient" in regard to coins, it is important to think about focus. Too many collectors have been attracted to the field of ancient coin collecting, purchased coins that they knew practically nothing about, and then found that those coins were really a white elephant in their emerging collections. The urge to rush out and buy a coin—any coin—is understandable, and we do not mean to discourage that enthusiasm, but stop for just a moment and think about the kind of coins that might appeal to you in the longer term.

Do ancients appeal to you because of their historical association? Are you attracted to famous personages of the past? Would you like a set of portrait coins of Alexander the Great? Do you like birds or animals? You name one and it probably appears on coins. We find hippopotami, storks, peacocks, lions, gazelles, elephants—a virtual menagerie. If you are fascinated by mythology or astrology, architecture, ships, weapons or armor, you're in luck. Maybe you just like things that are old—some collectors collect only archaic coins. The choices are countless, and you need not decide at this moment, but be aware that focus becomes essential at some point, even for the rich and famous. In the meantime, indulge yourself, buy a coin or two, even attend an auction if you can, but try to avoid esoteric things that you may later regret buying.

There are about as many ways to collect ancient coins as there are collectors. One of the remarkable things about the hobby is the diversity of the coins themselves. In the following paragraphs a few possibilities are highlighted, but in the end each collector will find their own yellow brick road.

Most beginning collectors find Roman coins the easiest to understand, because the inscriptions are formed from latin letters. The Roman coin series also has the added advantage of a clear structure with a precise beginning and end. These coins are also collectable in sub-groups. Two obvious (and major) divisions are coins of the Roman Republic and coins of the Roman Empire. Another group, Roman Imperatorial coins, divides the two chronologically. The logical way to collect Roman coins is to assemble a complete set of the moneyers, or emperors, and possibly of their family members, who appear on coins. This is not much different than collecting U.S. coins by date. We know how many different types there are, as well as which ones are rare, and there is sufficient challenge in accumulating the entire "set." To collect Roman coins by emperor, one needs only a checklist and patience. A companion volume to this work (Ancient Coin Collecting III: The Roman World—Politics and Propaganda) outlines the field of Roman Coins in greater detail, but the introductory section in this volume is a place to start.

Sometimes, collections will cross over between the Roman Republican or Imperatorial and Imperial eras. For example, one might collect coins of the Twelve Caesars. In the early years of the second century AD, a Roman biographer by the name of Gaius Suetonius Tranquillus (usually referred to simply as Suetonius) wrote *The Lives of the Caesars*. This biographical history included 12 rulers, starting with Julius Caesar, and ending with Domitian. Because of the popularity of his work, this set of emperors—which have no other reason to be associated as one group—is regarded as somehow distinct from those who ruled after them. Julius Caesar is not even regarded as an Emperor of Rome, but that matters little to collectors who want the coins of the "Twelve Caesars". Other typical collecting areas include coins of certain "dynasties." In some cases, the descendants of an emperor ruled for a considerable period of time. For example, the emperor Septimius Severus ruled from AD 193 to 211, but his last surviving descendant (Severus Alexander) ruled until 235. Altogether, there are 14 different personalities represented on coins of the Severans—making a nice little collection in itself. Similar sets of coins can be collected representing the families of Constantine the Great, and others.

Topical collections are also popular among collectors of Roman coins. These include coins which have the same topic as a common feature. For example, coins with military themes on the reverse, or coins picturing architectural monuments. Many collectors specialize in coins with camp gates on the reverse. Another popular theme is coins bearing clasped hands. The "Fallen Horseman" motif of the post-Constantinian era has a loyal following. Some collectors specialize in coins of a single denomination. Others collect only coins of a particular metal. Some specialize in coins of a particular geographic area, like Roman Britain. We could go on and on, the possibilities are endless.

Notice that in the paragraph above, the word "specialize" appears frequently. The hardest thing for a new collector to do, yet one of the things that becomes inevitable, is to focus on a particular aspect of ancient coinage. The field is simply too vast for even the most dedicated enthusiast to deal with. To place this in perspective, the author is a collector (by die variety) of Roman coins from the ancient city of Anazarbus (southern Turkey). The collection is limited only to this one city, which was not a particularly large or important city in the ancient world. Coins were struck at this place from about 19 BC until AD 253. During this period, the number of die varieties exceeds 1,250. Keep in mind, this is only one of the multitude of mints which struck coins in ancient times.

A collector normally specializes in one area or another because of some innate appeal. Reading about the ancient world, and looking at a wide variety of ancient coins will help develop this awareness. Don't feel trapped into collecting anything particular, just because it is conventional. Part of the fun of collecting is outlining your own collecting parameters.

Greek coins, in contrast to the Roman, are often collected as works of art. Roman portraiture—especially from the first century BC to the first century AD—is certainly artistic, but the masters of classical art were the Greeks. The pinnacle of Greek numismatic art is found at the end of the fifth century BC in Sicily and southern Italy. During this period, artists of great fame created images on coins that are to this day considered masterpieces. These coins are avidly collected, as are most coins of the Greek classical period. For the collector of modest means, Greek bronze coins often offer the work of master die-engravers at a fraction of the cost that one would expect for comparable silver coins. The topical collector also has a wide array of choices in the Greek series. Portraits of gods and goddesses, mythological figures, dynastic sets, and coins of the various wars, are just a few of the many choices.

The Roman Provincial series offers a similar variety of choices, but some are so obvious that they have become virtually a series unto themselves. Coins of Roman Egypt, for example, fall within the category of Roman Provincial Coins, but the series is so large and so avidly collected, that there are books specializing in this topic alone. Roman "city-coins" of the Holy Land form another series that is similar in this respect. The Romans installed "client-kings" in many of their newly conquered possessions, and the collecting of coins struck in the names of these kings is a popular field. Many of the Roman Provincial cities struck coins with intricate themes on exceptionally large flans. These are not only popular, but generally quite expensive when in high grade.

Romaion (Byzantine) coins are collected much like Roman coins in the sense that there is a coherent set of rulers with a beginning and end. Still, there are many subdivisions within this field. Overall, Romaion coins are not as popular among collectors as their Greek and Roman forerunners, therefore prices for equivalent rarities are substantially less. In addition to mainstream portrait collecting, some collectors specialize in period collecting. Coins of Heraclius and his family, for example, are popular. Another popular period is that of the Palaeologan emperors. Type coins are also collected with relish in this series, because many bear portraits of Christ and the saints. The sack of Constantinople by Crusader armies in 1204 created several subsidiary collecting areas. The Latin Kingdom which took over the city, an exiled Romaion empire in Nicaea, a family branch in Trebizond, and exiles in Thessalonica all left a numismatic legacy. Romaion gold coins are among the least expensive ancient gold coins, and can often be purchased in exceptional condition for under $300.

There are many peripheral cultures which struck coinage during the periods of the Greeks, Romans and Romaioi. Actually, no one has yet devised an acceptable category to link these coins. We refer to them as Non-Classical coins, only because the term "classical," by dictionary definition implies Greek and Roman. Some of the coins that fall into this category are listed earlier in this volume. They are not an insignificant body of coins by any means. The Persians, for example, ruled an empire equal to that of the Greeks—and their successors, the Parthians, kept the Roman army at bay for centuries. The Sasanians, successors to the Parthians, were more than a match for the late Romans and the Romaioi, and controlled all of the Middle East for large periods of time. They eventually were displaced by the rise of Islam. Jewish coinage and the coinage of various tribes and kingdoms from Arabia to North Africa constitute significant collecting areas. From Northern Europe to the Black Sea, we also find coins from impressive cultures.

It is impossible for the novice collector of ancient coins to absorb all of the information that has been compiled by numismatists over the years. Therefore, for the average collector, it is important to take one step at a time and learn as much as is comfortable about a favored group before pressing on to broader areas. It is very easy to become overwhelmed. Talking to other collectors and dealers will make the choices much easier as the options become clear.

At some point, many of us wonder what it would take to form a really important collection. The importance of a collection cannot be measured solely by quality or quantity. Rather, an imporant collection is one that earns widespread respect for having accomplished something of purpose and value. Almost any theme can lead to an important collection if it adds to our overall knowledge and appreciation of numismatics as an art and science, or provides insights that enrich other disciplines. The difference between a satisfying accumulation of pretty coins and an important collection is that the latter will serve the hobby in a broader sense. A collection by die of the entire output of one city or state would constitute an assembly of significant importance—but only if the resulting information were published.

The most difficult task for many is to narrow the parameters of a collection to a point where it will serve a unity of purpose. This is not something that others can or should do for you, as it goes right to the very core of why we collect. Of course, there is no rule that says that every collector must form an important collection. Many people will enjoy collecting without the slightest care as to how others perceive their effort. After all, ancient coin collecting is first and foremost a hobby and a recreational activity. But if one does secretly harbor the desire to build a collection of importance, it may be helpful to evaluate the overall purpose before acquiring a wealth of material that might not have a place in the ultimate plan.

If you are already overwhelmed, and need a simple path to explore, this section is written for you. It is very limited in scope, but it should at least get you into the collecting mode without making any dramatic mistakes. Since the topics which follow are generally popular among a wide audience, they will also be relatively marketable if the need should arise. It is almost always better to sell coins of a coherent group than to try to sell a handful of totally unrelated types.

Almost every beginning collector of ancient coins starts assembling a set of "something" because it is a comfortable way to start. That is why the Penny Books for U.S. coins are sold in practically every hobby store in the country. All you have to do is find the coin that fits the hole. Well, you can do that with ancient coins as well, and the next few pages will show you how. Whether it's a set of rulers, a topical area, or just oddities, you can easily define a narrow collecting field that will allow you to have fun while you are learning. Of course you can ignore the suggestions that we have provided, because they are really there only to stimulate your thinking about how to collect. Create your own topical area if you like, or select some particular aspect of ancient history that appeals to you, but by all means—**Focus!**

Among the most common of ancient coins on the current market are the coins of Constantine the Great and his family. Recent hoards from this period, found in Britain and Bulgaria, have produced a great many choice specimens.

Constantine became Emperor of Rome in AD 307 and is remembered for his military successes and his founding of the new capital of Constantinople. Even more so, he is remembered as the first Christian emperor. The Edict of Serdica, issued by Constantine and his co-rulers in AD 311, legalized Christianity as a state religion.

The coins of Constantine are very inexpensive and can easily be found in extremely fine condition. A beginning collector might build an attractive set of the coins of Constantine and his family (mother, wife and four children) for about $75 per coin on average or about $500 total (less in lower grades). This would essentially be a high-grade portrait set, so the primary objective would be to select coins with relatively large and attractive portraits. As Caesar (heir to the throne), Constantine's image appears on a large bronze coin of the denomination known as "follis." However, his coins struck as emperor were struck on a reduced standard. The flan, and consequently the portrait, is smaller. As the years of his reign passes, the standard was further reduced leaving bronze coins of only a fraction of the size. We have included in this grouping a coin of Constantine as emperor, which is

Constantine I
AE-Follis
EF, smooth brown patina
estimated value $75-100

Helena
Mother of Constantine
AE-Follis
EF, smooth brown patina
estimated value $75-100

Fausta
Second Wife of Constantine
AE-Follis
EF, smooth brown patina
estimated value $75-100

Crispus
Son of Constantine
AE-Follis
EF, smooth brown patina
estimated value $50-75

readily obtainable in high grade.

Constantine was married first to Minervina, but no coins were issued in her name. They did produce a son however, by the name of Crispus, who was elevated to the rank of Caesar in AD 317. Constantine's second marriage was to Fausta, the daughter of Maximian. By her, he had three sons: Constantine II, Constans, and Constantius II. He also struck coins in honor of his mother, **Helena**, who was canonized by the church as finder of the "true cross" of Christ.

Coins of Fausta, and Helena are somewhat harder to find than the coins of Constantine's sons, and will cost a bit above the average. Coins of Crispus, Constantine II, Constans and Constantius II should be very easy to find in good grades with attractive portraits. They should cost a bit less than the average.

Constantine also struck coins for his nephews Delmatius and Hanniballianus. His sons struck a coin in honor of his step-mother, Theodora. Three more nephews, Nepotian, Constantius Gallus and Julian, struck coins on their own behalf at a later date. All of these coins could be added to a growing collection, perhaps along with a coin of his father, Constantius Chlorus and one of Claudius Gothicus, from whom Constantine claimed to be descended.

In low grade, coins of the type illustrated may cost only $10 or $15 each,

Constantine II
Son of Constantine
AE-Follis
EF, smooth brown patina
estimated value $50-75

Constantius II
Son of Constantine
AE-Follis
EF, smooth brown patina
estimated value $50-75

Constans
Son of Constantine
AE-Follis
EF, smooth brown patina
estimated value $50-75

but they will certainly bring next to nothing at resale. If that is not a concern, shop for the best you can find at that price level and enjoy the coins as a recreational purchase. If you want to get back a part of the value when you ultimately trade up, buy coins with strong details, good centering and beautiful patinas. They exist and are worth searching for.

210

As an expansionist empire, Rome was at war with its neighbors more often than not. It should be no surprise that their military campaigns, especially the successful ones, were heralded on coins. Actually, a few unsuccessful ones were touted as well, but that's just part of the never-changing game of politics. The formula was fairly standard over a long period of time. The vanquished foe, always a "barbarian", was depicted in mourning beneath a Roman trophy. Sometimes one barbarian is depicted, sometimes more than one. Presumably, the greater number alluded to more than one campaign or to more than one foe in the same campaign.

Julius Caesar, 46-45 BC, AR denarius
Gallia and a Gaulish captive mourning

Titus, AD 72, AR denarius (x1.5)
Judaea in mourning

Some of the campaigns, like that of Julius Caesar in Gaul, or the Flavians in Judaea, are well documented, others are obscure and may in fact be known to us only because of the appearance on coinage. Antoninus Pius, during his campaign in Britain built a monumental wall across the island as a defense against northern tribes—part of which still stands today.

There are enough different campaigns represented by this motif on Roman coinage that it can form a productive series to collect. Although many of these types are common, there are also enough rare types to allow some real challenge. One benefit of selecting a thematic approach like this to collecting is that it is possible to create a very interesting and educational display for sharing with others.

Domitian, AD 81-96, AV aureus
Germania in mourning

Antoninus Pius, AD 138-161, AE As
Britannia in mourning

Homer Portrayed on Coins

Marvin Tameanko, a collector from Canada, has an incredibly fertile and encyclopedic mind when it comes to themes portrayed on ancient coins. He has written many fascinating articles on the subject, and never seems to run out of ideas. We have included here one of the thematic areas that he has written about, in order to give the reader some sense of the various directions that collecting interest might take.

COINS PORTRAYING HOMER:

Tameanko, M. "The importance of Homer's writing led to his representation on the coinage of Greek city states," *The Celator*, May 1991.

M.T.

In addition to the portrayal of gods, goddesses, rulers and heros, ancient coins sometimes portray poets and scholars. Some of the personages included in this list would be Pythagoras, Sappho, Homer, Hipparchus, Anaxagoras, Heraclitus, Herodotus, Zenophon and Hippocrates. Homer is perhaps the best known on this list of memorables because of his epic poems, the *Iliad* and the *Odyssey*, which relate the story of the Trojan War and its aftermath. For detailed information about the coins and their significance see the article cited above. The following chart is provided only to demonstrate the scope of this interesting "mini topic," which forms a small but wonderful collection.

---

1. **IOS,** AR-Didrachm, ca. 300 BC,Obv. Bearded bust of Homer, r. (SG 3103)
2. **IOS,** AE-20mm, 2nd-1st c. BC, Obv. Bearded head of Homer, r. (SG 3104)
3. **IOS,** AE-17mm, 2nd-1st c. BC, Obv. Bearded head of Homer, l. (SG 3105)
4. **IOS,** AE-19mm, 1st c. AD, Obv. Head of Homer, r., wearing tainia (SGI 4876)
5. **COLOPHON,** AE-18mm, 2nd-1st c. BC, Rev. Homer std. l. holding scroll (SG 4357)
6. **COLOPHON,** AE-28mm, AD 244-249, Rev. Homer std. r. holding scroll (SGI 4007)
7. **SMYRNA,** AE-19-23mm, 2nd-1st c. BC, Rev. Homer std. l. (SG 4571-75)
8. **AMASTRIS,** AE-20mm, AD 96-192, Obv. Bearded head of Homer, r. (SGI 4885)
9. **AMASTRIS,** AE-26mm, 2nd c. AD, Obv. Bearded hd. r. (Wadd. 170,32, rev. unpub.)
10. **AMASTRIS,** AE-28mm, AD 96-192, Obv. Bust of Homer, r. (Waddington 171,42-43)
11. **AMASTRIS,** AE-21mm, 2nd c. AD, Obv. Bust of Homer, r. (Waddington 170,32)
12. **AMASTRIS,** AE-21mm, 2nd c. AD, Obv. Bust of Homer, r. (Waddington 170,34)
13. **AMASTRIS,** AE-21mm, 2nd c. AD, Obv. Bust of Homer, r. (Waddington 170,35)
14. **AMASTRIS,** AE-18mm, 2nd c. AD, Obv. Bust of Homer, r. (Waddington 170,36)
15. **AMASTRIS,** AE-21mm, 2nd c. AD, Obv. Bust of Homer, r. (Waddington 170,37-39)
16. **AMASTRIS,** AE-28mm, 2nd c. AD, Obv. Bust of Homer, r. (Waddington 171,40)
17. **AMASTRIS,** AE-25mm, 2nd c. AD, Obv. Bust of Homer, r. (Waddington 171,44)
18. **AMASTRIS,** AE-25mm, 2nd c. AD, Obv. Bust of Homer, r. (Waddington 172,45)
19. **CHIOS,** AE-16mm, 1st - 2nd c. AD, Rev. Homer std r. unrolling scroll (SGI 4962)
20. **NICAEA,** AE-17mm, AD 175-177, Rev. Bust of Homer, r. (sim. to Waddington 430,249)
21. **CYME,** AE-23mm, AD 96-192, Rev. Homer std. r. (*Historia. Numorum.* p. 554)
22. **TEMNUS,** AE-18mm, AD 96-192, Rev. Homer std. r. (*Historia. Numorum.* p. 557)

Famous People of the Ancient World

Famous figures have always been an attraction to the general populace. Even in antiquity, authors like Plutarch and Suetonius wrote biographical sketches about people who were fascinating to them. A glance at the covers of magazines on any newsstand will confirm that our fascination with famous people continues today. Many famous people of the past are represented on ancient coins, and not all of them are political personalities. On the facing page, for example, is a long list of coins that portray Homer, and before that a section about coins of Constantine the Great. On the following page, is a sample of coins bearing the portrait of Alexander the Great. There are too many famous figures to include a list here, but assembling that list will be part of the fun of collecting this topical area. Below are just a few of the possibilities.

Philetairos
Progenitor of the
Pergamene Kingdom
282-263 BC
(on a coin of Attalos I)

Vercingetorix
Chief of the Averni
Gaul, ca. 52 BC
(on a coin of
L. Hostilius Saserna)

Nero
Emperor of Rome
AD 54-68

Shapur I (The Great)
Sasanian Kingdom
AD 241-272

Boudicca
Queen of the Iceni (x1.5)
Britain, ca. AD 61

Heraclius
Romaion Emperor
AD 610-641

Throughout history many important leaders and conquerors have idealized Alexander the Great. His image alone commanded so much respect, that its use brought legitimacy of a fashion to those who flattered his memory. Portraits of Alexander may even be seen on coins struck by the Romans. They make an interesting and collectable series.

To the left, Alexander is featured on a silver tetradrachm struck in his own name at the Babylon mint. The type is of Herakles wearing the scalp of a lion, but the features are clearly those of Alexander. The transition from representation of Herakles to Alexander took place during Alexander's lifetime and marked the beginning of Hellenistic portraiture.

Alexander wears an elephant-skin headdress on a silver tetradrachm struck by his general Ptolemy as Satrap of Egypt (ca. 323 BC). Ptolemy retrieved Alexander's body and had it transported to Egypt, where it remained on display for many centuries.

Alexander is diademed with the horn of Zeus Ammon, on a silver tetradrachm struck by his general Lysimachos, as King of Thrace (323-281 BC). This is considered to be one of the most accurate likenesses of Alexander.

Alexander wears a horned helmet on a silver tetradrachm issued at Susa (Persia), by his general Seleucus, King of Syria and the East (ca. 312-280 BC). During the Middle Ages, Alexander was referred to in Persia as the legendary "Dhul Qarnayn" (The two-horned).

Athletic Events

The hosting of games was serious business in the ancient world because they usually were held in honor of a deity or of a ruler. It was considered a privilege and important games were usually marked by the contemporary issue of commemorative coins. Illustrated here is a bronze from Perinthus in Thrace. It depicts an athlete preparing himself for participation in the games held in honor of the emperor (Septimius Severus). Participants competed in the nude, and their bodies were covered with olive oil. After the event, the oil was scraped off with a curved wooden stick. This post event action is also depicted on some ancient coins.

AE 25mm (x1.5) AD 193-211
Perinthus, Septimius Severus
rev: Athlete reaching into a jar for
oil, preparatory to an event
in the Severen Games

Wrestling is one of the oldest sports still active today. The olympic wrestling matches of antiquity were encumbered by fewer rules than contestants abide by today. Aside from gouging and biting, all else was pretty much fair game. A series of silver staters struck at the city of Aspendos on the Pamphylian coast of Asia Minor bear scenes of great variety where two contestants try to punch, twist, trip and kick each other to facilitate a take down.

The coins with athletic themes are called "Agonistic" types after

Aspendos, ca. 400-370 BC
AR stater

the Greek god who presided over such affairs. In addition to depictions of the actual athletic events, which include horse races, javelin throwing, discus throwing, and others, the coins often depict the prizes associated with the games being celebrated. These may include palm branches, crowns, armor and other honors. Sometimes the emperor himself would attend the games and there are scenes on some Roman Provincial coins which appear to depict the emperor awarding prizes to the victorious athletes. We provide more information, and a useful bibliography about athletics on ancient coins, in Volume IV of this series.

Animals on Coins

Animal lovers will find an extraordinary array of subjects depicted on ancient coins. From domestic pets to exotic wild animals, an entire book could easily be devoted to the subject. The subject is so popular that John and Janet Twente, both retired professors from the University of Missouri, have built a business selling ancient coins with animal motifs. From Pomeranian dogs to scorpions, the list is incredible. Presented here, for example, are a few coins portraying elephants—just one of the many possible themes.

Ptolemaic Kingdom:
Biga of elephants, on a gold stater of Ptolemy I, as King of Egypt, 305-285 BC.

Carthaginian:
Siculo-Punic silver half-shekel from Sicily during the Carthaginian occupation ca. 213-210 BC.

Roman Imperatorial:
Silver denarius of Julius Caesar, 49-48 BC.

Seleukid Kingdom:
AE Serrate 22mm, Antiochos VI, Syria, 145-142 BC.

Roman Empire:
AE As of Antoninus Pius, AD 138-161.

Caracalla and Julia Domna
AD 212-217
Markianopolis, AE 28mm
Aesculapius with serpent staff

Although the serpent entwined staff imagery has antecedents in the ancient Near East, it became popular in Greek culture and was adopted by the Romans—making its way through time to our own era. The Greek tradition is universally regarded as the basis of medicinal art and science. And, fortunately for us, the coins of the Greeks and the Romans bear wonderful allusions to this tradition. There were many centers of cult worship throughout the ancient world at which Aesculapius was venerated. Among them, some of the more important were Epidaurus, Cos, Cnidus, Pergamon and Aegeae. Not only did people go to these places to honor the deified healer, the sites themselves were generally regarded as being great healing centers. Springs and baths, meditative rooms, and hospital-like treatment complexes were administered by a caste of priests who were supposedly descended from Aesculapius. The art of healing was a secret that was passed from father to son.

Although the cadeuces is a device that appears frequently on ancient coins, the modern medical symbol of the winged and serpent entwined cadeuces does not seem to have been related to medicine in antiquity. Apparently, a misconception in the early 20th century led to its adoption by the medical fraternity. There are, however, a great number of coins, both Greek and Roman, with allusions to medicine in some form. The subject is covered in great detail, and is well illustrated, by R.G. Penn in *Medicine on Ancient Greek and Roman Coins*. (London, 1994).

Regal coinage, AE 18mm
Pergamon, 282-133 BC
Aesculapius feeding serpent

Astrology

Astronomy and Astrology, to the ancients, were the same thing. Their study of the skies and the behavior of celestial bodies was motivated by a belief that the movement of the planets affected the affairs of man. This belief was so thoroughly embedded in the minds of people that astrological symbols were well understood and appear frequently on ancient coins.

The Moon in Cancer
Antoninus Pius
AD 138-161
AE Drachm, Alexandria

Solar eclipse in Sagittarius
Nasir al-Din Artuq Arslan
AH 599 / AD 1201-39
AE Dirham, Mardin

Luna and Taurus
Castulo Spain
AE 18mm, ca. 50 BC

Phoenix
commemorates the end of the
3rd Sothic Cycle
Antoninus Pius, AD 138/9
Alexandria, Billon Tetradrachm

Caesar's Comet
Augustus, 27 BC - 14 AD
AR Denarius

Sol / Luna
L. Lucretius Trio
AR Denarius, 76 BC

Collecting Damaged Coins

Collectors are usually keen to obtain things a bit unusual. Fortunately, a variety of discarded treasures can often be found in dealer "junk boxes". These might include mint errors like brockages or flip-over double strikes. Because the resulting image can be quite crude, these are often thought to be damaged, and undesirable.

Another form of damage that many dealers and collectors reject is graffiti on coins. The scratching of letters onto the surface of a coin after it enters circulation is in the minds of most collectors an abomination. However, in antiquity it was not an uncommon practice. In fact, graffiti can sometimes have a charm of its own. Often, the marks are letters which form a name or an abstract idea. One gold solidus that found its way to me several years ago bore the graffiti MAPTYP—which spelled the word *Martyr* in Greek. Whether this was a reference to the Christian faith or merely to a personal name is uncertain, but the scratched out letters unquestionably provoked interest in what would otherwise have been a rather mundane coin. It eventually became the subject of a David Vagi article in *The Celator*.

As a sign of public condemnation of the memory of a displaced ruler, the image of that ruler was sometimes defaced on his coinage. After the murder of Geta by his brother Caracalla, Geta's memory was publicly purged in a "Memoriae Damnatio". Certain coins of the brothers Caracalla and Geta are often found with Geta's image scratched off of the surface. These "damaged" coins are understandably of interest to collectors.

Yet another form of damaged coin which often appears in junk boxes is the "cut coin" which we mentioned earlier in this book. These coins were intentionally divided to create lower denominations which were in short supply at the time. The incidence of this phenomenon is particularly high among the coins of Syria and the Levant.

Stratonikeia in Caria, AD 39mm
Caracalla and Geta, AD 211-212
with head of Geta erased in Damnatio Memoriae

Coins with holes in them are heavily discounted in value by most collectors and dealers alike. Aesthetically, this is understandable. But emotionally, the fact that a coin was holed can have a certain appeal. Take, for example, the anonymous bronze folles of the Romaioi struck in the eleventh century AD. These issues are often found with holes at the periphery, which were obviously used to affix the coin as a pendant. When hung, the coin typically lines up in such a way as to exhibit the portrait of Christ. The hole itself becomes of less importance than the reason for which it was created—turning a utilitarian object like a coin into an aesthetic and emotional object of beauty or reverence.

There are many other forms of damage or alteration which might to some appear as a major detraction and to others as something intriguing or desirable. Coins have at times been hammered into squares or rectangles and used as weights. They have been used for all sorts of personal adornment or building decoration. Many have been made into earrings, belts and finger rings. Some have even been used industrially as bushings or bearings. They may appear as fused and coral encrusted lumps from an underwater excavation, or as highly polished cuff links.

Sometimes, coins were hammered flat and engraved with a design or a name. This became a particularly popular activity in the 19th century and are commonly referred to as "Love Tokens". We also find examples of this from antiquity, as illustrated by the engraved coin of Nero illustrated below. This was apparently so common an occurrence during the reign of Tiberius that he passed strict laws with the imposition of draconian penalties for the defacement of a Roman coin. Obviously those laws were relaxed before the reign of Nero, or Titus Calpurnius Diadumenus would have thought twice before advertising his defiance so blatantly.

Nero, AD 54-68, AE sestertius
Holed and engraved, possibly for personal
identification (i.e. a Roman "dogtag")?

Odd and Curious

Oddities have always been a popular collecting topic and ancient coins offer a plentiful supply. Even when coins were available, these symbols of value were exchanged between peoples of the ancient world.

Celtic gold Ring Money, 1st millennium BC. 20mm, 9.05 gm.

AE Cast hexas of Akragas, ca. 450 BC. Eagle on one side, crab on the other. Denomination marks on the flat top.

Olbia, bronze arrowhead money Ca. 6th - 5th century BC from the Black Sea area

Celtic tin Wheel Money, 1st century BC. 24mm, 3.22 gm.

Olbia, AE Dolphin money ca. 5th - 4th century BC, 2.17 gm.

Queen T'amar, Georgia AD 1184-1213 Normally struck on irregular planchets

Akragas, AE Uncia ca. 450 BC, Eagle's head and Crab Claw.

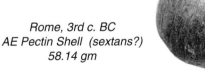

Rome, 3rd c. BC AE Pectin Shell (sextans?) 58.14 gm

Other Topical Collecting Areas

The number of topical areas that one might consider for collecting ancient coins is limited only by one's imagination. Some are immediately obvious, but others are quite innovative. Listed below are some of the topical areas that, in addition to those already touched on, collectors are actually known to have taken an interest in:

- Aging process in portraits.
- Alexander tetradrachms by mint.
- Anepigraphic coins.
- Animals of every variety.
- Archaic coins.
- Architecture.
- Armor and weapons.
- Artists signatures.
- Astrological figures and representations.
- Barbarous imitations.
- Camp gate reverses.
- Cities of the Greek world.
- Clasped Hands as a symbol of concord or marriage.
- Corinthian-type staters by mint city.
- Countermarks.
- Cut coins (used for change).
- Dynastic coins (Ptolemaic, Seleucid, etc.).
- Error coins of every sort.
- Fractions of standard denominations.
- Games of the ancient world.
- Historical commemoratives.
- Legionary or military references.
- Maps on coins.
- Maritime themes.
- Monograms.
- Mythological themes.
- Narrative scenes.
- Numbers on coins.
- Roman Emperors by Portrait.
- Roman Republican coins by moneyer or type.
- Time as a concept and theme.
- Travel.
- Works of art (statues or paintings, etc.) depicted on coins.
- And many many more!

Storing Coins

The author's first experience with storing ancient coins was in Germany in the 1960s. It was typical then, to visit a dealer's office (in a quiet residential neighborhood) and be shown coins. The stock was stored in trays which fit nicely into a magnificent wooden cabinet. Each coin was nested on felt in a circular cutout—no 2x2 flips—and was accompanied by tags brown with age and written in the most delightful script. It was a genteel and emotional experience—a perfect setting for the enjoyment of artifacts from antiquity.

Today, an acceptable system of storing coins usually involves a compromise between aesthetics, security and accessibility. Security is not only necessary in a physical sense, but also in the sense of avoiding dangerous contamination. One of the contaminants most often faced by collectors is sulphur. The safest form of storage, from the standpoint of avoiding contamination, is the old standard 2x2 chemically neutral (sulphur free) paper envelope. The envelopes may be stored in cardboard boxes made especially for the purpose. This, unfortunately, is also the least aesthetic and least functional method of storage. Coins stored this way are difficult to view since they must be removed from the envelopes. One must also avoid contamination caused by cardboard boxes in which these envelopes are stored, since some boxes may not in themselves be sulphur free. The effect of sulphur contamination is that coins will darken and the discoloration may not be even—in other words, the coins may become stained.

The clear plastic 2x2 "flips" that one finds at all coin supply stores are very functional, but they also have some limitations. Flips made of Mylar are inert and do not interact with the metallic composition of a coin, or deteriorate through natural processes. The downside of these flips is that they are very brittle and tend to break if handled frequently. Poly Vinyl Chloride (PVC) flips are much more pliable, and therefore are popular among dealers who have to transport their stock and show their coins frequently. The disadvantage of this product is that PVC can degrade over time and release hydrochloric acid in a gaseous state. This can cause corrosion on a coin if the condition is not spotted and the flip replaced. Don't panic if you have some or all of your coins in PVC flips, the breakdown does not occur rapidly, and is usually not noticeably harmful to ancient coins. If you remove a coin from a PVC flip and can see a ring on the plastic where the coin previously was, then the flip should be replaced.

PVC and Mylar flips have one pouch for the coin and another to hold a descriptive insert. The 2x2 paper inserts that accompany coins in these flips may also contain traces of sulphur. Even if the coins do not come into direct contact with sulphur contaminated paper, fumes can accumulate in a sealed container and migrate to pouches containing coins. Therefore, it is prudent to use sulphur-free inserts if you plan to store coins for an extended period without observation. The boxes made to store 2x2 flips come in both cardboard and plastic varieties. The plastic boxes are sure to be sulphur and PVC free.

Coin trays are a desirable storage alternative if one has the space to store and display them. While boxed coins can easily be transported to or kept in a safe deposit box or small safe, trays of coins are more difficult to transport and secure. The "Abafil" type cases, which self-store in their own box, are better in this respect—but are still far from a perfect solution. The hard plastic cases with plastic trays and a clear plastic cover are apparently inert, but are also harder to store than 2x2 boxes. For those with internal security and space, wood trays are an age-old tradition. Not all woods, however, are safe. The beautiful hardwoods that are used in furniture often release fumes that are destructive to the surface of a coin. Oak is especially corrosive to lead and copper. The woods of choice among museums with coin trays are tropical hardwoods, like mahogany which is very stable. Inert tray liners are often used with wood trays to further isolate the coins. Wool (felt) can tarnish silver so it is not recommended as a liner, but other textiles and polyethylene foam are acceptable. Covers are not necessary on these trays, and are actually discouraged because they restrict the free circulation of air which might remove contaminating fumes. If covers are preferred, glass or a hard clear acrylic plastic seems to be a reasonable and safe choice.

2x2 PVC "flips" are the most popular method for short term storage, particularly when coins are likely to be removed often for examination

Abafil cases, made in Italy, provide an attractive and safe storage option for ancient coins. Trays come in varied sizes and will fit in most home safes.

If you choose to store ancient coins in PVC flips, it would be a good idea to check them frequently, and replace any flips that exhibit signs of breaking down (look for a light ring or cloudy circle on the plastic where the coin was laying). Remember, the more your coins have a chance to breathe clean fresh air, the healthier they (like us) will be.

Another consideration of storage, is the order in which coins will be arranged. Most modern museums have taken to arranging coins in trays, by mint. This is a useful way to organize coins if one is studying local history or monetary reform. It makes political and art historical research more difficult, however. Most collectors arrange Roman and Byzantine coins chronologically, by emperor and then by mint. Greek and Roman Provincial coins are usually arranged geographically, by issuing authority. This geographical arrangement was devised by Jan Eckhel in the 18th century and is still widely used today. The accepted order starts in the northwest corner of the Mediterranean and progresses easterly around the sea through the Middle East to Egypt and then continues westerly through North Africa back to the Atlantic coast. Most auction catalogs and major reference works are arranged in this fashion. In recent years, there has been some movement away from the Eckhel system. For example, the comprehensive *Roman Provincial Coinage* (RPC) departs from convention and catalogues the coins of North Africa in sequence with those of Southern Italy and Sicily—in other words, before the coins of mainland Greece, Asia Minor and the Levant. One disadvantage of the Eckhel system is that coins of cities like Corinth and its colonies are extremely difficult to study as a group because of their geographical separation.

Some collectors and dealers arrange their Greek and Roman Provincial coins alphabetically by city—which at least enjoys the virtue of simplicity, if not academic approbation.

225

One sure way to generate a lot of heat in any discussion with ancient coin collectors, is to mention the term "slabbing." Seasoned collectors react very negatively to the thought of sterilizing ancients in a sheath of plastic.

Slabbing is a practice developed by dealers in U.S. and modern world coins whereby a specimen is graded and certified, then encased in a sealed plastic holder (slab) with a certification number and the grade affixed. This supposedly provides an absolute determination of authenticity and grade, which theoretically benefits the collector. Next to slabs, the most popular device on the market is the slab-cracker, which is used to break open slabs so that coins can be resubmitted in the expectation of improving their "certified" grade. At the same time, a grading system emerged in which numeric grades expanded the range of possible grade assignments, supposedly making the grade more definitive. To collectors of ancient coins, who are used to absolute subjectivity in grading, this is pure folly. It is truly a different mindset.

Aside from the issue of micro-grading, which means nothing to a collector of ancient coins, there is the very real issue of accessibility. Collectors of ancient coins are generally fond of handling their coins. Part of the nostalgia of collecting something old is the emotion that an artifact stirs as one holds it and contemplates its journey through time. This is something that collectors of modern proof and mint coins must avoid, because nature has not had time to build that protective coating we refer to as patina. A fingerprint on a proof coin sends shivers up the spine of a U.S. coin dealer. In 1991, a certification service in the U.S. announced that they planned to offer certification and slabbing services for collectors of ancients. The reaction within the fraternity was akin to rebellion. Because of the uncertain market, and some technical problems with the plastic housing itself, the idea was dropped and lay dormant for several years. However, another firm known as Independent Coin Grading Company (ICG) continued to develop the concept of slabbed ancients. Today, ICG offers authentication, certification and slabbing service for certain types of ancient coins. In fact, there have been recent auctions in which all of the ancient coins offered were slabbed.

The slabbing of ancient coins is primarily a marketing tool to get ancient coins into the hands of people who would otherwise have no comfort level with them. It is understandable that some collectors who are aesthetically attracted to coins from antiquity will be ill at ease with the rather loose controls which exist in the ancient coin market. An authentication and certification gives at least the illusion that value is real and not just perceived. However, there is more to the issue than simply the encasement of a coin in plastic. There is a sort of mystique among antiquarians that recalls the age of enlightenment and a nostalgia that does not lend itself to plastic entombment. Few things are more rewarding to an ancient coin collector than holding a piece of ancient history in hand and being able to pass it from person to person around a room enjoying the reactions that it evokes.

Although the arguments proffered by both supporters and critics of slabbing are passionate, the final choice boils down to personal preference. As an alternative to slabbing, it seems that the education of new collectors would help prepare them to deal effectively with the ancient coin market and to develop that comfort level necessary to enjoy the hobby without fear of authentication or grading issues. That, of course, is one of the aims of this book.

It seems that there are endless debates over many aspects of ancient coin collecting, and one of them concerns the question of cleaning coins. There are some collectors who will clean everything and some who will clean nothing. Some believe that any alteration to the condition of a coin, other than that produced by nature, is undesirable.

The truth of the matter is that there are very few ancient coins on the market today that have not been cleaned at some time or other. Cleaning should not degrade the value of a coin if it is done properly. Museums clean the coins in their collections, archaeologists clean the coins they find, metal detector enthusiasts clean the coins they dig up—why shouldn't collectors clean coins?

The joy of admiring, or owning, an ancient coin is mainly a product of its beauty or historical importance. If the piece is so encrusted that the image is not discernable, it is certainly not enjoyable as a work of art, and probably not as a piece of history.

It is easy to spot a poorly cleaned coin. Silver coins that have been overcleaned turn a hideous chrome-like color, while bronze coins that have been stripped turn an ugly red or brassy yellow. The biggest danger in cleaning is to overclean. Once a coin's surface is disrupted it is impossible to bring it back to a natural state. The decision whether or not to clean a coin should be made with due caution. If it is a coin that you cannot afford to lose, DON'T CLEAN IT! If, on the other hand, it is an encrusted lump that has seen better days, or the patina looks like main street after the spring thaw, what value is it as is?

Cautions considered, we will assume that the coin *needs* to be cleaned. Before doing anything, wash the coin in plain warm water to remove ordinary dirt. City dwellers should be cautious about using tap water that is probably chlorinated. In every case, distilled water is the coin cleaner's best friend. It is cheap, totally inert, readily available at any grocery store, and you cannot make a mistake by soaking a coin too long in distilled water. The main disadvantage of distilled water is that it is incredibly slow. If you have a sonic cleaning device, that may speed up the process somewhat, but be careful not to overdo it. We have heard horror stories about crystallized coins disintegrating in a sonic cleaner. Although distilled water alone may not completely eradicate chlorides, even with repeated baths, it is by far the least intrusive and most practical remedy for the amateur collector.

Our next consideration is the type of metal. Gold coins are very soft and scratch or abrade easily. Silver coins are harder, and bronze coins are very hard. The patinas that form on these metals also exhibit relative degrees of hardness and need to be handled appropriately. Patina is a coating formed through oxidation over a very long period of time. Gold itself may or may not oxidize (another debate), but the trace impurities in a gold coin do. Therefore, even gold coins can have a patina. Silver oxides are not very hard, but copper oxides, sulphates, chlorides and carbonates can be very hard and difficult to remove. So, before doing anything to the coin, think about the likely effect of your actions.

There are many age-old recipes for home cleaning. One method for cleaning silver coins is to place them in a small metal pan with a half inch or so of water in which is dissolved a tablespoon of Cream of Tartar. Bring the water to a boil, remove the coins and (after allowing them to cool) brush gently with a toothbrush, then rinse in distilled water. Another method is to wrap the coin(s) in aluminum foil with a generous coating of lemon juice. Check every few hours and remove them when the desired effect is achieved. It may be necessary to remove dirt and dissolved oxides with a very soft brush as the cleaning progresses. In extreme cases, an overnight bath may be necessary. As always, rinse thoroughly in distilled water after cleaning. The citric acid works slowly and is relatively gentle with the surface of a gold or silver coin. It does not work as well on bronze coins as it tends to make the surface (patina) gooey.

Bronze coins may be cleaned of dirt and light encrustations with a small brass bristle brush of the type sold for brushing suede leather products. Brush gently and examine the coin often to check progress. In source countries, it has long been a standard practice to batch soak ancient coins in olive oil to remove dirt and encrustation. Olive oil contains a plethora of unfriendly ingredients and should be avoided.

If the surface of a coin is basically smooth and clean, but there are small encrustations present, the preferred method of cleaning is mechanical. One of the important considerations is that the person doing the cleaning use a magnifier which allows 3-D viewing. This can be in the form of a binocular microscope, a jeweler's headband, or a large platform glass that leaves room below it to work. It is difficult to judge pressure or depth of the cleaning tool using a monocular glass, and scratching of the surface is inevitable. As for the tool, one of the best substances is bamboo. Cut a sharp point on the end of a bamboo slip and gently use it to lift encrustations off the surface. Do not use metal objects, like dental pick and scalpels, unless you are prepared to do major surgery—at the risk of a lost patient. As always, practice on a junker of a coin before tackling any work on a precious collectable.

A light green powder, usually residing in a spot of corrosion or pitting, may be a sign of bronze disease. This destructive condition is the result of chlorides being formed from copper in the coin. The powder can be picked out or brushed away, but it will certainly return. If left unattended, bronze disease can literally eat away the metal of a coin to nothing. The only way to prevent spread of the disease is to remove the chlorides and seal the surface against infiltration of air. As usual, there are debates over the most effective method to treat bronze disease, including the use of complicated sounding compounds like benzotriazole-ethanole, sesquicarbonate or dithionite. This approach is best left in the hands of experts as some of these compounds are carcinogenic. A totally safe and easy approach for the amateur is simply to soak the coin in distilled water until the chlorides are completely removed. Use De-ionized water, or better yet tripled distilled HPLC grade $H2O$, this will remove all the cations/anions out of the copper chloride/iron chloride contaminants that are the cause of bronze disease. The higher grade water, produced by reverse osmosis membrane filtration, works much faster than regular distilled $H2O$. When the normal "salts" in $H2O$ are removed, it aggressively attracts cation/anion salts from nearby objects. Distilled water is carried on the shelf of practically every grocery store and comes in two varieties—plain distilled and de-ionized or super-distilled. The latter, as its name implies, is more pure and the cost differential is negligible. If you don't have access to de-ionized water, just use distilled water, and change it more frequently. One should never use tap water, especially from a chlo-rinated source.

This process requires long soakings, we may be talking months in severe cases, with frequent changes of water (every few days). It is best to brush the surface of the coin gently each time the water is changed. One way to track the success of this method is to add a little silver ni-trate to the used water after changing it. If chlorides are present the contaminated water will turn a white milky color. If you don't happen to have access to silver nitrate, just give the soaking process plenty of time. When all of the exfoliation appears to have stopped, heat the coin in an oven at low temperature, about 200-250 degrees for several hours. This will help drive out any lingering gases. Overheating may destroy the patina on a coin, so don't crank up the temperature thinking more is better. Coins retain heat for quite a long time, so be careful handling coins that have been heated. Then, after it cools, coat the coin with a thin application of Renaissance Wax or acrylic floor wax. The object is to prevent air and moisture from reentering the inner recesses of the coin. Renaissance Wax is a brand name for a product marketed out of Britain. It is preferred over acrylic floor wax because it does not leave a shiny film. One collector reportedly went to the extreme of sealing problem coins in a vacuum with an appliance of the type sold for pre-serving food. Of course part of the joy of collecting ancient coins is the ability to touch something of great antiquity. Encapsulating them re-moves this option. The hard dark green encrustations that one often finds on an ancient coin are not bronze disease and do not cause a problem.

Sometimes encrustations on the surface of a bronze coin adhere so tightly that they cannot be pried off. In this case, more serious efforts are required. Small spots may often be softened by application of the commercial bathroom cleaners designed to remove lime. Use a Q-tip and apply the undiluted liquid sparingly. If the encrustation will not come off, the easiest remedy is to strip the entire surface of the coin. This can be done by immersion in any of a number of caustic cleaners including dilute acids. Sulphuric acid is preferable, but is dangerous to work with and is not recommended for the inexperienced. A 10% solution of acid is usually sufficient to strip a coin's surface to bare metal. After soaking in any acid or caustic chemical, be sure to give the coin a long bath in distilled water to neutralize it. A little baking soda in the water will help neutralize acids, but don't use too much or you will be cleaning *it* off the coin next.

A stripped ancient coin is really unattractive. Natural toning is slower than the bureaucracy of most nations, but can be speeded up somewhat by oxygen enrichment. This may be as simple as exposure to the warming rays of direct sunlight. Placing the coin in a south facing window can help but it will take many months and maybe years to develop a natural tone. So some collectors may choose to tone the coin down a bit with a chemical oxidizing agent. There are commercial formulas designed expressly for this purpose. Check with your local coin supply center, or any craft store that stocks supplies for people who make their own stained glass items. Art supply houses are another source of metal conditioners. Liquid patina comes in a variety of colors and is easy to apply. Don't expect it to look like Mother Nature's best —it won't! If all else fails, *powdered sulphur* is easily obtainable at any drug store and rubbed onto the surface of a warm coin it will produce a black toning. In addition to sealing the surface, a very light coat of microcrystalline wax, like Renaissance Wax, applied by rubbing between thumb and forefinger, will help remove the flatness of a cleaned and toned coin.

Remember, the suggestions here are extreme measures for coins that have really serious problems. More coins are ruined by cleaning than are helped, so be careful and practice on your junkers first. There are a couple workshops in Europe that do a spectacular job of stripping and repatinating coins. An acquaintance that was invited to visit one of them remarked that it was a virtual science lab, white jackets and all.

When a coin is completely stripped and repatinated, the work done on it falls into the realm of restoration rather than cleaning or preservation. Again, a debate rages over the acceptability of restoration. Professional restoration has been done on metal objects in museums for centuries and is considered appropriate by most. The real problem with restorations in the collector community is not that coins with serious problems are restored, but that the coins might at some later date be sold without disclosure of that restoration. Poorly restored coins are seldom a problem, the condition is easily recognized and buyers can be forewarned. Skillful restorations, however, can be very deceptive. Epoxy fillers and shoe polish to smooth the surface, machine tooling and smoothing to enhance detail and paints to obscure problems, are a few creative ways that coins have been "improved." A coin that has been carefully "doctored" may initially fool another collector or dealer, and be traded as original. During the 19th century, it was commonplace for collectors to have a coin enhanced by engraving new hairlines to replace those naturally worn, or to heighten relief by removing some of the metal from the vacant fields of a coin. Those coins are still circulating within the collector community, and are not that uncommon. It always pays to look carefully at a coin's surface, and if you have any doubts or concerns about it being altered, ask the seller outright.

Given the choice, it is usually better not to clean a coin beyond a simple washing or light brushing. If it *is* necessary to clean it, use extreme caution and accept the possibility that you may damage the coin beyond repair. From a commercial point of view, patina is a major determinant in price. One should never destroy original patina unless it is absolutely unavoidable.

By far, the question asked most often by observers who have never seen ancient coins before is: How do you know they are real? The answer that one normally hears is both true and unsatisfying at the same time. Dealers who have handled thousands upon thousands of ancient coins will usually claim simply to have developed an "eye" for fakes. Actually, there is a little more to it than that. Knowledge of minting practices and an awareness of previously detected fakes helps the dealer or collector to deal with this perennial problem. With practice, the average collector can become quite good at ferreting out bad coins.

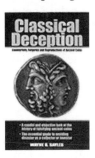

In 2001, as a sequel to our series of six introductory books about *Ancient Coin Collecting*, we wrote a monograph titled *Classical Deception*. Many people think of it as Ancient Coin Collecting VII. This book approaches the question of authenticity from several perspectives. It presents an historical overview with vignettes of many famous forgers of the past. It introduces the tools of the numismatist and explains how they are used to gauge the authenticity of a coin. And, it offers practical advice on how to limit one's risk of being victimized by the forger.

There are basically three kinds of fakes. Those made in ancient times to be used in commerce are actually counterfeits. Those produced in modern times for tourist consumption or artistic appreciation are generally considered reproductions. Those which were purposely made to deceive the collector are forgeries. All three may fool the uninitiated.

Contemporary counterfeits, those coins produced during ancient times either as a result of deceit or necessity, were intended to duplicate a coin whose acceptance was already established. While they may have fooled an uneducated populace, these fakes seldom matched the quality of the official coins that they were copied after. Today, they are actually quite collectable. There is continuing debate over whether some of these crude types might actually have been produced by official mints during periods of siege or political disruption. They may be cast, struck or plated copper (fourrée) and are seen in copper, silver or gold. One common method of counterfeiting coins in antiquity was to take genuine coins and impress them into

Ancient forger's mold of a coin of Constantine the Great

233

Ancient forger's mold, ca. 8th century AD.
Made of green limestone and containing a
crude imitation of an Ummayad gold dinar

clay to make a mold. Then the mold was fired and the two halves bound together while molten metal was poured into the mold. The terracotta molds from this activity are often found in archaeological excavations, especially in northern Europe and in Egypt where the practice was most widespread.

Tourist Fake of an
Alexander tetradrachm

Tourist fakes are generally very crude casts of rare, famous or impressive types. Common fakes include, but certainly are not limited to, Syracusan decadrachms and tetradrachms, Alexander and Athenian tetradrachms, Seleukid tetradrachms and the large diameter Romaion (Byzantine) folles of Justinian. They often have a powdery gray or green "patina" and a very porous look. Only the most naive really expect that these coins are genuine when they buy them, but the entertainment value of buying from the children that scurry about ancient sites offering these "treasures" is too much for many to pass up.

The key to determining authenticity of any specimen is to understand how the coin type was originally made. It is not too difficult to make a piece of metal look old, but it takes quite a lot of skill to faithfully copy the processes used by the ancients. There are several things that one should take into consideration when judging the authenticity of an ancient coin.

In antiquity, some coins were cast, some were struck, and some were struck on cast planchets. Obviously, coins that typically were struck should not show signs of being cast. Contemporary counterfeits made by throwing casts of real coins are often found along with genuine ancient coins—proof that they circulated, and were apparently accepted as genuine (or at least as tradable). Cast copies are nearly always beyond normal weight tolerances (usually light), so a sensitive scale (.01 gram accuracy) is a useful tool for the authenticator of precious metal coins. Bronze coins generally varied too much in weight to make weight analysis meaningful. To obtain normal weights one can check comparable specimens in major auc-

234

tion catalogues or published collections. It happens that the vast majority of genuine ancient coins were produced by being struck at a mint rather than being cast. Therefore, one of the first things to examine in a coin is evidence of casting.

The process of casting requires that a mold be made of each side of a coin. The two molds are then fastened together and molten metal is poured into the void. This requires an opening along the edge of the mold, through which the metal can be poured. Three notable features characterize this process. An appendage of metal from the pouring must be removed from the cast coin, a seam where the two molds are joined must be filed down, and the surface of the coin will inevitably be pitted from the existence of microscopic air bubbles that rest on the surface of the mold. On modern centrifugal casts, where the mold is spun in a centrifuge while it is cast, bubbles are less apparent. The telltale marks of casting are usually identifiable with a high power magnifying glass, but on gold coins they are less obvious. File marks on the edge of a coin are not necessarily a sign of casting, for example, the coin might have been mounted at one time in jewelry, with solder or indentations having been filed down. Nevertheless, file marks are not a good sign and they certainly degrade the value of a coin. The pitting of surfaces is not in itself a guarantee of casting either. Normal corrosion can leave pit marks that look very much like casting bubbles. The combination of the two, however, is pretty condemning. Another typical characteristic of cast coins is an overall soft look. Detail is not sharp, and the coin looks like a photo out of focus. On a struck coin, not only should detail be sharp but the minute stress lines that radiate from the carved portions of the die should be visible.

What if the coin type was originally cast at the mint? Early Roman Republican bronzes, for example, were cast rather than struck. Testing for signs of casting won't help in this case—but Mother Nature does. Patina forms on the entire coin, not just on the surface. Therefore, an original patina on the edge of the coin means that the coin could not have been filed,

"Paduan" by Giovanni Cavino 1500-1570
imitating AE sestertius of Aelius

235

and could not have been cast in modern times. If a coin that was normally cast has been cleaned, it should be treated as suspect since there is no way of determining authenticity short of destructive analysis. Patina is generally a good indicator of age. As mentioned above, there are modern labs that can produce amazing patinas, but they are noticeably uniform in color and consistency. Chocolate Brown and Sicilian Green (a deep green/black) are the two most common varieties. Don't mistake encrustation for patina. One of the oldest tricks in the business is to bury fakes in animal waste to "age" them. In some cases, entire hoards of fakes have been known to be buried for years in the hope that they would deceive unwary dealers and collectors.

The Renaissance of classical interest in the 15th and 16th centuries led some antiquarians to produce medals of ancient style and bearing ancient motifs. The center of this activity was at Padua and the artistic medals of this type are referred to generically as "Paduans". Some of the Paduans were cast from molds and others were struck from dies. The artistic quality varies from issue to issue, but some of these pieces were created by great masters of the Renaissance and are extremely collectible today.

British Museum Electrotype
19th century, by Robert Ready

Another duplicating process, popular in the past century, uses the science of electrolysis. These copies are called "Electrotypes." Like casts, they also have a seam on the edge and their weights will be incorrect. A whole series of British Museum coins were reproduced in this fashion and sold as study pieces. Some were stamped with the initials BM or of their inventor, Robert Ready, (RR) on the edge. Still, they find their way into boxes and bags with genuine coins and can be a problem for the novice. If a normally expensive coin shows up in a junk box, look it over carefully before counting your blessings.

Not all fakes are cast. Within the past ten years we have seen a great increase in the number of struck fakes coming into the market. The first struck fakes intended for the collector market were probably among the Paduans mentioned above, so the idea is far from new. Famous forgers like Becker, Christodoulo and several unidentified "schools" struck ancient coin types in the 19th century, and others like Peter Rosa (1926-1990) produced "Scholar Copies" in the 20th century. Rosa's copies were produced in a variety of mediums including plaster, base metal, copper, lead, silver-plated lead uniface, and pure silver. The dies were created mainly from casts of coins in the British Museum and other

Work of Carl Wilhelm Becker
ca. 1820 forgery of an
AR Denarius of Trajan
(restitution series)

museum collections. Rosa also reproduced "Becker" counterfeits (a forgery of a forgery, and still saleable!), and ran a business out of Staten Island under the name "Becker Reproductions." Some of his early pieces were stamped "copy" in tiny letters on the edge of the coin. A few of these were cast rather than struck. Rosa fakes are typically identifiable by their very flat and smooth fields, which are a result of cold striking (he struck them on his kitchen table using a hydraulic automobile jack).

The main characteristic of less sophisticated struck fakes is the style of engraving. Few artists today can match the excellence of Greek and Roman die-engravers. As a result, the portraits and lettering look strange to the experienced eye.

Since these coins usually come out of the source countries along with genuine coins (this is called salting the hoard) they sometimes pass as genuine. In today's market, any freshly cleaned silver with unusual portraits or epigraphy should be examined closely.

Modern struck copy
Brutus, AR denarius
Bulgarian School

One would think that these fakes would consist mainly of rare varieties and coins of higher value, but that is not always the case. A recent hoard of small Greek silver coins, known in the hobby as the "Black Sea Hoard", was loaded with fakes which were offered on the market for as little as $8.00 each. Fake silver coins of the Roman emperor Gordian III, have also been sold at about that price level. A wide variety of modern die-struck fakes, produced in Bulgaria in pure silver, have been offered in quantities for about $8-10. Remember, eight dollars may not seem like much to a resident of the industrial west, but it is a whole lot more to someone in Turkey or Bulgaria—and there are substantial numbers of these, not just two or three coins.

Of course there have also been examples of high quality die-struck

Black Sea Hoard Fakes
Apollonia AR diobol (x1.5)
Bulgarian School

237

fakes, which were highly priced as well. The *Bulletin on counterfeits,* formerly published by the IAPN's International Bureau for the Suppression of Counterfeit Coins and now published in cooperation with the American Numismatic Association is a periodical notice of current problem areas. Certainly, there are fakes in the market, and in museums today, that remain undetected—but don't panic!

Every collector should learn the basics of coin production that help to reveal obvious fakes. Having done this, the collector's best hedge against the danger of forgeries is the dealer. Every reputable dealer of ancient coins will guarantee, in writing if you prefer, the authenticity of coins sold—without limitation. If your dealer refuses to do so, you can choose not to buy the coins, it's that simple. Part of the price you pay for an ancient coin compensates the dealer for his or her knowledge and expertise. That should include the acceptance of risk on the dealer's part when it comes to authenticity. If you buy a coin through some other source, you take the risk yourself.

Sometimes one will desire an independent opinion as to the authenticity of a coin. Unfortunately, the authentication services of the American Numismatic Association were officially discontinued in 2002. In a public statement accompanying the announcement, the ANA official previously overseeing this service noted that it was no longer viable because the number of submissions did not generate the revenue necessary to sustain it. This is ironic, since the field of ancient coin collecting has seen a huge increase in forgery of entry level collector coins in recent years. If the service was ever needed, it is needed even more now. Part of the rationale for disbanding the service was a feeling among ANA Museum committee members that the professional grading services are offering authentication services as well. The commercial certification companies concentrate mainly on the slabbing of modern coins and only a very limited number of ancient coin types fall into this category. Actually, few collectors of ancient coins are advocates of slabbing anyway, so the point is moot.

The abdication of ANA from the authentication scene leaves only a few choices to the collector. David R. Sear currently operates an independent Ancient Coin Certification Service which can be accessed through http://DavidRSear.com or by mail to P.O. Box 7314, Porter Ranch, CA, 91327. Of course addresses are always subject to change, and books generally outlive all of us, so this information is tentative. The Independent Coin Grading Service (ICG) authenticates certain classes of ancient coins, but only as part of their certification service which slabs submissions. The IGC website is http://www.icgcoin.com. The ANA Certification Service, was divested from the ANA in 1990 and became part of Amos Press, the owners of Coin World newspaper. ANACS does not advertise a service of authenticating ancient coins, but they have reportedly done so on special occasions.

In any case, the collector who wants to have an ancient coin professionally authenticated is faced with few choices. The most difficult consideration for many is that a coin priced at less than $100 is hardly worth the cost of authentication. Sadly, this is the price range that many of the recent forgeries from Eastern Europe fall into. Experienced dealers will often give a non-binding personal opinion about a coin's authenticity if they are presented with the coin in person at a convention and are not busy serving customers. However, this can easily backfire on a dealer. So, don't be surprised if you get some serious hedging. The best protection a collector can obtain is to buy from an experienced and established dealer who guarantees authenticity without limitation. Reliability and integrity are ALWAYS worth the few dollars more that you might have to pay in fair compensation.

Because of the above limitations, some Internet collectors have taken the task of authenticating coins and ferreting out sellers of forgeries upon themselves. At least three Internet chat lists have been established for the purpose of discussing forgeries of ancient coins. As well intentioned as this effort is, there are some potential problems. At first blush, this collector-helping-collector approach seems perfectly rational and agreeable. However, it is dangerous to paint this issue with such a broad brush. In reality, self-appointed "guardians" can become overly righteous and zealous in their pursuit of perceived wrongdoers. This is a dangerous path to walk, since errors in judgement may well result in the public condemnation and slander of innocent parties. It should be kept in mind that there are no prerequisites of education or experience to offer opinions on an Internet chat list. Just like repetitive advertising, the frequent appearance of a name on such lists builds a certain level of familiarity and comfort level. It is a false assumption, but one is easily led to believe that those who have much to say are the most knowledgeable. Institutional lists are better controlled in this respect than private lists, but none of the lists are very actively policed. To make a long story shorter, we need to identify forgeries, and to educate new collectors. But this is something that needs to be done in a careful and professional manner.

Just as there are no prerequisites required to offer an opinion on a chat list, there are no prerequisites to become a dealer. The industry is totally unregulated and anyone can become a dealer simply by advertising themselves as such. In such a loosely organized world, it behooves the buyer to look carefully at the track record and credentials of the seller. Unscrupulous dealers prey on human nature by offering deals that are "too good to be true". This is the first ingredient of a scam, and the prudent collector will have their antennae tuned carefully when this circumstance arises.

Grading of ancient coins is much less precise than the grading of modern coins. Although an ancient coin may have very little wear, it can be covered with a thick patina or encrustation which in effect cancels that detail and makes the coin less appealing—or in some cases *more* appealing. It is not unusual to find subjective terms associated with the grade of an ancient coin. For example: terms like *Choice* VF, *Superb* EF, *Toned* VF, *Good* Fine, *Near* VF, etc. etc. Grades are also commonly embellished with terms like "good for the type," "rare this nice," "perhaps the finest known" and a creative host of others. If one were to list all of the descriptive adjectives used to grade an ancient coin, there would probably be as many different grades as there are for U.S. coins.

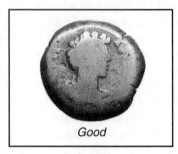

Good

Practically speaking, there are only four grades to be concerned with—Good, Fine, Very Fine and Extremely Fine. "Mint-state" does not have much appeal as a description for an ancient coin, although the French term *Fleur de Coin* (FDC) has a certain ring. When a coin is better than EF, we won't quibble over the technicalities. One experienced cataloguer recently listed a coin as "Choice EF (as struck - FDC)." Get the point? Coins grading less than Good are basically uncollectable, except as fillers.

Fine

Very Fine

Included on the following page is a list of the commonly found grades. We hesitate even to attempt a description of each grade, since the entire issue is so subjective. If a coin is beautiful, a third of a grade up or down is not going to matter. If it is not beautiful—ditto. So why should we split hairs over the issue?

Extremely Fine

Grade is primarily an indicator of wear, and coins graded Good or lower will be very worn. Coins graded Fine will generally retain some detail in the motif, and legends will be mostly readable. A Very Fine coin's legends should be fully readable, and the subject should be clearly recognizable, with moderate wear. An Extremely Fine coin will exhibit very little wear, even on the highest relief points, and all legends will be sharp and clear.

The amount of wear on an ancient coin is not nearly as important as the coin's "eye-appeal." A damaged, off-center, encrusted specimen should not be valued as EF, no matter how many hairlines are visible! Likewise, a poorly cleaned coin may be much less appealing than its technical grade would suggest. Wear is a natural condition, and should not be viewed as a major distraction if the coin is otherwise attractive. Still, wear does to a large degree determine grade. The examples shown here are only a relative guide, but they will give the reader a sense of what to expect of a coin graded at each level.

Subjective Grades
(commonly seen in sale catalogues)
Poor
Fair
About Good
Good
Good Plus
Very Good
About Fine
Fine
Fine Plus
About Very Fine
Very Fine
Very Fine Plus
About Extremely Fine
Extremely Fine
Extremely Fine Plus
Superb Extremely Fine
Mint State (FDC)

Aside from the technical aspects of grading, there are philosophical and practical considerations to weigh when evaluating grade. The number of ancient coins that survive in really spectacular grade is much smaller than the market for such specimens. Collectors have always been fond of well-preserved coins, but in recent years there has been an influx of new collectors who have been pre-conditioned by the modern coin market. They expect, and will settle for nothing less than, choice Extremely Fine (mint-like) specimens. What this inevitably leads to, is a collection of freshly cleaned and sparkling hoard coins rather than a thoughtful collection of ancient works of art. Grade becomes a substitute for beauty, and connoisseurship becomes unimportant. To some, this is justifiable, and they will not be dissuaded. It is more rewarding, however, to seek coins of true beauty, than to seek coins of the highest technical grade.

Having participated in countless auctions over the years, the author never ceases to be amazed at the process of selection exhibited by bidders. When four or five coins of the same type are offered in sequence, the one that inevitably brings the highest price is the first of the group, and this is usually the coin of the highest technical grade. It is also, in many cases, among the least artistic of the lot. What this suggests, is that collectors (and some dealers) are not really buying coins as works of art. Grade is relatively easy to judge, but connoisseurship takes more sensitivity, training and practice. Even though a dealer may fully understand the difference between grade and beauty, the present market (price aside) will probably absorb a "mint-state" example much faster than a beautiful VF. This drives the competition, and the decision, when it comes time to choose one specimen for stock. From an art lover's perspective, this seems unjust. But actually, it is a blessing. It lets art lovers pick from wonderful examples without fighting the grade mania of our age.

The beginning collector cannot expect to become a connoisseur overnight, but it helps to understand that grade is not *everything* in determining the desirability of an ancient coin. Illustrated below are photos of a few specimens that have been sold at auction in the past few years. All are exceptionally attractive coins, with lovely toning and patinas, yet their estimated values are quite reasonable. This is because their technical grade is only VF (more or less). Actually, coins of this grade are still buyable at these prices. They are, in this author's opinion, the best buy on the ancient coin market today.

Grade is important, make no mistake about it. It is particularly important in certain types of coins. The price differential between coins graded nice VF and EF in a signed Decadrachm or scarce Aureus may easily be a multiple of three or more. A similar upgrade with common Romaion (Byzantine) solidi would be very inexpensive. Is the differential worth the price? You be the judge!

Some VF coins of exceptional appeal

L. Procilius
AR Denarius, 80 BC
est. value $150

Aelius, AE
AD 136-138
Alexandria,
est. value $150

Bruttium,
282-203 BC
AE Sextans,
est. value $150

Justinian I, AD 527-565
AE 1/2 follis,
Antioch Mint,
estimated value $75

Severina
AD 270-275
AE Denarius,
est. value $100

Measuring and Weighing Ancient Coins

A coin can be measured in more ways than one might think. The most commonly encountered measurement is its diameter. Historically, the English have measured diameter in inches, the French and other Europeans in millimeters, and numismatists have over the years developed some unique systems of their own. Among these is the famous *Mionnet Scale*. Between 1807 and 1837, the acclaimed numismatist T.E. Mionnet produced a monumental 16-volume catalogue attempting to list all known Greek and Roman coins. Instead of measuring each coin precisely, Mionnet developed a scale with pre-established sizes numbered 1 through 19 (see facing page). This scale was used frequently by 19th and early 20th century numismatists, especially in describing Greek and Roman Provincial coins. Roman Imperial coins were normally described by denomination only, since the sizes of common denominations were fairly standard and well known. Another arbitrary system came into use by numismatists to describe various bronze coins of the Late Roman Empire for which the denomination is uncertain. These coins are classified as First, Second, Third or Fourth Brass or AE 1,2,3, 4 respectively. The AE 1 refers to coins over 25mm in diameter, AE 2 to coins between 25 and 21mm, AE 3 to coins between 21 and 17mm, and AE 4 to coins less than 17mm in diameter. Today, diameter is almost universally measured in millimeters and lacking a proper denomination, coins are referred to by the metal (AV=Gold, AR=Silver, AE=Bronze) and the diameter in millimeters, e.g. AE-22 for a bronze coin of 22 millimeters diameter.

With modern coins, measuring the diameter is a simple affair. But many ancient coins, by the nature of their production, are shaped in odd ways. How does one measure the diameter of an oblong coin? Remarkably, there is not a standard approach to this common problem. Cataloguers usually describe within the introduction to a work the method that they used to determine diameter of coins listed. Some record the widest part of the coin, others take an average of the measurements at the widest and narrowest points, still others record both readings. Since the diameter of ancient coins of the same type and denomination can—and usually does—vary significantly, the utility of a precise reading is questionable. Accuracy to the nearest millimeter is certainly adequate for most collector purposes.

The thickness of a coin is seldom recorded unless the cataloguer is doing so to make a particular point. Occasionally, a coin of a type with typically uniform module will appear struck on an unusually thick planchet. This might prompt a recording of the coin's thickness.

The accurate weight of a coin can in some cases be of greater importance than the diameter. Particularly in the case of coins struck in precious metals, the weight and purity was usually controlled very closely at the

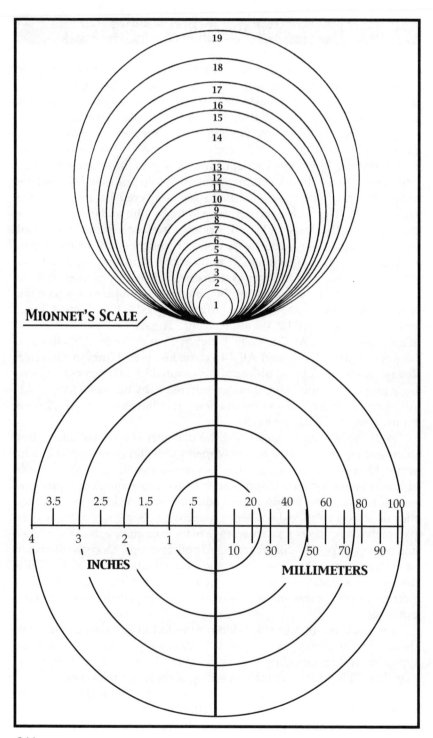

MIONNET'S SCALE

INCHES

MILLIMETERS

mint. Therefore, we know about what to expect for the weight of an Attic tetradrachm or a Roman denarius, etc. When the actual weight of a coin does not fall within reasonable proximity of the expected weight, there may be cause to suspect that the coin is not an authorized mint issue. The alternatives could be an ancient fourree (a precious metal coin with a base metal core) or a modern forgery. Having said that, there are several legitimate factors that can affect the weight of a perfectly genuine coin. Some coins were clipped around the edge in antiquity, by unscrupulous money changers to remove precious metal. The degree of wear on a coin can have a dramatic effect on its weight. The circumstances of a coin's preservation can also affect weight. Some coins lose metal (and weight) through various forms of corrosion while in the earth. Cross sectional analysis has shown that a high percentage of ancient coins suffer a loss of internal density over time. All of these possibilities should be considered when questioning the underweight condition of a coin. In other words, don't jump to a hasty conclusion just because a specimen is under normal weight for its type. This is simply one piece of data to be evaluated, not in itself a basis for authentication or condemnation.

There are basically two types of scales that can be used to weigh coins. The old standard balance scale, with a good set of weights, is still an accurate and inexpensive tool. It is possible to buy a small portable version of the balance scale and set it up wherever one might find a need. Modern digital scales are the ultimate in convenience, and have become much less expensive than in the past. Some models capable of measurement accuracy to .01 gram are advertised for less than $100. For the collector who is really into metalurgy, American Numismatic Society Numismatic Notes and Monographs # 154, *Metrological Tables*, by Earle R. Caley, provides handy conversion charts between grains, grams, pennyweight, scruples, troy ounces and carats.

A more sophisticated, and somewhat more difficult, measurement is that of a coin's specific gravity. This is the measurement of a coin's density compared to that of water. The specific gravity of gold is 19.3 and silver is 10.55. Therefore, one can determine the purity of a coin's metal and compare it to a known standard for the type being measured. With a coin that is not relatively pure gold or silver, it is important to know in advance what the expected specific gravity should be, because debased coins are naturally going to produce a specific gravity of less than that for pure metal. One can determine the amount of debasement in a particular type from the measurement of several like specimens, or from previously published statistical information in numismatic journals and studies. A description of the process, and a diagram of a simple weighing device, is included in *Classical Deception* (p. 102) and in an article by Dr. Charles E. Weber in *The Celator* (Dec. 1998).

Die Studies

As we explained in the earlier section about how ancient coins were made, most were hand struck from carved dies. Due to the pressures involved in manufacturing coins, dies often broke or simply wore out and needed to be replaced. The anvil die, which was in a fixed position, normally outlasted several punch dies. When a punch die was removed from service and a new punch die was used in combination with the existing anvil die, a situation arose whereby two different punch die varieties share a common anvil die image. Of course the same condition worked in reverse, except less frequently.

Die pairing can also be a product of internal mint control procedures. In antiquity, dies were strictly controlled at the mint, with each die being carefully accounted for to prevent the theft of dies and counterfeiting of coins. At the end of a shift, mint workers would turn their dies in to the mintmaster, who would log and secure them until the next work period. In some cases, obverse and reverse dies were apparently stored as pairs, and we see evidence of long production runs from a limited number of die sets. In other cases, the obverse dies seem to have been stored together in one box and the reverse dies together in another box. The issuing of dies to workers at the start of each work period would in that case have resulted in a random pairing. This would not affect the total number of coins produced, but it would greatly increase the incidence of obverse/reverse die links. Even so, a detailed study of a very large sample group can lead to fascinating conclusions.

The study of die links and sequence of issue can provide very useful information to the historian. Once the chronology of a series is properly organized, changes in denomination, weight or purity may shed important light on the economic conditions of that time. This firmly grounded scientific data, in a discipline often reliant on subjective reports, is very useful and dependable. Although tedious to develop and even more tedious to analyze, die studies are a powerful research tool.

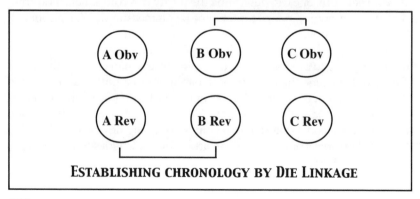

ESTABLISHING CHRONOLOGY BY DIE LINKAGE

ANCIENT COINS AS WORKS OF ART
Reflections of Time and Place

I n the briefest of terms, art on coinage tends to reflect a conservative view of society in the place and time it was struck. Archaic Greek art is characterized by a stiffness and frontal approach that to the modern eye appears crude and stylized. Proportions are often irregular and perspective is either lacking or flawed. Their world was not one of spontaneous action or progressive thinking.

Aside from a few transitional pieces, the advent of the Classical Period with its wonderfully sculptural images was quite abrupt. The defeat of Persia lifted the entire psyche of the Greek people and the mid fifth century is marked by spectacular success in all of the arts. It was the golden age of Pericles. During this time the Parthenon was finished, and the great statues of Olympia and Athens were sculpted by Pheidias. Greek coinage of the Classical Period, especially from Sicily and Magna Graecia (southern Italy), dramatically reflects this blossoming artistic achievement.

A school of master engravers, who worked on commission for competing patrons, left us not only their remarkable images but also their names. Notwithstanding two thousand years of subsequent effort, no die engravers have ever exceeded their virtuosity. The names Kimon and Euainetos, Myron and Herakeidas, Eukleidas, Eumenes, Sosion and Phrygillos still command the respect of all who gaze upon their work. Many books have been written about the masterpieces of Greek numismatic art, and there can be no argument that these artists are unparalleled. But, how many of us will ever own one of the masterpieces? Fortunately, there is more than enough beauty in the rest of the series to satisfy most of us. However, if we are going to collect these coins as works of art we should develop some appreciation for what it is that makes them different from each other or special artistically.

Catana, Sicily
ca. 410 BC
signed by
Euainetos

The Hellenistic Period is characterized by a shift from idealism to realism. Figures become more lithe and proportions are less compact. Sculptural details are much softer overall. The focus of Hellenistic art is on sensual emotion rather than idealization.

There are some interesting examples of coinage struck during the period of transition from Classical to Hellenistic. One of these is the series of silver staters struck by the Opuntians from Lokris in Central Greece. The reverse of these coins, which were issued from 369 to 338 BC, depicts a lunging warrior clad only with helmet and shield. This figure is the legendary Ajax, son of Oileus, who figured prominently in Homer's Iliad.

To digress for a moment, this is not the Ajax who mourned the death of his friend Achilles, but another, called Ajax the Lesser (lesser in size, that is). In some ways, this Ajax was even more important than the famous one. During the sack of Troy, he burst into the sanctuary of Athena and defiled Cassandra (a priestess, and daughter of King Priam) at the sanctuary altar. According to Homer, Athena was so enraged by this atrocity that she enlisted the help of her brother Poseidon in wreaking havoc on the Greek fleet as it sailed off in victory. The resulting storm sent Odysseus wandering for another ten years and provided good action for a sequel to Homer's story. Ajax was killed by a thunderbolt as he taunted the gods.

Canon of
Polycleitus

Canon of
Lysippus

Back to Lokris—early issues of the Lokrian stater depict Ajax as a stocky and muscular figure with the classical proportions that art historians refer to as the "Canon of Polycleitus." This canon was a very carefully defined set of measurements which all artists adhered to. Later issues of the same coin depict Ajax as a more sinewy and graceful figure with Hellenistic proportions following the "Canon of Lysippus." Lysippus was the successor to Polycleitus in fame and fortune and he was primarily responsible for the movement from Classicism to Hellenism as far as artistic style is concerned. Alexander the Great would allow no artist but Lysippus to carve his likeness in stone.

The point of this illustration is that ancient coins tend to reflect the changes in art that occurred over time. To appreciate coins as works of art one does not need to study the work of Sicilian engravers. The place to start is with books about ancient art in general. The same changes that occur in sculpture and vase painting, are traceable in coinage of corresponding periods. This is also true of Roman art and the style of representations on Roman coins. As cultural changes are reflected in monumental sculpture, we find the same changes taking place in numismatic portraiture. By examining the coins of the Greeks, Romans or any other culture which left behind images, we can observe changes that may not be so obvious in the written histories of these people. What we see on the coins is exactly what the artists themselves left us.

A Question of Style

The word *style* is a poorly understood and widely misused term in the field of ancient numismatics. It appears frequently in sale catalogues as a part of the subjective grade. That is, a coin will be described as "great style" or even worse, "best style." This is a meaningless description, because it suggests that style is a measurable feature of the coin's overall appearance.

Style is simply the manner of representation of any subject. It is a function of time and place, and it reflects the artist's view of his world. A style may be creative, or imitative; sculptural or crude; realistic or barbarous—but it cannot be "great" unless we specify that it is great in the opinion of the commentator. Then the term simply means that one person likes this style better than some other style. Since style is basically a reflection of taste, these comments do not belong in a general description of any form of art, including an ancient coin. The thought that cataloguers are most often trying to convey, is that the *execution* of a die has merit. If the celator applied his tools in a competent and skilled manner, regardless of style, the result of his work is a product of greater artistic appeal. This requires an aesthetic judgement that considers whether the essence of the subject has been adequately conveyed. This all has to do with the design of the coin and the skill of the artist engraving that design onto the die—not with the style. The style of art on coins has varied over the many centuries that coins have been struck, just as other forms of art have changed.

Within Greek numismatic art, we find three major categories which may be regarded as styles: Archaic, Classical and Hellenistic. Archaic art is characterized by rigid angular designs, especially of the human body where muscles are pronounced and proportions are unrealistic. A common feature seen on archaic coins is an almond shape to the eye that is drawn frontally, rather than in perspective. Classical art is very sculptural by comparison. It has more of a three-dimensional look. Features are rounded and proportions are more realistic. Perspective, rather than being ignored, is a point of great concern. The eye is drawn in profile, and experimen-

Archaic Greek Tetradrachm from Scione

Classical Greek Decadrachm from Syracuse

tation with facing heads and bodies in motion is common. During the Classical Period, people were idealized and made to look like gods. The Hellenistic Period reflects an opposing view, where gods were made to look like people. Human representations are more relaxed or fluid, and proportions are less formal. The idealism of the Classical age gives way to a more practical and realistic world view. Portraiture develops into a popular and sophisticated form of art, with a focus on accurate portrayal.

Roman numismatic art is quite different from that of the Greeks. The mindset of Roman citizens was perfectly suited to the veristic (truthful) representation of their own physical features. Portraiture, therefore, is one of the primary components of Roman art. First century portraits are so veristic, in fact, that warts, bumps, goiters and defects of every kind are found on the portraits of emperors. This vanity began to fade in the late second century, as more spiritual philosophies took hold. By the middle of the third century, little effort was made to portray the emperor in anything close to a realistic fashion. Many of the portraits produced during this period look so much alike that, without inscriptions, the coins would be difficult to identify. Later Roman coinage, with rare exceptions, is devoid of any recognizable portraiture. True, we sometimes can tell one coin from the other by virtue of the emperor's image, but we should not believe that they really looked like that.

Romaion art is very spiritual. Portraits of the emperors are intended only to give the essence of the ruler's authority, not to emphasize his personal presence in any way. The low relief of Late

Hellenistic Greek tetradrachm
from Pergamum

1st century Roman sestertius
of Vespasian

4th century Roman follis
of Maximinus II

Romaion follis
of Justinian I

250

Roman and Romaion coins in general is a further extension of this philosophy of not bringing attention to the mortal aspects of the emperor. Romaion art has a style of its own. Although often thought of as crude, this is not really the case. The art on Romaion coins is purposeful, not simply a reflection of unskilled artists. Contemporary ivory sculpture provides proof that the artists of that day were skilled in sculptural art, they simply chose not to design coins in this manner.

Illustrated below are a few examples of good execution and poor execution within a particular style of coinage. Which do you prefer?

Athens
AR - Tetradrachm
ca. 400 BC

Larissa
AR - Drachm
ca. 350 BC
(enlarged)

Diocletian
AE - Follis
ca. AD 300

251

CONCLUSION
A Boatload of Crusoes

We prefaced this book with an observation by David Sear that ancient coin collectors suffer from the "Robinson Crusoe Syndrome." It has been our objective throughout to leave footprints in the sand, so that the collector, either as a beginner or one that for too long has been isolated, can more easily find their way to enjoyment of the hobby. We have not intended this to be a comprehensive study in any respect. To do so, and still touch on the myriad aspects of ancient coin collecting, would require more than a lifetime effort.

Fortunately, the isolation of the past is fading. Where antiquarians once walked alone, we now find excellent company. This is all the more remarkable in light of the dwindling numbers of new enthusiasts, but it clearly reflects the impact of our new age. Communication is becoming so fast and easy, and information is disseminated at such a rapid pace, that we are almost faced with the opposite problem. We have access to so much information today that we are unable to digest it all. This is not really a disadvantage to the collector whose focus is in a well-defined area. We can follow more sales, deal in a broader market, seek information from major libraries, bounce our ideas off more collectors, and actually publish our results (even as amateurs) in a variety of places. It is truly a collector's world. The key to greater success in this environment is *specialization*. As generalists, we can only scratch the surface of what is possible. By introducing the hobby on a very broad but superficial plane, our intention has been to make specialization that much easier.

This book is followed by a series of complementary monographs dealing with each of the main collecting areas defined herein: Greek Coins, Roman Coins, Roman Provincial Coins, Romaion Coins and Non-Classical Coins of the Ancient World. Again, these are not definitive references, but rather provide a continuing set of footprints that the collector can follow toward better understanding of the nature of various collecting specialties. It is not nearly as important to know everything about a field as it is to know where to find everything that you need in that field.

We hope that you will enjoy collecting ancient coins, that your path will be a smooth one, and that you will have wonderful experiences along the way. As your interests become more clear, and your expertise develops, we hope that you will share that learning with other collectors through articles, talks, round-table discussions, exhibits and just friendly chats. The fraternity of ancient coin collectors has always been recognized as a group of some stature in the collecting world. Simply by expressing an interest in antiquity, and demonstrating a willingness to learn about different cultures, you have become a member.

APPENDIX

Our intention has been to make this book a handy reference that the collector will want to keep close by and consult often. Therefore, the material has been organized in a way that lends itself to "snapshot" extraction. Wherever possible, charts have been used to condense information and make it easier to reference. The tables in this appendix are also presented for the purpose of quick consultation.

Common Abbreviations

Adv	Advancing
AD	Anno Domini (year of our Lord)
AE	Bronze or copper
ANA	American Numismatic Association
ANS	American Numismatic Society
Ant	Antoninianus
AR	Silver
Aul	SNG Von Aulock
AV	Gold
AVF	About Very Fine, same for AVG, AF, AEF etc.
B	Born
BC	Before Christ
BCE	Before Common Era
BMC	*British Museum Catalogue*
BMCRE	*British Museum - Coins of the Roman Empire*
BN	Billon
C	Cohen, *Monnaies Sous L'Empire Romain*
Ca	Circa = about
CE	Common Era
Cf	Confer = compar
Ch	Choice
C/M	Countermark
Coll	Collection
Cop	SNG Copenhagen
Corr	Corroded or corrosion
Cr	Crawford
Cuir	Cuirassed
D	Died
Den	Denarius
Diad	Diademed
DOC	*Dumbarton Oaks Catalogue*
DR	Draped
EF	Extremely Fine
EL	Electrum

Enc	Encrustation
Et al	et alii = and others
Ex	Exergue; also ex: as formerly belonging to ....
F	Fine
FDC	Fleur-de-coin (mint state)
Ff	And pages following
Fig	Figure
G	Good
Gm	Grams
Hd	Head
Hld	Holding
L	Left
Laur	Laureate
Lev	SNG Levante
Lt	Light
Mm	Millimeters
MWI	Mitchiner, World of Islam
NC	*Numismatic Chronicle*
Obv	Obverse
OC	Off Center
P	Poor
Pb	Lead
Pl	Plate
Por	Porosity; or Price on request
R	Right
R1-R5	Rarity 1 to Rarity 5, with 5 being the highest degree
Rad	Radiate
Rev	Reverse
RIC	Mattingly et. al., *Roman Imperial Coinage*
RSC	Seaby, *Roman Silver Coinage*
SB	Sear, David R. *Byzantine Coins and Their Values.*
Scr	Scratch
SG	Sear, David R. *Greek Coins and Their Values.*
SGI	Sear, David R. *Greek Imperial Coins and Their Values*
SNG	Sylloge Nummorum Graecorum
SR	Sear, David R. *Roman Coins and Their Values*
SRM	Sear, David R. *Roman Coins and Their Values*, Millennium Edition
S/S	Spengler/Sayles, *Turkoman Figural Bronze Coins ...*
SNR	*Swiss Numismatic Review*
Std	Seated
Stg	Standing
Sup	Superb
Supp	Supplement
Syd	Sydenham, *Coinage of the Roman Republic*
T/V	Thurlow/Vecchi, *Italian Cast Coinage*
Var	Variety
VG	Very Good
VF	Very Fine

GLOSSARY

The words listed here are terms that one might encounter in this book or find used in typical auction or sale catalogues featuring ancient coins:

Accession: Reference to a ruler having attained the position.

Acropolis: High city, usually a citadel or temple site.

Acrostolium: Decorative extension on the prow of a ship.

Adlocutio: Emperor addressing the troops.

Adventus: The arrival of the emperor.

Aedicula: Small shrine containing a cult statue.

Aegis: Goatskin, bearing the image of Medusa, worn over the chest or arm as a form of protection.

Agonistic: Pertaining to athletic competitions.

Alkidemos: Protector of the people.

Amphora: Two-handled jug used to store and transport wine.

Ampyx: Woman's headband tied above the forehead.

Androsphinx: Sphinx with a male bust.

Anepigraphic: No inscription, as on the obverse of a coin.

Anguipede: A fantastic creature with snake-like legs.

Ankh: Circle with a cross below, meaning "life".

Anonymous: Not bearing the identifying mark of any magistrate or ruler.

Antiquarian: One who studies or deals in objects from ancient times.

Aplustre: The upward curved stern of a ship (also aphlastron).

Aqueduct: Raised channel used to carry water.

Aquila: An eagle, often appearing on Roman standards.

Archaic: Very early, e.g. the earliest period of Greek art.

Archiereus: Head priest.

Argentum: Silver. Abbreviated AR.

Argenteus: Silver coin of 1/96 lb. introduced under the tetrarchy.

Arete: Greek personification of virtue or excellence.

Armeniacus: Title awarded for victory over the Armenians.

Asiarches: Ruler of Asia.

Aspergillum: Vessel for sprinkling water at religious ceremonies.

Astragalos: Knuckle bone of an animal, used like dice.

Atargatis: Goddess worshipped in Syria.

Attis: Phrygian Great Mother goddess.

Attribute: Associated element which helps to identify a figure.

Attribution: Interpreting and recording the details of a coin's legends and symbols, and placing it in the proper context.

Augur: Roman priest specializing in divination (predictions).

Autokrator: Sole ruler, (Imperator) title on Roman provincial coins.

Autonomous: Independent, not under another's rule.

Baal: Semitic deity sometimes equivalent to Zeus.

Baetyl: Stone worshipped as divine, mainly in Eastern cultures.

Banker's Mark: Small punch mark used to test a coin.

Bare: Without ornamentation, as in bareheaded (no crown).

Belos: Minor river god.

Bibliophile: Book lover (collector).

Biga: Chariot drawn by two animals.

Bilingual: In two languages, usually pertaining to coin inscriptions.

Billon: Base metal and precious metal mixture.

Bi-Metallic: Monetary system of two metals, as in gold and silver coins.

Bipennis: Double headed axe.

Bourse: The sales floor of a coin show or convention.

Boustrophedon: Inscription turning back on itself as an ox plowing.

Bracteate: Thin coin, struck on only one face.

Brockage: Mis-struck coin; same design on both sides, one incuse.

Bucephalus: The name of Alexander's favorite horse.

Bucranium: The horned head or skull of a Bull.

Bust: Portrait of a person which includes the shoulders.

Cachet: Personal mark affixed by a collector, like a countermark.

Caduceus: Staff of Hermes, often winged or wound with two snakes.

Caesar: Title bestowed on the heir to the Roman throne.

Caliga: Boot worn by soldiers, after which Caligula was nicknamed.

Caritas: Affection or high esteem.

Caryatid: Column carved in the shape of a female figure.

Celator: Artist who carved dies for the striking of coins.

Censor: Roman official responsible for the census and public contracts.

Centaur: Mythological creature, half man, half horse.

Cestus: Boxer's glove.

Chimaera: Monster killed by Bellerophon and Pegasus.

Chiton: A Greek common outer garment similar to the Roman tunic.

Chlamys: Greek short cloak worn by the military, Latin paludamentum.

Christogram: A monogram of superimposed letters X-P = "Christ"

Cippus: Boundary pillar.

Cista Mystica: Basket containing a snake, used in Dionysiac rituals.

Cistophorus: Coin issued in Roman Asia with Cista Mystica motif.

Cithara: Greek lyre.

Clio: The muse of history.

Clipping: Removal of precious metal from a coin's edge.

Consul: Annual appointment as chief magistrate, shared between two.

Contorniate: Large Roman coin-like medallion.

Cornucopiae: Horn of plenty, symbol of abundance.

Cornuacopiae: Plural of cornucopiae

Countermark: Small punch mark used by the mint to re-tariff a coin.

Cruciger: Bearing a cross.

Curule Chair: Seat of honor reserved for the highest Roman officials.
Daemon: Spirit or minor deity.
Damnatio Memoriae: The condemnation of one's memory.
Dea: Feminine of Deus, a goddess.
Debasement: Lowering a coin's value by reducing weight or purity.
Demos: Personification of the governing political body or the people.
Denomination: Assigned value of a particular coin.
Devictus: Conquered.
Dextrarum Iunctio: Hands clasped as in a scene of marriage or concord.
Diadem: Royal headdress of eastern origin, often made of stringed pearls.
Die: Engraved stamp used to transfer an image to a coin.
Die-axis: Relative position of the obverse to reverse die during striking.
Die Link: Two coins whose obverses or reverses share a common die.
Discobolus: Discus thrower.
Distaff: Yarn spinner's staff.
Divus: Divine, as Deus = a god. Feminine Diva.
Double Strike: Error caused by successive blows on the same planchet.
Duovir: Governing body of two men.
Drachm: The basic unit of coinage at many Greek cities.
Echidna: Serpent tailed female monster, mother of the Lernian Hydra and the Nemean Lion.
Electrotype: A method for making reproductions of coins.
Electrum: Alloy of gold and silver.
Eleutheria: Greek personification of freedom.
Epigraphy: Inscriptions or deciphering of inscriptions.
Etrog: Citron fruit.
Exagium: A standard weight used for testing the weight of coins.
Exergue: Space at the bottom of a coin's image, often below a baseline.
Fasces: Wooden rods tied in a bundle and carried by Lictors.
Field: Part of the coin's surface not occupied by the main design.
Fillet: A plain ribbon or band, used sometimes as a tie or decoration.
Flan: Blank piece of metal upon which a coin is struck (planchet).
Fleur de Coin: FDC, the flower of coinage, mint condition.
Fourrée: Plated coin with a copper core; contemporary counterfeit.
Fulmen: Thunderbolt.
Funeral Pyre: Place of cremation.
Genius: Spirit (daemon), as Genio Populi = Spirit of the People
Germanicus: Title awarded for victory over the Germans.
Graces: Three minor goddesses or personifications of beauty and charm.
Graffito: Writing scratched on a coin, plural is graffiti.
Griffin: Monster, half lion, half eagle.
Hadad: Syrian god, consort of Atargatis.
Hammered: Struck by hand with a hammer.
Harpa: Short sword of Perseus with a hooked blade.

Hasta: Roman spear.

Hastati: Armored spear-bearing troops in the Roman front line.

Head: Portrait of a person which does not include the shoulders.

Hemi - -: Half. As in hemidrachm or half drachm.

Himation: Greek outer cloak, Latin pallium.

Hippocamp: Sea creature, half horse and half fish.

Hoard: Group of coins found together, usually buried for safekeeping.

Humanism: The Renaissance movement to study classical culture.

Imperator: Title of acclaim for victories achieved, also used as a praenomen (first name) by emperors from the later 1st century on.

Imperatorial: Coins issued by Roman generals in the late Republic.

Incuse: Design which is recessed into the surface of a coin.

Inscription: The legend, or words on a coin.

Intaglio: Engraved into the surface (negative) as in a coin die.

Interregnum: Period between the end of an authority's reign and the accession of a successor.

Invictus: Unconquered.

Jugate: Side by side, as with heads superimposed one upon the other.

Kalathos: Basket shaped like a vase.

Kandys: Outer robe of a Persian king.

Kantharos: Greek cup with long side handles.

Kausia: Soft flat hat, usually Macedonian or Persian.

Kerberos: Three headed dog which guarded the entrance to Hades.

Kharosthi: A script of Western India, seen on Indo-Scythian coins.

Kithara: Ancient Greek lyre.

Koinoboulion: Personification of the Common Council.

Krater: Large bowl used to mix wine with water.

Kylix: Flat drinking bowl.

Labarum: Roman military standard or ensign.

Lagabolon: A short curved stick used by shepherds or hunters.

Laureate: Crowned with a wreath made from leaves of laurel.

Lares: Deities of private homes and agricultural land.

Lebes: Cauldron, usually supported on a tripod.

Legati: Senior officers in the Roman army, appointed by the Senate.

Legend: Inscription or words on a coin.

Legion: A division of the Roman army numbering about 4,200 men.

Lictor: Bodyguard or police force attending a magistrate.

Limes: Military frontier roadway.

Lituus: An augur's wand.

Loupe: A small magnifying glass.

Lulav: Palm branch used in the Jewish Feast of the Tabernacle.

Lyre: Stringed musical instrument with a rounded sound box.

Macellum: Roman market building.

Maenad: Female companion of Dionysos.

258

Manus Dei: The hand of God.

Mappa: Cloth napkin used to start races, a consular attribute.

Mater: Mother.

Medusa: One of the gorgons, killed by Perseus.

Melqarth: Phoenician equivalent of Herakles.

Mint: Workplace where money was made.

Mint-mark: Letters indicating the mint at which a coin was struck.

Modius: Roman grain measure holding about two gallons.

Module: Diameter of a coin.

Moneyer: Individual recognized by the ruling power as having authority to strike coins for circulation as legal exchange.

Monogram: A shorthand form of name composed of linked letters.

Mule: Coin from the striking of two dies that are not related.

Mural Crown: Turreted headdress worn by city goddesses and Cybele.

Murex: Shellfish used to produce purple die.

Myriad: Greek, literally meaning 10,000.

Nikephoros: Depiction of a god holding Nike (Victory).

Nimbus: An aureole or halo surrounding the head or body of a deity.

Obverse: "Head" side of a coin, usually with a portrait or main figure.

Octastyle: Building with eight columns visible.

Occultation: Passing of one heavenly body out of sight behind another.

Officina: Specific mint workshop.

Oikstes: City founder.

Oinochoe: Pouring cup for wine.

Omphalos: Stone at Delphi which marked the center of the earth.

Orichalcum: Brass alloy of 80% copper and 20% zinc.

Overstrike: A coin struck over a previously struck coin.

Palladium: Cult statue of Athena at Troy.

Pallium: Greek style cloak.

Paludamentum: Military cloak.

Pantheon: All of the gods of a people.

Parthicus: Title awarded for victory over the Parthians.

Patera: Flat bowl used for drink and sacrifice.

Pater Patriae: "Father of His Country"

Patina: Oxidation on a coin's surface, sometimes hard and shiny.

Pegasos: Winged horse, born from the blood of Medusa.

Penates: Gods of the inner household.

Peplos: Woman's robe which gathers in folds.

Personification: Portrayal of an abstract concept, like virtue or fidelity, in the form of a human.

Perspective: View where lines converge on a single vanishing point.

Petasos: Travelling hat, often seen on Hermes (Mercury).

Pharos: Lighthouse.

Phiale: Same as Patera.

Phoenix: Mythical bird that died in flames and was reborn from its own ashes.

Phrygian Cap: A soft pointed cap which folds at the peak.

Pilos: Felt cone-shaped cap, often worn by the Dioskuri.

Planchet: Blank piece of metal, ready for stamping as a coin (flan).

Polytheist: Believing in more than one god, as opposed to monotheist.

Pontifex Maximus: Chief priest and judge of religious questions.

Porosity: Spongelike surface condition.

Praetor: A Roman magistrate second in rank to a Consul.

Prefect: A Roman commander of allied troops.

Princeps: Leader.

Privy Marks: Secret markings used for mint control purposes.

Proconsul: Officer assigned to govern a province or command an army.

Propugnator: Defender.

Protesilaos: First Greek killed at Troy.

Provenance: Place of origin.

Pulvinar: A seat upon which offerings to the gods were placed.

Quadriga: Chariot pulled by four animals.

Quaestor: Junior magistrate in charge of financial affairs.

Quies: Rest.

Radiate: Wearing a crown with eminating points or spikes.

Rector Orbis: Ruler of the world.

Redux: Return. Also, rarely as Reditus.

Regina: Queen.

Regnal Dates: A dating system which starts with the first year of a ruler's accession and continues only as long as the reign.

Restitutor: Restorer.

Retrograde: Letters or numerals reading right to left.

Reverse: "Tail" side of a coin, opposite of obverse.

Rex: King

Romaioi: "Roman(s)" in the Greek language.

Romaion: "Of the Romans."

Roman Empire: Political structure of Rome from 27 BC to 476 AD.

Roman Imperatorial: Latter days of the Roman Republic, during which the titles Imperator and dictator were bestowed on powerful leaders.

Roman Republic: Political structure of Rome from 509 BC to 27 BC, although coins were not issued until ca. 289 BC.

Rostrum: Beaklike prow of a ship used for ramming. A speaking platform in the Roman Forum was called the Rostrum.

Sacer: Sacred.

Sakkos: Greek hair net.

Satyr: Male companion of Bacchus with horse's legs and tail.

Scyphate: Inappropriate term for concave Romaion (Byzantine) coins.

Scylla: Sea monster residing in the straits of Messina.

Semissis: Gold coin equal to 1/2 solidus, introduced by Constantine I.

Sibyl: Priestess with powers of prophesy.

Silphium: Extinct medicinal plant .

Simpulum: Ladle used ceremonially by the Roman pontifex.

Sistrum: Rattle used in the worship of Isis.

Solidus: Gold coin equal to 1/72 pound, introduced by Constantine I.

Sphendone: Decorated part of a hair band.

Sphinx: Winged creature with the body of a lion and head of a woman.

Spintria: A class of tessera bearing erotic scenes.

S.P.Q.R.: Senatus Populusque Romanus = The Roman Senate and People.

Stater: Principal denomination of certain Greek cities.

Stephane: Woman's diadem or crown.

Strigil: Curved stick used by athletes to remove oil from the body.

Sybil: Female prophet.

Syrinx: Musical pipe of Pan.

Talent: Greek monetary unit equal to 6,000 drachms.

Taras: Son of Poseidon, founder of Tarentum.

Tempus: Time, as in Temporum Felicitas = Happy Times.

Tesserae: A class of tokens, counters, etc. which are often coin-like.

Tiara: Distinctive headdress of the type worn by Armenian kings.

Triga: Chariot drawn by three animals.

Tainia: Flat ribbon worn in the hair, sometimes as a sign of distinction.

Thyrsus: Staff of Dionysos/Bacchus surmounted by a pine cone or bunch of ivy leaves.

Titular: Pertaining to the titles inscribed on a coin.

Tooling: Enhancement of features on a coin by use of mechanical devices.

Tranquillitas: Tranquility.

Tres Viri: Three magistrates that managed affairs of the Roman mint.

Tribunicia Potestas: Tribune of the People, charged with protecting the rights of the lower classes.

Triga: A three-horse chariot.

Trident: A fishing spear with three prongs.

Trireme: A warship with three banks of oars.

Triskeles: A circular device with three human legs joined at the center.

Trophy: Arms of an enemy displayed on a staff as a monument.

Type: Main design feature of a coin that distinguishes it from others.

Tyrant: In Greek, a person who rules without constitutional legitimacy.

Uniface: Coins struck on only one face.

Urbs: City.

Usurper: One who seizes power without legal right or authority.

Verdigris: A Green crust of copper sulfate or copper chloride.

Wappenmünzen: Modern name given to early Athenian silver coins.

Translation of Numismatic Terms

Most sale catalogues and monographs produced these days are designed to appeal to the English speaking market, since English is the most commonly spoken language in the Western World. However, the serious numismatist will undoubtedly encounter offerings and references in other languages. Some of the more familiar terms are listed below in the English form, with German and French equivalents. Individuals with access to the Internet will find free language translation programs that help tremendously. Also of great help is the Special Dictionary supplement to Henri Cohen's *Monnaies Sous L'Empire Romain*, which lists a multitude of words and phrases in six languages.

ENGLISH	GERMAN	FRENCH
above	oben	au dessus
advancing	gehend	allant
alone	allein	seul
altar	Altar	autel
anchor	Anker	ancre
animal	Tier	animal
arms	Waffen	armes
around	herum, rings umher	l'entour, autour
arrow	Pfeil	flèche
bare	nacte	nu
bearded	bärtig	barbu
bee	Biene	abeille
before	vor	avant
behind	hinter	derrière
below	unten	au dessous
between	zwischen	entre
bird	Vogel	oiseau
bow	Bogen	arc
boy	Knabe	garçon
branch	Zweig	branche
bridge	Brücke	pont
bridled	gezäumt	bridé

ENGLISH	GERMAN	FRENCH
bucranium	Ochsenkoph	bucrane
captive	Gefangener	captif
cast	gegossen	coulé
chest	Koffer	coffre
circle	Kreis	cercle
closed	geschlossen	fermé
coarse	grob	grossier
cock	Hahn	coq
conjoined	zusammengeschlossen	accolé
cornucopiae	Füllhorn	corne d'abondance
countermark	Gegenstempel	contremarque
covered	bedeckt	couvert
crescent	Halbmond	croissant
cross	Kreuz	croix
cuirassed	geharnischte	cuirassé
dagger	Messer	couteau
deified	vergöttert	divinisé
diademed	diademierte	diademé
die	Münzstempel	coin
dog	Hund	chien
draped	drapierte	drapé
eagle	Adler	aigle
earth	Erde	terre
edge	Rand	bord
emperor	Kaiser	empereur
face to face	einander ansehend	affronté
facing	gegenüber	en face
field	Feld	champ
fine	schön	beau
fish	Fisch	poisson
flower	Blume	fleur
forgery	Fälschung	falsification
fourree	gefüttert	défourré
galley	Galeere	galère

ENGLISH	GERMAN	FRENCH
giving	gebend	donnant
globe	Kugel	globe
goddess	Göttin	déesse
hair	Haare	cheveux
helmeted	behelmte	casqué
hippocamp	Seepferd	cheval marin
horned	gehörnte	cornuto
horse	Pferd	cheval
incuse	vertieft	en creux
ivy	Eppich	ache
king	König	roi
laureate	belorbeerte	lauré
last	letzer	dernier
left	links	gauche
lion	Löwe	lion
mint	Münzstätte	atelier monétaire
moon	Mond	lune
nearly	beinahe	peu près, presque
neck	Hals	col
nothing	nichts	rien
oak	Eiche	chêne
other	anderer	autre
owl	Eule	chouette
ox	Ochs	boeuf
partly nude	halbnackt	demi nu
peacock	Pfau	paon
pig	Schwein	cochon
plant	Pflanze	plante
plow	Pflug	charrue
purse	Geldbeutel	bourse
quadriga	Viergespann	quadrige
quiver	Köcher	carquois
radiate	mit Strahlenkrone	radié
raised	erhoben	élevé

ENGLISH	GERMAN	FRENCH
rare	selten	rare
raven	Rabe	corbeau
rider	Reiter	cavalier
right	rechts	droite
river god	Flussgott	divinité de fleuve
running	laufend	courant
sacrificing	opfernd	sacrifiant
scales	Waage	balance
seated	sitzend	assis
serpent	Schlange	serpent
shield	Schild	bouclier
ship	Schiff	bateau
short	kurz	court
shrine	kleiner Tempel	aedicule
silver	Silber	argent
soldier	Soldat	soldat
square	viereckig	carré
stag	Hirsch	cerf
staff	Stab, Stäbchen	bâton, baguette
standard	Banner,	bannière, enseigne
star	Feldzeichen	astre, étoile
sun	Sonne	soleil
torch	Fackel	flambeau
tree	Baum	arbre
uninscribed	ohne Schrift	anépigraphe
veiled	verschleierte	voilé
winged	geflügelt	ailé
with	mit	avec
without	ausserhalb	dehors
woman	Frau	femme
wreath	Kranz	couronne
year	J ahr	année
zodiacal	Tierkreis	zodiacal

Greek Pronunciation Guide

One problem that all beginning, and many longtime, collectors of ancient coins have is the pronunciation of words that are foreign to the modern ear. We include here a guide to the generally accepted English pronunciation of a few commonly heard and often abused Greek terms. This is not a guide to pronunciation in the ancient tongue, for that see Michael Marotta's article "The voice of classical Greek" (*The Celator,* Vol 10, No. 1, January, 1996). Rather, it is a very short guide to pronunciation of terms as you might expect to hear them in the fraternity and the marketplace. Within the phonetic equivalents, the letter O standing alone or followed by an S is pronounced long as in "ocean". When followed by another consonant it is short as in "pod". AI is pronounced with the A silent and the I long, as in "eye". Remember, being a product of convention rather than scientific study, these pronunciations are often corruptions of the technical or proper academic version that one would learn in a classical language course.

Aitolia	EYE-TOW-**LEE**-A
Achaia	AH-**KAI**-A
Akanthos	A-**KAN**-THOS
Akarnania	AH-KAR-**NANE**-EE-A
Akragas	AH-**KRA**-GAS
Antigonos	AN-**TIG**-OH-NOS
Apollonia	AP-O-**LOAN**-EE-A
Arkadian	ARE-**KAY**-DIAN
Astarte	AH-**STAR**-TAY
Basilios	BAH-**SIL**-EE-OS
Boeotia	BEE-**OH**-SHUH
Cherronesos	SHARE-O-**NEE**-SOS
Cilicia	SIH-**LIH**-SEEA or KEY-**LI**-KEEA
Corcyra	KORE-**KEE**-RA
Cyclades	KEE-**KLOD**-EES
Dikaia	DEE-**KAI**-A
Dodona	DOE-**DOAN**-A
Drachm	**DRAM**
Eleusis	EE-**LEV**-SIS
Epidamnos	EPP-EE-**DOM**-NOS
Eretria	AIR-EE-**TREE**-A
Euainetos	YOU-**AIN**-E-TOSE
Eukratides	YOU-**KRAH**-TI-DEES
Gela	**GAY**-LA
Halikarnassos	HAL-EE-KAR-**NAA**-SOS

Herakles	**HAIR**-AH-KLEES
Hermes	**HER**-MEES
Kamarina	KAM-A-**REE**-NA
Kephallenia	KEF-A-LA-**NEE**-A
Kibyra	**KEY**-BEER-AH
Kimon	**KEY**-MOAN
Knidos	**KNEE**-DOS
Lamia	LA-**MEE**-A
Larissa	LAR-**ISS**-A
Leontinoi	**LEE**-ON-**TEE**-NEE
Leucas	**LEV**-KAS
Lycia	**LICK**-EE-A
Lysimachos	LU-SEE-**MACH**-OS
Mamertini	MAM-ER-**TEEN**-EE
Maroneia	MAR-O-**NAY**-A
Messana	MESS-**AH**-NA
Morgantina	MORE-GAN-**TEE**-NA
Mytilene	MI-TIH-**LEE**-NEE
Naxos	**NOCKS**-OHS
Obol	**OH**-BOWL
Oiniadai	**EYE**-NAY-DIE
Opuntia	OH-**POON**-TEE-A
Paeonia	PEE-**OH**-NEE-A
Panormos	PAN-**OAR**-MOS
Pantikapaion	**PAN**-TI-KUH-**PAY**-ON
Peloponnesos	PELL-O-**POAN**-EE-SOS
Ptolemy	**TOLE**-EH-MEE
Pyrrhos	**PEER**-OHS
Romaioi	ROW-**MY**-OY
Segesta	SAY-**GUESS**-TAH
Seleukid	SEL-**LOO**-KID
Selinus	SELL-**EE**-NOOS
Sikyon	**SICK**-EE-ON
Smyrna	**SMEER**-NA
Stater	**STAY**-TER
Thasos	**THAH**-SOS
Thessalian	THESS-A-**LEE**-AN
Thessalonica	THESS-A-**LOAN**-EE-KA
Thourioi	**THUR**-EE-EYE
Troas	**TRO**-AHS
Tyche	**TIE**-KEE
Zakynthos	ZAH-**KIN**-THOS
Zeus	**ZOOS**

Roman Pronunciation Guide

The correct pronunciation of Latin words, like the Greek words of the preceding section, is a matter of some confusion and disagreement among scholars, let alone collectors. Most collectors are really not too concerned with technical accuracy; they are more concerned with avoiding the strange looks that sometimes are generated by an unconventional pronunciation. As the old saying goes, "When in Rome, do as the Romans do". Metaphorically, that means, "When mixing with collectors, pronounce numismatic terms like your peers". So, a German collector might find it conventional to pronounce Caesar as **KI-SAR,** while an American collector pronounces it **SEE-ZAR.** It is fruitless to argue the merits of one over the other, because convention will undoubtedly prevail anyway.

Strangely enough, Roman provincial coins sometimes help us to figure out what contemporary pronunciation of some words or names was like. For example, Roman Provincial coins often spell the name of Julia **MAESA** as **MAICA.** This makes it fairly clear that the AE sounds like a long I. Conversely, the lunate sigma is comparable to the S in Latin or English. As a very rough rule of thumb, in Latin words, the letter I is pronounced like a long E. The letter A is pronounced like the A in "father", and the letter U is pronounced like the double O in "food". The vowels E and O follow more or less standard English usage, except that E sometimes is pronounced like the A in "game". When two vowels appear together (a diphtong) the sound is slurred over or elided. For example, ae becomes AH-EE or when pronounced quickly it becomes a long I like in ice. Au becomes AH-OO or ow like in "now". Of course this is tremendously oversimplified.

For a thorough discussion on pronunciation of Roman terms for numismatists, see Frank S. Robinson's article "A pronunciation guide to Roman coins," (*The Celator*, Vol. 9, No. 1, January, 1995), or the Internet article by Scott Rottinghaus on http://forvmcoins.hypermart.net. The following guide does not reflect proper Latin, but rather a loose conventional pronunciation with an admittedly American bias. Just remember that EVERYONE has a little uncertainty about pronunciation, so don't feel inadequate if you butcher a word here or there. The guides provided here are nowhere near complete, and are not intended to be. They will give the reader a general sense of how Greek and Roman names are typically pronounced and will set the stage for more effective dialogue between collectors.

Aegis	**EE**-JIS
Aelia Flacilla	**AY**-LEE-A FLA-**SILL**-A
Aes	AH-EES (**ICE**)
Aesculapius	ICE-KU-**LAH**-PEE-OOS
Anastasius	AN-A-**STAY**-SEE-OOS
Annona	A-**NOAN**-A
Arcadius	AR-**KADE**-EE-OOS
Ariadne	AIR-EE-**ODD**-NEE
As	**AHS**
Augustus	AWE-**GUS**-TOOS
Aurelius	OW-**RAY**-LEE-OOS
Aureus	**OW**-RAY-OOS
Basiliscus	BOS-ILL-**ISS**-KOOS
Biga	**BEE**-GA
Caduceus	KAH-**DOO**-SEE-OOS
Caesar	**CEE**-SAR (KAY-SAR in Latin)
Caligula	CA-**LIG**-YOU-LA
Caracalla	CAR-A-**CAH**-LA
Carinus	CAR-**EE**-NOOS
Carus	**CAR**-OOS
Commodus	**COMM**-O-DOOS
Crispus	**KRIS**-POOS
Cuirass	**CURE**-AHSS
Denarius	DEN-**ARE**-EE-OOS
Diadem	**DYE**-A-DEM
Diocletian	DEE-O-**CLEE**-SHUN
Domitian	DOE-**MI**-TEE-AN
Drusus	**DREW**-SUS
Dyrrhachium	DEER-**OCK**-EE-OOM
Elagabalus	ELA-GA-**BAL**-OOS
Eudoxia	YOU-**DOAKS**-EE-A
Eugenius	YOU-**GEEN**-EE-OOS
Felicitas	FELL-**EE**-SEE-TAS
Fides	**FEE**-DES
Gaius	**GUY**-OOS
Galba	**GALL**-BA
Galerius	GAL-**ERR**-EE-OOS
Galla Placidia	**GAL**-A PLA-**SID**-EE-A
Gallienus	GAL-EE-**ANE**-OOS
Geta	**GAY**-TA
Glycerius	GLI-**SEER**-EE-OOS
Gnaeus	**GNAY**-OOS
Gratian	**GRAH**-TEE-AN

Grave	**GRAHV**
Hadrian	**HAY**-DREE-AN
Honorius	ON-**OAR**-EE-OOS
Johannes	JOE-**HAN**-EES
Jovian	**JOE**-VEE-AN
Julius Nepos	**JOO**-LEE-OOS **NEE**-POSE
Justitia	JUS-**TEET**-SEE-A
Laelianus	LAY-LEE-**AN**-OOS
Laetitia	LAY-**TEET**-SEE-A
Leontius	LEE-**ON**-TEE-OOS
Licinius	LI-**SIN**-EE-OOS
Litra	**LEE**-TRA
Lituus	**LIT**-OO-OOS
Lucius	**LOO**-SHE-OOS
Macrinus	MAC-**REE**-NOOS
Maesa	**MY**-SAH
Magnentius	MAG-**NEN**-TEE-OOS
Majorian	MAH-**JOAR**-EE-AN
Mamaea	MAH-**MY**-AH
Martinian	MAR-**TIN**-EE-AN
Maximianus	MAX-IM-EE-**AN**-OOS
Maximus	**MAX**-EE-MOOS
Nero	**NEAR**-O
Nerva	**NUR**-VA
Numerianus	NOO-MER-EE-**AN**-OOS
Otho	**O**-THO
Palladium	PAL-**LADE**-EE-OOM
Pax	**POX**
Pileus	**PEE**-LEE-OOS
Pius	**PIE**-OOS
Pompey	**POM**-PEE
Poppaea	POP-**PYE**-A
Probus	**PRO** BOOS
Procopius	PRO-**COPE**-EE-OOS
Pulcheria	PULL-**CARE**-EE-A
Quadrans	**KWAD**-RANS
Regina	RAY-**JEEN**-A
Romulus	**ROM**-YOU-LOOS
Salonina	SOL-O-**NEE**-NA
Septimius	SEP-**TIM**-EE-OOS
Sestertius	SES-**TUR**-SHUS
Severus	SEV-**AIR**-OOS
Salus	**SAH**-LOOS

Sirmium	**SIR**-MEE-OOM
Siscia	**SIS**-KEE-A
Tessera	**TES**-ER-A
Theodosius	THEE-O-**DOE**-SEE-OOS
Tiberius	TIE-**BEER**-EE-OOS
Togate	**TOE**-GATE
Titi	**TEE**-TEE
Titiana	TEE-TEE-**AH**-NA
Titus	**TIE**-TOOS
Trajan	**TRAY-JAN**
Vabalathus	VAH-BAH-**LAH**-TOOS
Valens	**VAL**-ENS
Verina	VER-**EE**-NA
Vitellius	VIE-**TELL**-EE-OOS
Vespasian	VES-**PAY**-SEE-AN
Vexillum	VEX-**ILL**-OOM
Vetranio	VEH-**TRAN**-EE-O
Volusian	VO-**LOO**-SEE-AN
Zeno	**ZEE**-NOE
Zenonis	ZEE-**NOAN**-ISS

General Bibliography

The following bibliography lists works which have either been consulted in preparation of this volume or serve a general readership. Because the author has chosen not to footnote each reference in the text, this bibliography includes some titles which were only mentioned in passing. The field of ancient coin collecting is served by a substantial corpus of literature and the omission here of any particular work bears no reflection on its utility or lack thereof.

Alsop, Joseph. *The Rare Art Traditions,* Princeton University Press, 1982.

Bowder, D. ed. *Who Was Who in the Roman World,* Oxford, 1980.

Burnett, A. *Coinage in the Roman World,* London, 1987.

Butcher, Kevin. *Roman Provincial Coins: An introduction to the Greek Imperials,* Seaby, London, 1988.

Cooper, Denis R. *The Art and Craft of Coinmaking: A History of Minting Technology.* London, 1988.

Cox, Dorothy Hannah. *A Third Century Hoard of Tetradrachms from Gordion,* University of Pennsylvania, 1953.

Duruy, *History of Greece and of the Greek People,* four two-part volumes, Boston, 1890.

Duruy, *History of Rome and of the Roman People: From its Origin to the Invasion of the Barbarians,* eight two-part volumes, Boston, 1894.

Forrer, Leonard. *The Art of Collecting Coins.* London, 1955.

Franke, Dr. Peter R. and Irini Marathaki. *Wine and Coins of Ancient Greece,* Athens, 1999.

Giacosa, G. *Women of the Caesars. Their Lives and Portraits on Coins.* (Milan), 1977.

Grant, Michael. *From Imperium to Auctoritas, A Historical Study of the AES Coinage in the Roman Empire, 49 B.C.-A.D. 14,* Cambridge, 1946.

___. *Roman Anniversary Issues: An exploratory study of the numismatic and medallic commemoration of anniversary years 49 B.C.-A.D. 375,* Cambridge, 1950.

Harl, Kenneth W. *Coinage in the Roman Economy, 300 BC to AD 700,* Baltimore and London, 1996.

Head, B.V., *Historia Numorum,* (reprint) Chicago, 1967.

Hill, Philip V. *The Monuments of Ancient Rome as Coin Types,* London, 1989.

Icard, S. *Dictionary of Greek Coin Inscriptions,* (reprint) 1968.

Jex-Blake, K. (tr.) *The Elder Pliny's Chapters on the History of Art .* Ares, Chicago, 1982..

Junge, Ewald. *The Seaby Coin Encyclopaedia,* London, 1992.

Kent, J.P.C., M. Hirmer and A. Hirmer. *Roman Coins,* London, 1978.

Kroh, Dennis. *Ancient Coin Reference Reviews,* Ormond Beach, FL 1993.

Ladd, R. *The Illustrated Grading guide to Ancient Numismatics*, Anaheim, 1977.

MacDonald, George. *The Evolution of Coinage*, Cambridge, 1916.

Mattingly, Harold. *Roman Coins From the Earliest Times to the Fall of the Western Empire*, London, 1928.

Millar, F. *The Roman Near East, 31 B.C. - A.D. 337*, Cambridge and London, 1993.

Miller, Michael F. *Classical Greek and Roman Coins: The Investor's Handbook*, Altara Group, 1982.

Penn, R.G. *Medicine on Ancient Greek and Roman Coins*, London, 1994.

Scarre, Chris. *Chronicle of the Roman Emperors*, New York, 1995.

Smith, William. *Dictionary of Greek and Roman Antiquities*, 2nd ed. Boston, 1865. and *Dictionary of Greek and Roman geography*, two volumes, Boston, 1865.

Stevenson, S. *A Dictionary of Roman Coins*, (reprint) 1982.

Sutherland, C.H.V. *Roman Coins*, London and New York, 1974.

Toynbee, J. *Roman Historical Portraits*, London, 1978.

___. *Roman Medallions*, ANS NS 5, New York, 1944.

Technical Bibliography

The following bibliography lists specialized references which are commonly used in the numismatic trade. It is organized alphabetically by standard abbreviation, within general cultural classifications. The utility of this arrangement will become apparent to the collector who attempts to decipher cryptic abbreviations on coin flip inserts or in dealer catalogue descriptions.

GREEK BIBLIOGRAPHY

ACNAC	**Ancient Coins in North American Collections.** American Numismatic Society. New York.
ADM	M. Thompson. **Alexander Drachm Mints II, Lampsacus and Abydus,** ANSNS19, New York, 1991.
AJN	**American Journal of Numismatics.** American Numismatic Society. New York.
Akarca	A. Akarca. **Les Monnaies Grecques de Mylasa.** Paris. 1959.
Amandry	M. Amandry. **Le Monnayage d'Amathonte.** (Amathus) Amathonte I pp. 57-76. Paris. 1984.
___, Lebedos	M. Amandry. **Les Tetradrachmes Frappés a Lébédos,** in Kraay-Mørkholm Essays. Louvain. 1989.
AMNG	**Antiken Münzen Nord-Griechenlands.** Berlin. 1898-1935.
AMUGS	**Antike Münzen und Geschnittene Steine.**
Anokhin	V.A. Anokhin. **Monetoe delo Bospora.** Kiev. 1986.
ANS NNM	**American Numismatic Society Numismatic Notes and Monographs.** New York.
Anson	L. Anson. **Numismata Graeca.** 6 Vols. London. 1911-1916.
Arslan-Lightfoot	M. Arslan and C. Lightfoot, **Greek Coin Hoards in Turkey,** Ankara, 1999.
Ashton	R. Ashton. **'Rhodian Coinage and the Colossus,"** in RN 1988, pp. 75-90.
Asyut	M. Price & N. Waggoner. **Archaic Greek Silver Coinage: The Asyut Hoard.** London. 1975.
Atlan	S. Atlan. **Sidenin Milattan önce V ve IV Yüzyil Sikkeleri Üzerinde Arastirmalar.** (Side). Ankara. 1967.
Babelon, Traité	E. Babelon. **Traité des Monnaies Grecques et Romaines.** 9 Vols. Paris. 1901-1932. (Reprinted)
Balcer	J.M. Balcer. **The Early Silver Coinage of Teos.** SNR XLVII pp. 5-54. Bern. 1968.
Baldwin, Chios	A. Baldwin. **The Electrum and Silver Coinage of Chios.** New York. 1915.
___, Lampsacus	A. Baldwin. **The Electrum Coinage of Lampsakos.** New York. 1914.
Barron	J.P. Barron. **The Silver Coins of Samos.** London. 1966.
Basel	H.A. Cahn et al. **Griechischen Münzen aus Grossgriechenland und Szilien.** Basel. 1988.
BCD Corinth	Numismatik Lanz, **Münzen von Korinth: Sammlung BCD,** Auction 105, München, 2001.

274

BCD Euboia	Numismatik Lanz, **Münzen von Euboia: Sammlung BCD,** Auction 111, München, 2002.
Bellinger, Troy	A.R. Bellinger, **Troy, the Coins,** Princeton, 1961.
Bérend, Rhodes	D. Bérend. **"Les Tetradrachmes de Rhodes de la première périod, 1er partie",** in SNR 51, Bern, 1972.
Betlyon	J.W. Betlyon. **" A New Chronology for the Pre-Alexandrine Coinage of Sidon",** ANSMN 21, New York, 1976.
BMC	Various authors. **Catalogue of Greek Coins in the British Museum.** 29 Vols. London. 1873-1927. (Reprinted)
Bodenstedt	F. Bodenstedt. **Die Elektronmünzen von Phokaia und Mytilene.** Tübingen. 1981.
Boehringer	E. Boehringer. **Die Münzen von Syrakus.** Berlin and Leipzig. 1929.
___, Chron.	C. Boehringer. **Zur Chronologie mittelhellisticher Münzserien 220-160 c.Chr.** Berlin, 1972.
___, Leontini	C. Boehringer. **"Die Münzgeschichte von Leontini in klassicher Zeit"** in Studies Price.
Bopearachchi	O. Bopearachchi. **Monnaies Gréco-Bactriennes et Indo-Grecques.** Paris. 1991.
Boston	A. B. Brett. **Catalogue of Greek Coins, Boston Museum of Fine Arts.** Boston. 1955.
Boston(C)	M. Comstock. **Greek Coins 1950-1963, Boston Museum of Fine Arts.** Boston. 1964.
Brunetti	L. Brunetti. **"Nuovi Orientamenti sulla Zecca di Taranto,"** in RIN 1960, pp. 5-132.
Burgos	A. Burgos. **La Moneda Hispanica desde sus Origenes Hasta el Siglo V.** Vol.1. Madrid. 1987.
Burnett	A. Burnett. **The Enna Hoard and the Silver Coinage of the Syracusan Democracy,** in SNR 62, pp. 5-26.
Cahn-Knidos	H.A. Cahn. **Knidos-Die Münzen des Sechsten und des Fünften Jahrhunderts v. Chr.** AMUGS IV. Berlin. 1970.
___, Naxos	H.A. Cahn. **The Coins of the Sicilian City of Naxos.** Basel. 1940. (Reprinted)
Calciati	R. Calciati. **Corpus Nummorum Siculorum: La Monetazione di Bronzo.** 3 Vols. Italy. 1983-87.
Calicó	X. and F. Calicó. **Catálogo de Monedas Antiguas de Hispania.** Barcelona. 1979.
Carridice	I. Carridice. **Coinage and Administration in the Athenian and Persian Empires.** BAR 343. Oxford. 1987.
Clerk	M.G. Clerk. **Catalogue of the Coins of the Achæan League.** London. 1895.
De Callataÿ	F. de Callataÿ. L'Histoire Des Guerres Mithridatiques Vue Par Les Monnais. Louvain-La-Neuve, 1997.
Deppert-Lippitz	B. Deppert-Lippitz. **Die Münzprägung Milets vom Vierten bis Ersten Jahrhundert V. Chr.** Aarau. 1984.
Desneux	J. Desneux. **Les Tétradrachmes d'Ankanthos,** in Revue Belge. Brussels. 1949.
Dewing	L. Mildenberg and S. Hirter. **The Dewing Collection of Greek Coins.** ACNAC 6. N.Y. 1985.
Dittrich	K. Dittrich. **Ancient Coins from Olbia and Panticapaeum.** London. N.D.
Essays Hersh	A. Burnett et. al. **Coins of Macedonia and Rome, Essays in honour of Charles Hersh,** London, 1998.

Essays Robinson	C.M. Kraay and G.K. Jenkins. **Essays in Greek Coinage Presented to Stanley Robinson,** Oxford, 1968.
Favorito	E. Favorito. **The Bronze Coinage of Ancient Syracuse.** Boston. 1990.
Fischer-Bossert	W. Fischer-Bossert. **Chronologie DerDidrachmenprägung von Tarent 510-280 v.Chr,** Berlin, 1999.
FlorNum	H. Nilsson, Ed. **Florilegium Numismaticum: Studia in Honorem U. Westermark.** Stockholm. 1992.
FS Price	R. Ashton, S. Hurter (Hrsg.), Studies in Greek Numismatics in Memory of M. J Price, London (1998).
Furtwängler	A.E. Furtwängler. **Monnaies Greques en Gaule.** Typos III. Fribourg. 1978.
Gabrici	E. Gabrici. **La Monetazione del Bronzo nella Sicila Antica.** Palermo. 1927. (Reprinted)
Gaebler	H. Gaebler. **Die Antiken Münzen von Makedonia und Paionia.** AMNG III. Berlin. 1906, 1935.
Gorini	G. Gorini. **La Monetazione Incusa della Magna Grecia.** Milan. 1975.
Greenwell	W. Greenwell. **The Electrum Coinage of Cyzicus.** London. 1887.
Grunaeur	S. Grunaeur. **"Die Münzprägung der Lakedaimonier",** AMUGS VII, Berlin, 1978.
Gulbenkian	E.S.G. Robinson and M.C. Hipólito. **A Catalogue of the Calouste Gulbenkian Collection of Greek Coins.** 2 Parts. Lisbon. 1971, 1990.
Gutman	F. Gutman and W Schwabacher. **Tetradrachmen und Didrachmen von Himera (472-409 v Chr),** in MBNG 47, pp. 101-144. Munich. 1929.
Head	B.V. Head. **On the Chronological Sequence of the Coins of Ephesus.** London. 1880. (Reprinted)
Heipp-Tamer	C. Heipp-Tamer. **Die Münzprägung der Lykischen Stadt Phaselis in Grisischer Zeit,** Saarbrüker, 1993.
Heiss	A. Heiss. **Description Générale des Monnaies Antiques de l'Espagne.** Paris. 1870. (Reprinted)
Herrmann	F. Herrmann. **"Die Silbermünzen von Larissa in Thessalien,"** in ZfN 35 (1925), pp. 1-69.
Herzfelder	H. Herzfelder. **Les Monnaies d'Argent de Rhegium.** Paris. 1957.
HN Italy	N.K. Rutter. **Historia Numorum Italy,** London, 2001.
Holloway	R.R. Holloway. **The Thirteen-Months Coinage of Hieronymos of Syracuse.** Berlin. 1969.
Holloway/Jenkins	R.R. Holloway and G.K. Jenkins. **Terina.** Bellinzona. 1983.
Houghton	A. Houghton. **Coins of the Seleucid Empire from the Collection of Arthur Houghton.** ACNAC 4. New York. 1983.
___, Seleucia	A. Houghton. **"The Seleucid mint of Seleucia on the Calycadnus"** in Kraay-Mørkholm Essays.
Houghton & Spaer	A. Houghton and A. Spaer. **"New Silver Coins of Demetrius III and Antiochus XII at Damascus",** in SM 157, Bern, 1990.
Hunterian	G. MacDonald. **Catalogue of Greek Coins in the Hunterian Museum, Glasgow.** 3 Vols. Glasgow. 1899-1905. (Reprinted)
Ierardi	M. Ierardi. **"Tetradrachms of Agathocles of Syracuse",** in AJN 7-8, New York, 1995-1996.

Imhoof-Blumer	F. Imhoof-Blumer. **Kleinasiatische Münzen,** Wien, 1901 (reprinted).
Jameson	R. Jameson. **Monnaies Greques Antiques.** 4 Vols. Paris. 1913-1932. (Reprinted)
Jenkins, Gela	G.K. Jenkins. **The Coinage of Gela.** Berlin. 1970.
Jenkins	G.K. Jenkins. **"The Electrum Coinage at Syracuse,"** in Essays Robinson. Oxford. 1968.
Jenkins & Lewis	G.K. Jenkins and R.B. Lewis. **Carthaginian Gold and Electrum Coins.** London. 1963.
Jenkins, SNR	G.K. Jenkins. **Coins of Punic Sicily,** in Swiss Numismatic Review. Bern. 1971-1978.
JIAN	**Journal International d'Archéologie Numismatique.** Athens. 1898-1927.
Johnston	A. Johnston. **The Coinage of Metapontum, Part 3.** ANSNNM 164. New York. 1990.
Kleiner-Noe	F.S. Kleiner and S.P. Noe. **The Early Cistaphoric Coinage.** Numismatic Studies 14. N.Y. 1977.
Konuk	K. Konuk. **"The Early Coinage of Kaunos",** in Studies Price.
K/M Essays	G. Le Rider et al. eds. Kraay-Mørkholm Essays. **Numismatic Studies in Memory of C.M. Kraay and O. Mørkholm.** Louvain-la-Neuve, 1989.
Kraay, ACGC	C. Kraay. **Archaic and Classical Greek Coins.** London. 1976.
Kraay	C. Kraay. **The Archaic Coinage of Himera.** Naples. 1984.
Kraay-Hirmer	C. Kraay & M. Hirmer. **Greek Coins.** New York. 1966.
Kroll	J.H. Kroll. **The Athenian Agora Volume XXVI: The Greek Coins.** Princeton. 1993.
Laffaille	**Collection Maurice Laffaille-Monnaies Grecques en Bronze.** Bàle. 1990.
Le Rider, Crete	G. Le Rider. **Monnaies Crétoises du V au I Siécle av J.C.** Paris. 1966.
Le Rider, Philip	G. Le Rider. **Le Monnayage d'Argent et d'Or de Philippe II.** Paris. 1977.
Lind.-Kovacs	H. Lindgren & F. Kovacs. **Ancient Bronze Coinage of Asia Minor and the Levant.** San Mateo. 1985.
Lindgren II	H. Lindgren. **Ancient Greek Bronze Coins: European Mints.** San Mateo. 1989.
Lindgren III	H. Lindgren. **Ancient Greek Bronze Coins.** Quarryville. 1993.
Lorber	C. Lorber. **Amphipolis-The Civic Coinage in Silver and Gold.** Los Angeles. 1990.
Lorber Hoard	C. Lorber. **"A Hoard of Facing Head Larissa Drachms",** in SNR 79, Bern, 2000.
Mabbott	H. Holzer. **The T.O. Mabbott Collection Part 1. Coins of the Greek World.** N.Y. 1969.
MacDonald	D. MacDonald. **The Coinage of Aphrodisias.** London. 1992.
Malloy	A.G. Malloy. **The Coinage of Amisus.** New York. 1970.
Mamroth	A. Mamroth. **"Die Silbermünzen des Königs Perseus,"** in ZfN 38 (1928), pp. 1-28.
May, Abdera	J.M.F. May. **The Coinage of Abdera, 540-345 BC.** London. 1966.
May, Ainos	J.M.F. May. **Ainos, Its History and Coinage.** London. 1950.
May, Damastion	J.M.F. May. **The Coinage of Damastion.** London. 1939.

Mazard   J. Mazard. **Corpus Nummorum Numidiae Mauretaniaeque.** Paris. 1955-1958.

McClean   S. Grose. **Catalogue of the McClean Collection, Fitzwilliam Museum.** 3 Vols. Cambridge. 1923-1929. (Reprinted)

Milbank   S.R. Milbank. **The Coinage of Aegina.** NNM 24. New York 1924.

Milne   J.G. Milne. **Colophon and its Coinage.** NNM 96. N.Y. 1941.

Mionnet   T. Mionnet. **Description des Médailles Antiques, Grecques et Romaines.** 7+9 Vols. Paris. 1806-1837. (Reprint: Graz, 1972-3)

Müller, Africa   L.Müller, C.T. Falbe, J.C. Lindberg. **Numismatique de l'Ancienne Afrique.** Copenhagen. 1860-1862. (Reprinted)

Müller   L. Müller. **Numismatique d'Alexandre le Grand; Appendice les Monnaies de Philippe II et III, et Lysimaque.** Copenhagen. 1855-58. (Reprinted in English)

Mushmov   N. Mushmov. **Antichnitie Moneti na Balkanskitiia Poluostrov i Monetite Tsare.** Sofia. 1912.

Naville   L. Naville. **Les Monnaies d'Or de la Cyrénaïque.** Geneva. 1951.

Newell   E.T. Newell. **The Coinage of Demetrius Poliorcetes.** London. 1927. (Reprinted)

Newell, ESM   E. Newell & O. Mørkholm. **The Coinage of the Eastern Seleucid Mints from Seleucus I to Antiochus III.** New York. 1978.

Newell, WSM   E. Newell & O. Mørkholm. **The Coinage of the Western Seleucid Mints from Seleucus I to Antiochus III.** New York. 1977.

Newell, Tyre   E. Newell. **Seleucid Coins of Tyre: A Supplement.** NNM 73. New York. 1936.

Newell, LSM   E. Newell. **Late Seleucid Mints in Ake-Ptolemais and Damascus.** NNM 84. New York. 1939.

Newell, SMA   E. Newell. **The Seleucid Mint of Antioch.** New York. 1917.

Niggler   **Sammlung Walter Niggler.** Bank Leu, Münzen u. Medaillen AG. Zürich and Basel. 1965-1967.

Noe   S. Noe. **The Coinage of Metapontum.** New York. 1927-31. (Reprinted)

NNM   **Numismatic Notes and Monographs.** American Numis–matic Society. New York.

NumChron   **Numismatic Chronicle.** Royal Numismatic Society. London. 1838-.

NumCirc   **Spink's Numismatic Circular.** London. 1892-.

Pegasi   R. Calciati. **Pegasi.** Mortara. 1990.

Picard   O. Picard. **Chalcis et la Confédération Eubéenne.** Paris. 1979.

Pick   B. Pick & K. Regling. **Die Antiken Münzen von Dacien und Moesien.** AMNG Vol. 2. Berlin. 1912.

Pixodarus   R.H.J. Ashton et. al. **"The Pixodarus Hoard"** in Coin Hoards IX, London, 2002.

Ployart   B. Ployart. **Choix de Monnaies Gauloises.** Paris. 1980.

Pozzi   S. Pozzi. **Catalogue Monnaies Grecques Antiques.** Geneva. 1921. (Reprinted)

Price   M.J. Price. **The Coinage in the Name of Alexander the Great and Philip Arrhidaeus.** London. 1991.

Randazzo	C. Arnold-Biucchi. **The Randazzo Hoard.** ANS Numis–matic Studies 18. New York. 1990.
Ravel	O. Ravel. **The "Colts" of Ambracia.** NNM 37. New York. 1928.
Ravel	O. Ravel. **Les "Poulains" de Corinthe.** 2 Vols. Basel. 1936-1948. (Reprinted)
Raymond	D. Raymond. **Macedonian Regal Coinages.** NNM 126. New York. 1953.
RIN	**Revista Italiana de Numismatica e Scienze Affini.** Milan. 1888-.
RN	**Revue Numismatique.** Paris. 1836-.
Robinson-Clem.	D.M. Robinson and P.A. Clement. **The Chalcidic Mint and the Excavation Coins found in 1928-1934.** Excava–tions at Olynthus IX. Baltimore. 1938.
Rogers	E. Rogers. **The Second and Third Seleucid Coinage at Tyre.** NNM 34. N.Y. 1927.
Rosen	N. Waggoner. **Early Greek Coins from the Collection of Jonathan P. Rosen.** ACNAC 5. New York. 1983.
Rutter	N.K. Rutter. **Campanian Coinages 475-380 BC.** Edinburgh. 1979.
Sachs	K.S. Sachs. **"The Wreathed Coins of Aeolian Myrina".** in ANSMN 30, New York, 1985.
Scheers S-M	S. Scheers. **Monnaies Gauloises de Seine-Maritime.** Rouen. 1978.
Schönert-Geiss	E. Schönert-Geiss. **Die Münzprägung von Maroneia.** Berlin. 1987.
Seleucid Coins	A. Houghton and C. Lorber. **Seleucid Coins, A Compre-hensive Catalogue,** Part I (2 vols.) New York, 2002.
Seltman	C.T. Seltman. **The Temple Coins of Olympia.** Cambridge. 1921. (Reprinted)
Seyrig	H.Seyrig. **Notes on Syrian Coins.** NNM 119. New York. 1950.
SG	D. Sear. **Greek Coins and Their Values. Vol. 1 Europe. Vol. 2 Asia & Africa.** London.1978-79.
SNG Alpha Bank	**Sylloge Nummorum Graecorum, Greece II. The Alpha Bank Collection. Macedonia I: Alexander I - Perseus,** Athens, 2000.
SNG Ashmolean	**Sylloge Nummorum Graecorum, Ashmolean Museum, Oxford.** London. 1962-69.
SNG ANS	**Sylloge Nummorum Graecorum, American Numis-matic Society.** New York. 1969-.
SNG BM 1	**Sylloge Nummorum Graecorum, British Museum1: The Black Sea.** London. 1993.
SNG BM 2	**Sylloge Nummorum Graecorum, British Museum2: Spain.** London. 2002.
SNG Berry	**Sylloge Nummorum Graecorum, Burton Y. Berry Collection.** New York. 1961-1962.
SNG Cop.	**Sylloge Nummorum Graecorum, Danish National Museum.** Copenhagen. 1942-. (Reprinted) + 2002 Supplement - Acquisitions 1942-1996.
SNG Delepierre	**Sylloge Nummorum Graecorum, Bibliothèque Na-tional.** Paris. 1983.
SNG Fitz.	**Sylloge Nummorum Graecorum, Fitzwilliam Museum, Cambridge.** London. 1940-1958.

SNG France 2	**Sylloge Nummorum Graecorum, France 2: Cilicie.** Paris, 1993.
SNG France 3	**Sylloge Nummorum Graecorum, France 3: Pamphylie, Pisidie, Lycaonie, Galatie.** Paris, 1994.
SNG France 5	**Sylloge Nummorum Graecorum, France 5: Mysie.** Paris, 2001.
SNG Helsinki	**Sylloge Nummorum Graecorum, Finland; Erkki Keckman-Karia.** Helsinki. 1994.
SNG Levante	**Sylloge Nummorum Graecorum, Switzerland; E Levante- Cilicia.** Bern. 1986.
SNG Lev Supp.	**Sylloge Nummorum Graecorum, Switzerland; E Levante- Cilicia: Supplement I.** Zurich. 1993.
SNG Lloyd	**Sylloge Nummorum Graecorum, Lloyd Collection.** London. 1933-1937.
SNG Lockett	**Sylloge Nummorum Graecorum, Lockett Collection.** London. 1938-1949.
SNG Morcom	**Sylloge Nummorum Graecorum, John Morcom Collection.** Oxford. 1995.
SNG München	**Sylloge Nummorum Graecorum, Staatlische Münzsammlung.** Munich. 1968-.
SNG Paris 2	**Sylloge Nummorum Graecorum, France 2: Cilicie.** Paris. 1993.
SNG Paris 3	**Sylloge Nummorum Graecorum, France 3: Pamphylie, Pisidie, Lycaonie, Galatie.** Paris. 1994.
SNG Paris 5	**Sylloge Nummorum Graecorum, France 5: Mysie.** Paris, 2001.
SNG Righetti	**Sylloge Nummorum Graecorum, Schweiz II.** Bern. 1993
SNG Spaer	**Sylloge Nummorum Graecorum, Israel I, The Arnold Spaer Collection of Seleucid Coins..** Jerusalem, 1998.
SNG Stancomb	**Sylloge Nummorum Graecorum, The William Stancomb Collection of the Black Sea Region..** Oxford, 2000.
SNG Tübingen	**Sylloge Nummorum Graecorum, Münzsammlung Universität Tübingen.** Munich. 1981-.
SNG Turkey 1	**Sylloge Nummorum Graecorum, Turkey 1: The Muharrem Kayhan Collection.** Istanbul, 2002.
SNG v. Aulock	**Sylloge Nummorum Graecorum, Sammlung Hans Von Aulock.** Berlin. 1957-1968. (Reprinted)
SNG von Post	**Sylloge Nummorum Graecorum, Sweden: Sammlung Eric von Post.** Stockholm. 1995.
SNR	**Schweizerische Numismatische Rundschau.** (Swiss Numismatic Review).
SPNO	**Studia Paulo Naster Oblata I: Numismatica Antiqua.** Leuven. 1982.
Strack	M.L. Strack and F. Münzer. **Die Antiken Münzen von Thrakien.** AMNG II. Berlin. 1912.
Studies Price	R. Ashton and S. Hurter. **Studies in Greek Numismatics in Memory of Martin Jessop Price.** London, 1998.
Svoronos	J. Svoronos. **Les Monnaies d'Athenes.** Munich. 1923-26. (Reprinted in English)
Svoronos, Crete	J. Svoronos. **Numismatique de la Crète Ancienne.** Paris. 1890. (Reprinted)
Svoronos	J. Svoronos. **Ta Nomismata tou Kratous ton Ptolemaion.** Athens. 1904-08.

280

Thompson   M. Thompson. **The Mints of Lysimachus,** in Essays Robinson, pp. 163-182. Oxford. 1968.

Thompson   M. Thompson. **The New Style Silver Coinage of Athens.** New York. 1961.

Troxell, Carians H.A. Troxell. **Carians in Miniature,** in Studies in Honor of Leo Mildenberg. Wetteren. 1984.

Troxell, Lycia   H.A. Troxell. **The Coinage of the Lycian League.** NNM 162. N.Y. 1982.

Troxell, Winged H.A. Troxell. **Winged Carians,** in Greek Numismatics and Archaeology. Wettern. 1979.

Troxell, Macedon H.A. Troxell. **Studies in the Macedonian Coinage of Alexander the Great.** ANSNS 21, New York, 1997.

Troxell/Spengler Troxell, Hyla A and W.F. Spengler. "A Hoard of Early Greek Coins from Afghanistan." *ANS Museum Notes 15,* 1969.

Tudeer   L.O. Tudeer. **Die Tetradrachmenprägung von Syrakus in der Periode der Signierenden Künstler.** Berlin. 1913.

Villaronga   L. Villaronga. **Nummum Hispaniae ante Augusti Aetatem.** Madrid. 1994.

Vlasto   O. Ravel. **The Collection of Tarentine Coins Formed by M.P. Vlasto.** London. 1947.

Von Fritze   H. Von Fritze. **Die Elektronprägung von Kyzikus,** in Nomisma VII. 1912.

Waddington, Rec. W. Waddington, E. Babelon & T. Reinach. **Recueil Général des Monnaies Grecques d'Asie Minuere.** Paris. 1904-25. (Reprinted)

Weber   L. Forrer. **The Weber Collection of Greek Coins.** 3 Vols. London. 1922-1929. (Reprinted)

Weidauer   L. Weidauer. **Probleme de Frühen Elektronprägung.** Fribourg. 1975.

West   A.B. West. **Fifth and Fourth Century Gold Coins from the Thracian Coast.** ANS NNM 4, 0. New York. 1929.

Westermark   U. Westermark. **Das Bildnis des Philetairos von Pergamon.** Stockholm. 1960.

West.-Jenkins   U. Westermark and K. Jenkins. **The Coinage of Kamarina.** London. 1980.

Williams   R.T. Williams. **The Confederate Coinage of the Arcadians in the Fifth Century BC.** ANS NNM 155. N.Y. 1965.

Williams   R.T. Williams. **Silver Coinage of the Phokians.** London. 1972.

Williams   R.T. Williams. **Silver Coinage of Velia.** London. 1992.

Work   E. Work. **The Earlier Staters of Heraclea Lucaniae.** NNM 91. New York. 1940.

Youroukova   Y. Youroukova. **The Coins of the Ancient Thracians.** Oxford. 1976.

ZfN   **Zeitschrift für Numismatik.** Berlin. 1874-1935.

Ziegler   R. Ziegler. **Untersuchungen zur Münzprägung von Anazarbos.** Vienna. 1993.

Zograph   A.N. Zograph. **Antichnye Monety.** Moscow. 1951. (English Trans. Oxford. 1977)

ROMAN PROVINCIAL BIBLIOGRAPHY
(See also Greek Bibliography)

Amandry   M. Amandry. **Le Monnayage des Duovirs Corinthiens.** Paris. 1988.

Bellinger   A. Bellinger. **The Syrian Tetradrachms of Caracalla and Macrinus.** New York. 1940.

Brin   H.B. Brin. **Catalogue of Judaea Capta Coinage.** Minneapolis. 1986.

Castelin   K.O. Castelin. **The Coinage of Rhesaena in Mesopotamia.** ANSMMN 108. New York. 1946.

Christiansen   E. Christiansen. **Coins of Alexandria and the Nomes.** London. 1991.

Curtis   Col. J. Curtis. **The Tetradrachms of Roman Egypt.** Chicago. 1957. (Reprinted)

Dattari   G. Dattari. **Numi Augg. Alexandrini.** Cairo. 1901. (Reprinted)

Demetrio   F. Feuerdant. **Collections Giovanni di Demetrio, Numismatique, Egypte Ancienne.** Paris. 1872.

Emmett   K. Emmett, Alexandrian Coins, Lodi WI, 2001.

Frankfurt   G. Förschner. **Die Münzen der Römischen Kaiser in Alexandrien-Historische Museum Frankfurt.** Frankfurt. 1987.

Geissen   A. Geissen. **Katalog Alexandrinischer kaisermünzen,** Köln (5 vols), Cologne, 1974-83.

Howgego   C.J. Howgego. **Greek Imperial Countermarks.** London. 1985.

Kadman Caesarea   L. Kadman. **The Coins of Caesarea Maritima.** Corpus Nummorum Palaestinensium Vol 2. Jerusalem. 1957.

Kadman Akko   L. Kadman. **The Coins of Akko Ptolemais,** Schocken, 1961.

Kindler   A. Kindler. **The Coinage of Bostra.** Warminster. 1983.

Köln   A. Geissen. **Katalog Alexandrinischer Kaisermünzen, Köln.** 5 Vols. Cologne. 1974-83.

Krzyzanovska   A. Krzyzanovska. **Monnaies Coloniales d'Antioche de Pisidie.** Warsaw. 1970.

Meshorer   Y. Meshorer. **City-Coins of Eretz Israel and the Decapolis in the Roman Period.** Jerusalem. 1985.

Metcalf   W.E. Metcalf. **The Cistophori of Hadrian.** New York. 1980.

Milne   J.G. Milne. **Catalogue of Alexandrian Coins in the Ashmolean Museum.** Oxford. 1927 (Reprint: London 1971).

Price & Trell   M.J. Price & B. Trell. **Coins and Their Cities.** London. 1977.

RPC I   A. Burnett, M. Amandry & P. Ripollès. **Roman Provincial Coinage.** Vol. 1. London and Paris. 1992.

RPC II   A. Burnett, M. Amandry & I. Carradice. **Roman Provincial Coinage.** Vol. II. London and Paris. 1999.

SGI   D. Sear. **Greek Imperial Coins and Their Values.** London. 1982.

Spijkerman   A. Spijkerman. **The Coins of the Decapolis and Provincia Arabia.** Jerusalem. 1978.

Sydenham   E. Sydenham. **The Coinage of Caesarea in Cappadocia.** London. 1933. (Reprinted and revised)

Vogt   J. Vogt. **Die Alexandrinischen Münzen.** 2 Vols. Stuttgart. 1924.

Voegtli   H. Voegtli. **Bilder der Heldenpenen in der Kaiserzeitlichen Griechischen münzprägung,** Basel, 1977.

| Wruck | W. Wruck. **Die Syrische Provinzialprägung von Augustus bis Traian.** Stuttgart. 1931. |

ROMAN BIBLIOGRAPHY

Alföldi	A.& E. Alföldi, C. Clay. **Die Kontorniat Medallions.** AMUGS VI. Berlin. 1976.
Alföldi	M.R. Alföldi. **Die Constantinische Goldpragüng.** Mainz. 1963.
Amandry	M.Amandry. **Le Monnayage des Duovirs Corinthiens,** Paris, 1988.
Babelon	E. Babelon. **Monnaies de la Republique Romaine.** 2 Vols. Paris. 1885.
Baldus	H.R. Baldus. **Uranius Antonius- Münzprägung und Geschichte.** Bonn. 1971.
Banti	A. Banti. **I Grandi Bronzi Imperiali.** 9 Vols. Florence. 1983-1986.
Banti & Simonetti	A. Banti and L. Simonetti, **Corpus Nummorum Romanorum,** (18 vols.), Florence, 1972+.
Bastien, Mag.	P. Bastien. **Le Monnayage de Magnence (350-353).** Wetteren. 1983.
Bastien, Post.	P. Bastien. **le Monnayage de Bronze de Postume.** Wetteren. 1967.
Bastien/Metz.	P. Bastien & C. Metzger. **Le Trésor de Beaurains (dit d'Arras).** Wetteren. 1977.
BMCRE	H. Mattingly et al. **Coins of the Roman Empire in the British Museum.** London. 1932-1962.
Bruun	Patrick Bruun. **Studies in Constantinian Chronology,** ANS NNM 146, New York, 1961.
Burnett	A. Burnett. **'The Coinage of Allectus: Chronology and Interpretation.,"** in Studies in the Coinage of Carausius and Allectus. London. 1985.
Campana	A. Campana. **La Monetazione degli Insorti Italici Durante la Guerra Sociale (91-87a.C.),** Modena. 1987.
Cayon	J. Cayon. **Los Sestercios del Imperio Romano.** Madrid. 1984.
CNR	A. Banti & L. Simonetti. **Corpus Nummorum Romanorum.** 18 Vols. Firenze. 1972-1979.
CRE Ash.	C.H.V. Sutherland & C.M. Kraay. **Catalogue of Coins of the Roman Empire in the Ashmolean Museum. Part I. Augustus.** Oxford. 1975.
Cohen	H. Cohen. **Description Historique des Monnaies Frappées sous l'Empire Romain.** 8 Vols. Paris. 1880-92. (Reprinted)
Crawford	M. Crawford. **Coinage and Money under the Roman Republic.** Berkeley and Los Angeles. 1985.
Crawford	M. Crawford. **Roman Republican Coinage.** 2 Vols. Cambridge. 1974.
Cunetio	E. Besly & R. Brand. **The Cunetio Treasure: Roman Coinage of the Third Century AD.** London. 1983.
Depeyrot	G. Depeyrot, Les monnaies dor de Diocletien à Constantin L (284-33 7), Wetteren (1995).
DOCLR	P. Grierson & M. Mays. **Catalogue of Late Roman Coins in the Dumbarton Oaks Collection.** Washington D.C. 1992.

283

Estiot	S. Estiot. **Tacito e Floriano.** Verona. 1987.
Giard, BN	J. Giard. **Bibliothèque Nationale, Catalogue des Monnaies de l/Empire Romain.** Paris. 1976-.
Gnecchi	F. Gnecchi. **I Medaglioni Romani.** 3 Vols. Milan. 1912. (Reprinted)
Göbl	R. Göbl. **Die Münzprägung des Kaisers Aurelianus.** Vienna. 1993.
Grünwald	M. Grünwald. **Die Römischen Bronze- und Kupfermünzen mit Schlagmarken im Legionslager Vindonissa.** Basel. 1946.
Haeberlin	E.J. Haeberlin. **Aes Grave; Das Schwergeld Rom und Mittelitaliens.** Frankfort. 1910. (Reprinted)
Harlan	M. Harlan. **Roman Republican Moneyers and Their Coinage, 63 B.C. - 49 B.C.,** London, 1995.
Hill	P.V. Hill. **The Coinage of Septimius Severus and his Family.** London. 1977.
Hill	P.V. Hill. **The Undated Coins of Rome AD 98-148.** London. 1970.
Hunter	A. Robinson. **Roman Imperial Coins in the Hunter Coin Cabinet, University of Glasgow.** 5 Vols. Oxford. 1962-82.
Kestner	A. Mlasowsky. **Die antiken Tesseren im Kestner-Museum Hannover.** Hannover. 1991.
Kestner	F. Berger. **Die Münzen de Römischen Republik im Kestner Museum Hannover.** Hannover. 1989.
Kraay	C.M. Kraay. **The Aes Coinage of Galba.** ANS NNM 133. New York. 1956.
Lacam	G. Lacam. **La Fin de L'Empire Romain et le Monnayage Or en Italie.** Lucern. 1983.
LRBC	R.A.G. Carson, P.V. Hill & J.P.C. Kent. **Late Roman Bronze Coinage.** London. 1978.
Mabbott	**The T.O. Mabbott Collection Part 2: Coins of the Roman World.** New York. 1969.
MacDowall	D.W. MacDowall. **The Western Coinages of Nero,** ANS NNM 161, New York, 1979.
Martin	P-H Martin. **Die Anonymen Münzen des Jahres 68 nach Christus.** Mainz. 1974.
Martini	R. Martini. **Una Collezione di Monete Romane Imperiali Contromarcate nel Gabinetto Numismatico di Locarno.** Milan. 1993.
Mazzini	I.G. Mazzini. **Monete Imperiali Romane.** 5 Vols. Milan. 1957-1958.
MIRB	W. Hahn. **Moneta Imperii Romani-Byzantinii.** Vienna. 1989.
PCR	R.A.G. Carson. **Principal Coins of the Romans.** 3 Vols. London. 1978-1981.
RIC	H. Mattingly et al. **The Roman Imperial Coinage.** 10 Vols. London. 1923-1994.
RSC	D. Sear et al. **Roman Silver Coins.** 5 Vols. London. 1978-1987.
SR	D. Sear. **Roman Coins and Their Values.** London. 1988.
SRM	D. Sear. **Roman Coins and Their Values.** Millennium Edition, London. 2000-2002.
Shiel	N. Shiel. **The Episode of Carausius and Allectus.** Oxford. 1977.

Sydenham	E. Sydenham. **The Coinage of the Roman Republic.** London. 1952. (Reprinted)
Szaivert	W. Szaivert. **Die Münzprägung der Kaiser Marcus Aurelius, Lucius Verus und Commodus.** Vienna. 1986.
T/V	B. Thurlow & I. Vecchi. **Italian Cast Coinage.** Dorchester. 1979.
Vagi	D. Vagi, **Coinage and History of the Roman Empire,** Sidney, Ohio, 1999.
WCN	D.W. MacDowall. **The Western Coinages of Nero.** ANSNNM 161. New York. 1979.

ROMAION (BYZANTINE) BIBLIOGRAPHY

Anoxin	B.A. Anoxin. **Monetnoe delo Chersonesa.** Kiev. 1977.
Bendall	S. Bendall. **A Private Collection of Palaeologan Coins.** Wolverhampton. 1988.
Berk	H. Berk. **Eastern Roman Successors of the Sestertius.** Chicago. N.D.
Berk	H. Berk. **Roman Gold Coins of the Medieval World 383-1453 AD.** Joliet. 1986.
BN	C. Morrisson. **Catalogue des Monnaies Byzantines de la Bibliothéque Nationale.** 2 Vols. Paris. 1970.
Boutin	S. Boutin. **Collection N.K. (Nadia Kapamadji)-Monnaies des Empires de Byzance.** 2 Vols. Maastricht. 1983.
DOC	A. Bellinger & P. Grierson. **Catalogue of Byzantine Coins in the Dumbarton Oaks Collection and the Whittemore Collection.** 3 Vols. Washington D.C. 1966-73.
Dochev	K. Dochev. **Moneti i Parichno Obrushenie v Turnovo XII-XIVv.** Turnovo. 1992.
Grierson	P. Grierson. **Byzantine Coins.** Berkeley. 1982.
Hendy	M. Hendy. **Coinage and Money in the Byzantine Empire 1081-1261.** Washington D.C. 1969.
Hendy, Studies	M. Hendy. **Studies in the Byzantine Monetary Economy c.300-1450.** Cambridge. 1985.
Hunt	Sotheby's. **The William Herbert Hunt Collection of Highly Important Byzantine Coins.** December 5-6, 1990; and **Important Byzantine Coins.** June 21, 1991. New York.
LPC	S.Bendall and P.J. Donald. **The Later Palaeologan Coinage.** London. 1979.
MIB	W. Hahn. **Moneta Imperii Byzantini.** 3 Vols. Vienna. 1973-81.
Ratto	R. Ratto. **Monnaies Byzantines et d'autres Pays Contemporaines.** Lugano. 1930. (Reprinted)
Ricotti-Prina	D. Ricotti-Prina. **La Monetazione Aurea delle Zecche Minore Bizantine dal VI al IX Secolo.** Rome. 1972.
Sabatier	J. Sabatier. **Description Générale des Monniaes Byzantines.** 2 Vols. Paris. 1863. (Reprinted)
Seyrig	J. Cheynet, C. Morrisson, W. Seibt. **Sceaux Byzantins de la Collection Henri Seyrig.** Paris. 1991.

SB	D. Sear et al. **Byzantine Coins and Their Values.** 2nd edition. London. 1987.
Tolstoi	I.I. Tolstoi. **Vizantiiskia Monety.** St. Petersburg. 1912-14. (Reprinted)
Whitting	P.D. Whitting. **Byzantine Coins.** New York. 1973.
Wroth(BMC)	W. Wroth. **Catalogue of the Imperial Byzantine Coins in the British Museum.** London. 1908. (Reprinted)
Wroth(BMCV)	W. Wroth. **Catalogue of the Coins of the Vandals, Ostrogoths and Lombards and of the Empires of Thessalonica, Nicaea and Trebizond in the British Museum.** London. 1911.(Reprinted as **Western and Provincial Byzantine Coins in the British Museum**)
Zacos	G. Zacos & A. Veglery. **Byzantine Lead Seals.** 2 Vols in 6 Parts. Basel & Bern. 1972-1984.

NON-CLASSICAL BIBLIOGRAPHY

AC	Y.T. Nercessian. **Armenian Coins and Their Values.** Los Angeles. 1995.
AJC	Y. Meshorer. **Ancient Jewish Coinage.** 2 Vols. New York. 1982.
Album	S. Album. **A Checklist of Popular Islamic Coins.** Santa Rosa. 1993.
Alexandropoulos	Jacques Alexandropoulos, **Les monnaies de l'Afrique Antique. 400 av. J.C. - 40 ap. J.C.**, 2000.
Allen/Nash	D.F. Allen & D. Nash. **The Coins of the Ancient Celts.** Edinburgh. 1980.
Alram	M. Alram. **Nomina Propria Iranica in Nvmmis.** IPNB Vol. 4. Vienna. 1986.
Anzani	A. Anzani. **Numismatica Axumita.** RIN III, Series 3, XXXIX (IV). 1926.
Babelon, Perses	E. Babelon. **Les Perses Achéménides.** Paris. 1893.
Balog	P. Balog. **The Coinage of the Ayyubids.** London. 1980.
Balog	P. Balog. **The Coinage of the Mamluk Sultans of Egypt and Syria.** N.Y. 1964.
Balog-Yvon	P. Balog & J. Yvon. **Monnaies a Légendes Arabes de l'Orient Latin,** in RN 1958, pp. 133-168.
Bates-Metcalf	M.L. Bates and D.M. Metcalf. **Crusader Coins with Arabic Inscriptions,** in A History of the Crusades, Vol.6 pp. 421-482.
Bedoukian CCA	P.Z. Bedoukian. **"Coinage of Cilician Armenia."** ANSNNM 147. N.Y. 1962.
Bedoukian CAA	P.Z. Bedoukian. **Coinage of the Artaxiads of Armenia.** RNS, London. 1978.
BMC Arab	S. Lane-Poole. **Catalogue of Oriental Coins in the British Museum.** 10 Vols. London. 1875-1890. (Reprinted)
BMC India	J. Allan & E.J. Rapson. **A Catalogue of the Indian Coins in the British Museum.** 3 Vols. London. 1908-1936. (Reprinted)
Carter	Martha L. Carter, Editor, **A Treasury of Indian Coins,** Marg Publications, Bombay (1994)
CCCBM	D. Allen. **Catalogue of Celtic Coins in the British Museum.** 2 Vols. London. 1987-1990.

286

De Callataÿ	F. de Callataÿ. **Les Tétradrachmes d'Orodès II et Phraate IV.** Paris. 1994.
De la Tour	H. De la Tour. **Atlas de Monnaies Gauloises.** Paris. 1892. (Reprinted)
De Morgan	Jacques de Morgan. **Manuel de Numismatique Orientale de L'Antiquite et du Moyen Age,** Obol International, 1923 (reprint: Chicago, 1979).
Edhem	I.G. Edhem. **Catalogue des Monnaies Turcomanes.** 1894. (Reprinted)
Forrer	L. Forrer. **Biographical Dictionary of Medallists, Coin, Gem and Seal Engravers 500 BC-AD 1900.** 8 Vols. London. 1902-1930. (Reprinted)
Foss	C. Foss. **"The Coinage of Tigranes the Great: Problems, Suggestions and a New Find,"** in NumChron 1986, pp. 19-67.
Frolova	N.A. Frolova, **The Coinage of the Kingdom of the Bosporus,** Oxford, 1979.
Göbl, Hunnen	R. Göbl. **Dokumente zur Geschichte der Iranischen Hunnen in Baktrien und Indien.** 4 Vols. Weisbaden. 1967.
Göbl, Kushan	R. Göbl. **Münzprägung des Kusanreiches.** Vienna. 1974.
Göbl, Sasanian	R. Göbl. **Sasanian Numismatics.** Braunschweig. 1971.
Hendin	D. Hendin. **Guide to Biblical Coins.** New York. 2001.
Hill	G.F. Hill. **Becker the Counterfeiter.** London. 1924. (Reprinted)
Hill Arabia	G. F. Hill, **The Ancient Coinage of Southern Arabia,** 1915 (Reprint: Argonaut, Chicago,1969)
INJ	**Israel Numismatic Journal.** Jerusalem. 1963-
Kazan	W. Kazan. **The Coinage of Islam.** Beirut. 1983.
MACW	M. Mitchiner. **Oriental Coins and Their Values: The Ancient and Classical World.** London. 1978.
Meshorer	Y. Meshorer. **Nabataean Coins.** Qedem 3. Jerusalem. 1975.
Meshorer, Aelia	Y. Meshorer. **The Coinage of Aelia Capitolina,** Jerusalem, 1989.
MIG	M. Mitchiner. **Indo-Greek and Indo-Scythian Coinage.** 9 Vols. London. 1975-1976.
Mildenberg	L. Mildenberg. **The Coinage of the Bar Kokhba War.** Salzburg, 1984.
Miles	G.C. Miles. **The Coinage of the Umayyads of Spain.** N.Y. 1950.
Miles	G.C. Miles. **The Coinage of the Visigoths of Spain.** N.Y. 1952.
Miles	G.C. Miles. **Coins of the Spanish Muluk al Tawa'if.** N.Y. 1954.
MNW	M. Mitchiner. **Non-Islamic States and Western Colonies.** London. 1979.
Munro-Hay	S.C. Munro-Hay and Bent Juel-Jensen. **Aksumite Coinage.** London. 1995.
MWI	M. Mitchiner. **The World of Islam.** London. 1977.
Nercessian	Y.T. Nercessian. **Armenian Coins and Their Values,** Los Angeles, 1995.
Paruck	F.D.A. Paruck. **Sasanian Coins.** New Delhi. 1976.

Pre-Kushana	O. Bopearachchi, A. ur Rahman. **Pre-Kushana Coins in Pakistan.** Karachi. 1995.
Prou	M. Prou. **Les Monnaies Carolingiennes.** Paris. 1892. (Reprinted)
Prou	M. Prou. **Les Monnaies Mérovingiennes.** Paris. 1896. (Reprinted)
Rapson	E. J. Rapson, **Indian Coins,** Indological Book House, India (1969)
Rtveladze	E. Rtveladze. **The Ancient Coins of Central Asia,** Tashkent (1987)
Rosenberger	M. Rosenberger. **The Rosenberger Israel Collection.** 4 Vols. Jerusalem. 1972-1978.
Rostovtsew	M. Rostovtsew & M. Prou. **Catalogue des Plombs de l'Antiquité, du Moyen Age et des Temps Modernes.** Paris. 1900.
Samaria Hoard	Y. Meshorer, S. Qeder. **The Coinage of Samaria in the 4th Century BCE.** Jerusalem. 1991.
Scheers	S. Scheers. **La Gaule Belgique: Numismatique Celtique.** Louvian. 1983.
Schjoth	F. Schjoth, **Chinese Currency/The Schjoth Collection at the Numismatic Cabinet of the University of Oslo,** Oslo (1929).
Schlumberger	G. Schlumberger. **Numismatique de l'Orient Latin.** Paris. 1878. (Reprinted)
Sellwood	D. Sellwood. **An Introduction to the Coinage of Parthia.** 2nd edition. London. 1980.
Senior	R. Senior, **Indo-Scythian Coins and History,** London (2001)
Senior, Hermaios	Robert C. Senior, **The Coinage of Hermaios and Its Imitations Struck By the Scythians,** London (2000)
Shore	F. Shore. **Parthian Coins and History-Ten Dragons Against Rome.** Quarryville. 1993.
SNG ANS 6	**Sylloge Nummorum Graecorum - The Collection of the American Numismatic Society - Part 6: Palestine - South Arabia,** NY, 1981.
SWW	D. Sellwood, P. Whitting, R. Williams. **An Introduction to Sasanian Coins.** London. 1985.
SNA Tübingen	L. Ilisch. **Sylloge Numorum Arabicorum: Tübingen. Palästina.** Tübingen. 1993-.
S/S	W.F. Spengler, W.G. Sayles. **Turkoman Figural Bronze Coins and Their Iconography.** Lodi. 1992.
Tomasini	W.J. Tomasini. **The Barbaric Tremissis in Spain and Southern France-Anastasius to** Leovigild, ANSNNM 152, New York, 1964.
Walker	J. Walker. **A Catalogue of Arab-Byzantine and Post-Reform Ommayyad Coins.** London. 1956.
Walker	J. Walker. **A Catalogue of Arab-Sassanian Coins.** London. 1941. (Reprinted)
Van Arsdell	R. Van Arsdell. **Celtic Coinage of Britain.** London. 1989.
Victoor	R. Victoor. **Roulles Celtes et Objets Assimilés.** Rosendaël-lez-Dunkerque. 1989.

Index

A

D

O

P

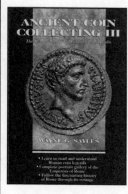